Exploring Black Sexuality

D1519575

Exploring Black Sexuality

Robert Staples

ROWMAN & LITTLEFIELD PUBLISHERS, INC.
Lanham • Boulder • New York • Toronto • Oxford

ROWMAN & LITTLEFIELD PUBLISHERS, INC.

Published in the United States of America
by Rowman & Littlefield Publishers, Inc.
A wholly owned subsidary of The Rowman & Littlefield Publishing Group, Inc.
4501 Forbes Boulevard, Suite 200, Lanham, Maryland 20706
www.rowmanlittlefield.com

PO Box 317
Oxford
OX2 9RU, UK

British Library Cataloguing in Publication Information Available

Library of Congress Cataloging-in-Publication Data

Staples, Robert.
  Exploring black sexuality / Robert Staples.
     p. cm.
  ISBN-13: 978-0-7425-4658-5 (cloth : alk. paper)
  ISBN-10: 0-7425-4658-6 (cloth : alk. paper)
  ISBN-13: 978-0-7425-4659-2 (pbk. : alk. paper)
  ISBN-10: 0-7425-4659-4 (pbk. : alk. paper)
  1. African Americans—Social conditions. 2. African Americans—Sexual behavior.
3. Sex customs—United States. I. Title.
  E185.86.S725 2006
  306.7089'96073—dc22   2005030691

Printed in the United States of America

⊗™ The paper used in this publication meets the minimum requirements of
American National Standard for Information Sciences—Permanence of Paper for
Printed Library Materials, ANSI/NISO Z39.48-1992.

To Dr. Alfred Kinsey,
whose scientific breakthrough made this book possible,
to Richard Pryor,
who provided a racial perspective that showed sexual
relationships could be fun if you didn't take them too seriously,
and to the memory of Alphonso Pinkney, 1930–2005.

Contents

Acknowledgments

During the thirty-five years of this book's evolution, a number of people contributed to its development and content. Although all the research and preparation was done in the United States, most of the writing was completed in Melbourne, Australia. I hold an appointment as visiting research fellow in the Centre for Australian Indigenous Studies at Monash University. My thanks to Professor Lynette Russell, director of the Centre, for the institutional support she provided, and to Diana Hettihewa for secretarial help and her friendly demeanor. All of the drafts and revisions were typed by the Publications Unit at Monash University under the direction of its manager, Ms. Laura Allen, and Ms. Beverly Higgins, her assistant. They served a greater function than word processors: their fast and accurate typing kept me constantly in a writing mode due to their fast completion rates.

I am grateful to Alan McClare, acquisitions editor, who very capably handled my manuscript, solicited reviews, and facilitated numerous aspects of publication. I thank Sheila-Katherine Zwiebel, production editor, who efficiently coordinated all the tasks of bringing this book to fruition. I am heavily indebted to her for getting the book out on schedule, for her attention to detail, and for answering e-mails in the middle of the night, something made necessary by my location in Melbourne, some eighteen hours ahead of the state of Maryland.

Among my academic colleagues I wish to thank Dr. Robert Hall of Northeastern University, who provided many helpful suggestions in the early stages of this book's development. Professor Paul Rosenblatt of the University of

Minnesota supervised my doctoral dissertation on Black sexuality and made many helpful comments over the years in correspondence and conversations. Dr. Rutledge Dennis read several chapters and offered insights in e-mails that I found useful.

A heavy debt of gratitude is owed to Dr. Ted McIlvena, President of the Institute for the Advanced Study of Human Sexuality in San Francisco. He very graciously allowed me access to the Institute's library with its vast collections of books, journals, and videotapes in the area of human sexuality. Jerry, the librarian was equally accommodating in the use of the library which is normally not open to the public. Finally, I am immensely thankful for Dr. Anthony Lemelle's help which I could not do without, assisting me in the writing and publication of the book.

Whatever is in the book was solely determined by this author. I am responsible for its content and any of its flaws.

Robert Staples, Professor Emeritus
San Francisco, 2006

Introduction

As I recently went through some of the major books on the Black family, what stands out consistently is how little attention is paid to dating and sexuality. Even in anthologies with twenty to forty separate articles, Black sexuality is ignored. While I know many of these scholars as colleagues and friends, it puzzles me why the curious silence on sexuality issues. In the 1980s when there was much concern about the problems of teenage pregnancy, research studies on teenage Blacks were conducted and were limited to those adolescent years. The AIDS crisis brought about a greater cross-section of Black sexual investigations in order to develop public policies and strategies to limit the spread of HIV. Thus, it was an opportune time to write a book on Black sexuality because there was an empirical database to draw upon. Having studied the subject for more than thirty years, I had an accumulated wisdom on the subject and the credibility to reach an audience of readers who may have been waiting for the first general work on this topic. Moreover, I was not dissuaded by the fears that prevented other Black scholars from its exposition.

That main fear is that giving visibility to the liberal sexual behavior of Afro-Americans will retard or hinder the movement toward racial equality in the United States. First, allegations of sexual promiscuity among Blacks is rarely in the public discourse because the society has advanced too much to deny any group its rights based on what transpires inside its bedrooms. Even gays, long the most stigmatized group, are finding that its sexual practices are irrelevant to attaining its civil rights. After decades as a student of race relations, it is clear that the United States is more concerned about capitalism and the ability to make profits than anything else. The sexual threat posed by Blacks, if publicly declared, is nothing more than a pretext to mask the competition for scarce resources. If all adult Blacks took an oath of celibacy today, some other cause would have to be invented as a roadblock to racial parity.

That does not mean the sexual threat is not real in the minds of millions of Euro-Americans. The white families who take their daughters out of public schools, which are racially mixed, when they reach puberty, those who move out of racially integrated neighborhoods into all-white enclaves, the millions of Euro-American women who suspect every Black male they encounter of wanting to rape them, all represent a veiled expression of the fear of Black sexuality. Yet, it is an uneasy fear to manifest in a public way. If they are not threatened in any kind of economic way, they will rarely take on a public character. Moreover, the sexual fear persists in the absence of any books on Black sexuality and a book on the subject that provides a balanced account is not likely to incite a sexual holocaust.

Meanwhile the stereotypes of Black sexuality are widespread even when counteracted by the empirical evidence. Somehow, Black males like Justice Clarence Thomas and boxer Mike Tyson became the poster boys for sexual harassment and date rape. Kobe Bryant may do the same for nonconsensual sex. Add to these men the highly publicized incident featuring singer Janet Jackson and we find a people representing 13 percent of the total population exemplifying the worst violations of America's moral code. When Janet Jackson allowed a portion of her breast to be bared during the Super Bowl half time, for ten seconds, it seemed as if Western civilization would implode before our very eyes. The person who claimed to be the most horrified was a Black man, one Michael Powell, the head of the Federal Communications Commission. Her actions may bring down a whole broadcast industry with her.

In the stranger than strange category, we have two other Black poster boys for child molestation and child pornography, Michael Jackson and R. Kelly. What is so odd about them representing pedophilia is that this type of crime is so rare in the Black community. Very few Blacks are involved in the production, selling, and viewing of pornography in general and almost none have been implicated in child pornography. Of course, there is a white celebrity, Peter Townsend, of the British rock band "The Who," also accused of viewing child pornography. We do not hear much about his case, maybe because he is British or even due to the lack of a hit record in the last twenty years. With the exception of Janet Jackson, who exposed a portion of her breast before one hundred million people, we might wonder why so many prominent Blacks are involved in these sexual scandals. Most cases of sexual harassment involve Euro-Americans because it is the rare Black male who resides in a high enough executive position to harass anybody. The overwhelming number of date rapes involves Euro-Americans because most white women date men of their race and it is that man who is most likely to rape her on a date. Maybe the sexual stereotypes of Afro-Americans give credence to these incidents, when they occur, and cause the media to pay attention.

When reflecting on the issue of human sexuality, I am inclined to focus on two forces that command public attention. One is that almost all sexual activity transpires in private. Other than our own sexual behavior, we do not know what is going on in the lives of our fellow citizens. Even in our own sexual conduct, we are not positioned well to get the best look at what we are doing. In the missionary position, she is looking up at his torso and he will be viewing her face and upper chest. This breeds inordinate curiosity when sex becomes public. And, it typically becomes public when there is a violation of the moral code. That is why local television news is replete with stories of sex crimes as are many local newspapers. While deploring the erosion of morals, we are excited by every graphic detail given us. There is probably no other subject so private that is given so much public exposure.

The other epiphany is how irrational our attitudes toward sex are. Freud pretty much told us that humans are "inherently irrational" and it is in the area of sexuality that this human tendency is most likely to be expressed. We have rationalized almost every form of human activity, at least in the developed world. That includes education, medicine, transportation, and commerce. Only in the realm of sexuality do we still permit the mysticism of religion to dominate. Certainly, the principles of science have been applied and are available in the Western world. Thus, we have ways to control conception, cure sexual diseases, etc. Yet, we attach so much importance to such a basic process involving genital penetration and ejaculation that we are not far removed from the Victorian era when they covered the legs of pianos to avoid sexual lust.

Freud and Marx

In writing this book, I am most influenced by the works of Marx and Freud on the subject of sexuality. I am not a disciple of either man and certainly do not agree with much of their theories. However, they seemed accurate in some of their basic assumptions. With Freud, it was his conclusion that the sex drive is a basic force in all humans constantly seeking expression. For him, it begins in childhood and has its trajectory determined by the experiences in the early ages. This sex drive, that he calls libido, has to be expressed

in some way and it is through the mental processes of repression and subli-
mation that it is controlled. To allow unfettered expression of the libido
would be to create a roadblock to the creation and maintenance of civilization. In particular, it was men that needed to be controlled lest they would
engage in sex with every woman possible.[1]

The significance of Freud, for me, is his interpretation of the power of the
sex drive, especially for men, in seeking its expression counteracted mostly
by the ego and superego, the latter constituting the moral values of society.
What we need to understand is when the moral order is undermined, the individual is freer to seek illegitimate outlets for his libido. Instead of the
legally wedded wife, it can be anyone from the child in one's household, the
"bad girl" in his environment, a prostitute, his best friend's wife, the girl next
door. The libido can be satisfied by any category of female and a litany of sex
scandals has eroded the moral basis of American society. Anyone conversant
with current events knows of the massive number of child sexual abuse allegations against organized religion, sexual harassment practices in the corpo-
rate world and the sins of political figures, one that wound up in the im-
peachment of a sitting president.

Freud prepared us for the consequences of the breakdown of the moral order. Karl Marx provided the theoretical foundation for the variations in sexual behavior based on the political and economic structure of society. We
must note here that both Freud and Marx were Eurocentric in their analysis.
It was Friedrich Engels who actually is credited with authorship of the book,
"The Origin of the Family, Private Property, and the State."[2] Marx however,
took notes and provided ideas for the book. Society, according to Engels, began with unregulated sexual transactions, where everybody was available to
everybody else. The implication is that not even the incest taboo had been
put into place. Society evolved from a situation where there was no private
ownership of land to a society where land was held in common, and marriages were polygamous for both men and women. The children belonged to
the women. With the development of private property, men had a need to
pass on their property to their rightful heirs. Thus, it became necessary for
the women only to be monogamous in order for men to be sure of their paternity. All these stages were also accompanied by certain technological innovations that made them possible.

Marx and Engels provided us with a relationship between economic structure and family relationships, whether they were correct about the specific
economic formations and the family types, we can never be sure. There is no
way to prove what happened thousands of years ago. However, it is possible
to see the relationships between the economic structure and sexual patterns.

Under the boom and bust cycles of American capitalism, women may feel the need for economic security. This leads to a bargaining process in which regularized sexual relations are leveraged in exchange for male economic support. The argument can be made that women no longer need male economic support. Yet, there can be a time lag whereby women still feel vulnerable in the fluctuations of American capitalism. They may feel responsible for the survival of the children and welfare reform has in many ways, yanked the safety net from them.

America Versus the World

If we look at American history, its moral code has mostly evolved in a progressive manner. The Europeans who settled in the southeastern part of the new world developed a double standard of sexual conduct. White women, of certain social classes, were not expected to have sexual relations until married and not to enjoy it within the context of marriage. Very lower-class white women and Black women were the ones selected for the white male's premarital sexual encounters. Along the eastern seaboard, the Puritans observed a single standard of sexual abstinence before marriage, for both men and women. Premarital sex was against the law, as was adultery, which carried serious penalties including death for adultery. Some states permitted men to kill their wives if caught in the act of adultery. Despite the harsh penalties, some violated the laws and paid the price. A common practice, for women impregnated before marriage, was to marry before the birth of the child. In some states, one of every four marriages involved a pregnant bride.

For changes in sexual patterns, we look to variations in the role of women. Kinsey found that almost 70 percent of American men had once had sex with a prostitute before marriage. The greatest change for women occurred among women born after 1900. By the time Kinsey and his colleagues did their monumental sexual study, they claimed that half of all American women had engaged in sexual activity before marriage.[3] In the 1950s, sex attitudes gradually were liberalized. Among whites, the men divided women up into legitimate and illegitimate sexual targets. Sometimes the legitimate sexual targets were women of a lower social class. In other cases, they were women in certain occupational categories such as nurses, secretaries, flight attendants, and waitresses. Or, they might be divorced or older women. The illegitimate sexual targets were the women saved for marriage. Gradually, most women became eligible for premarital coitus although residues of the good girl/bad girl dichotomy can still be found among a minority of men. When America is viewed from a foreign perspective, it is often seen as the

xvi   Introduction

most sexually liberal of countries. American women often had affairs in other countries, the United States was the producer of most pornography found around the world, distributed mainstream movies with sexual content, contained risqué lyrics in its music, and was regarded as the center of world decadence by other countries. It still has the highest rate of teenage pregnancy in the developed world. Yet, when they compare the most sexually liberal countries in the world, depending on the measures used, Britain, Sweden, even Brazil ranks ahead of Americans. A couple of factors may account for America's low standing. Neither of the above three countries have significant religious group participation in national politics. Both Britain and Sweden have substantial welfare benefits that may free women to indulge their sexual passions without worry about marriage and the economic support of a man.

Whereas Americans engaged in much angst over the ten-second view of a portion of Janet Jackson's breast, much of the developed and developing world laughed. Anyone who has traveled widely, watched television, knows that nudity is commonplace on the broadcast channels. In many cases, the channels showing the nudity are government funded. Sex education, abortion, contraceptives are widely available in developed countries, which may account for their lower rate of teenage pregnancies. Prostitution is legal and controlled in many of those countries. That means that sex industry workers get regular medical checkups.

In the United States, any number of religious groups and moral crusaders are pandered to by the Republican Party. Using their political influence, they have managed to sanitize the offerings on free to air television network channels, weakened the laws allowing women the right to choose whether to bring a child into the world, prevented public schools from offering practical sex education classes, instead pressuring them to offer courses advocating sexual abstinence. They have made the use of contraceptive measures by teenagers difficult to obtain by requiring them to receive parental permission. Moreover, they are not deterred by the saying, "let thee who is without sin cast the first stone." It is estimated that more than ten thousand children were sexually abused by Catholic priests. Some of the nation's most famous religious leaders have been implicated in consorting with prostitutes, raping a church secretary, supporting a mistress with church funds and other sins of the flesh.

Sex as Business

For years, we have been bombarded with estimates that the "sex" industry grosses more than two hundred and fifty billion dollars a year in the United

States. That figure includes only the most obvious use of sexuality, much of it illegal and, hence, not counted. America, however, has managed to sexualize almost everything we see. In the staid pages of the most respected newspapers are scantily clad women modeling lingerie and other provocative clothing. Even the news section manages to show us attractive women in photos accompanying stories of national disasters. What we may be shown is an attractive woman who lost her home in the disaster. Every year there are stories about a heat wave that cause them to show women in bikinis on the beach. Then, there is the multi-billon dollar advertising industry. Sex has long been used to sell everything from cosmetics to cars, coffee, and haute couture fashion. The trend has gone so far as to be labeled "porno chic."[4]

Young women are trained early to flaunt their sexuality in the interest of social approval. Beauty pageants for the very young are held all over America. The culture encourages them to market themselves as sexual beings, and then complains that women are being sexually objectified. It also decries the obsession of young men with sex when that is all they see around them. The fashion industry pushes the envelope with coquettish looks, raunchy poses, and voyeurism to seduce their target market for luxury goods. The feminists claim it is male sexism run amok that is responsible for these ad campaigns while others note that it is often women who run these ads, particularly in the fashion industry. Many women want to display their sexuality and do not see themselves as a victim—only a woman who is making a strong sexual choice.

Ironically, the Americans may be the more conservative practitioners of "porno chic." In other developed nations nude or scantily clad photos of women adorn the first and second pages of tabloid newspapers for no reason other than men—and some women—like to see them. In France, a clothing chain portrays a naked woman on all fours in a paddock alongside a sheep. Another clothing manufacturer shows the breast of a ruby-robed woman being groped by a man's hand.[5] Italy may have raised the sexualization of women to a new level when it accepted a one and one-half million dollar grant from the European Union to train young women to be television "bimbos." Apparently, barely clad women populate most Italian variety and game shows there. Young women are being trained to be the performers on those television programs.[6]

While the United States makes better use of women in its television programs, popular culture here is riddled with images of female sexuality. In the recording industry, only attractive, very sexual women seem to have hit records. Their music videos show them in sexually provocative clothes singing songs that promise hot passion on demand. The competition is such that an older, somewhat rotund woman, of average looks has almost no chance. Women in films complain that the only roles they are offered portray them as sex objects who are often marginal to the plot. It is not clear who, if anyone, pressures them to show up near naked at award shows. With few exceptions, if they want to sell millions of CDs, fill the movie houses, and keep the TV ratings up, they play the sexuality game.

Television is a breed apart from films and records because broadcast, free to air, television is more likely to engage in titillation than any raw sexuality. The commercials may be raunchier than the programs. That is a major reason that millions of Americans switched to cable television. Not only can you watch the theatrical films uncensored, there are programs that feature sexuality in all its dimensions, shows like "Sex and the City." For those who want to dispense with the idea of a plot or real acting, there are the playboy and spice channels that feature hardcore porno with the graphic penetration of genitals deleted. Cable programs with commercial sponsors may still censor the content of movies. About 80 percent of Americans now receive cable television and they are slowly approaching almost half the share of all television viewers.

Cable television, of course, has the advantage of being unregulated by government authorities. Given the desire of the American public, the status quo will likely remain unless there is a military coup. It means however, that only those who can afford cable television will be able to watch the most sophisticated and sexual fare available in American households. The other unregulated medium is the computer and its Internet. The Internet is estimated to have about 10 percent of the total pornography market, their sites grossing two billion dollars in revenue in 2003. They claim that about thirty-five million people visited porn sites in December 2003. A number of cottage industries have developed around pornography on the Internet because anyone with a camera and web connection can produce content quickly and cheaply. The advantage of the Internet is that consumers of pornography no longer have to go to dangerous, seedy parts of the city to get their dose of porn. The Internet is delivering it right into the homes of Middle America.[7]

In a Divided America

While millions decry the moral decay of the United States, the sexual revolution continues at an incremental pace. The AIDS crisis had a chilling effect for many and recent statistics show a reticence to exchange sexual partners casually in today's environment. At the same time, only 59 percent of adult Americans are married and living with their spouse. About five and one-half million households consist of unwed couples living together as part-ners and half of all newlyweds will have cohabitated before their marriage. Around one third of all children born in the United States are out of wed-lock. Although the figures are inconsistent, a range of 60–90 percent of mar-ried couples had affairs during their current marriage or a previous one. Of those who marry this year, more than half will have engaged in sex before age eighteen and more than 90 percent will have experienced sexual activity by the time they marry.[8]

The do-gooders are fighting a losing battle and can only hope to slow down the rate of increase, particularly among the young. In that regard, they appear to be having some success. When the Kaiser Family Foundation sur-veyed young adults aged sixteen through twenty-four, four of their five con-cerns were about sexual matters. Yet, concern about AIDS and HIV, teen pregnancy, etc., do not necessarily translate into abstinence before marriage or lifelong monogamy.[9] Groups have been collecting pledges from teenagers to remain virgins before marriage. More than 90 percent were not faithful to that pledge.[10] Some churches are enrolling their young, unmarried members in pre-marriage counseling programs where they agree to be counseled and to remain celibate until marriage. Even among the very religious, those vows are honored more in the breach.

If the fear factor in AIDS/HIV is deleted, it is likely that sexual permis-siveness will return to the level of the 1970s—at least among the young. As women gain economic independence, they will not want to rush into a mar-riage and child before reaching the age of thirty. Some, knowing their chances of a successful marriage are less than 50 percent, will not want to risk marriage at all. As women go, so will the sexual revolution. Some Pollyan-nas take pride in the historical fact that, by age sixty, 97 percent of men and 95 percent of women have married.[11] I doubt that those figures will be simi-lar for Generation Y when they reach the age of sixty. If a life-threatening disease could not kill off the sexual revolution, it is unlikely anything will in the short term.

Up to this point, I have not included any of the biological determinist theories of human sexuality. A popular aspect of those theories is that male/female variations in sex drives can be accounted for by genetic factors. The male's instinct for survival means he must propagate his genes as much as possible. That is why he seeks to have sexual relations, as much as possi-ble, with as many women as he can. Conversely, women can only propagate their genes through their own bodies. Moreover, their instinct for survival leads them to seek out a monogamous relationship with a man who can sup-port her and her brood.[12] Some studies have shown women to be more critical of the looks of potential rivals during their most fertile period. Another study revealed that women tend to dress in a more provocative way when they are ovulating.[13] Whatever the validity or influence of these physiological factors, I believe that they are superseded by cultural and social forces.

Plan of the Book

Although I have read the research and statistics on Black sexual patterns, they will be cited sparsely. Many of them will be inconsistent with each other because of sampling methods or wording of questions but a major reason is that people lie about sex more than anything else. When the former President Clinton was impeached for lying on a court deposition, a common refrain was that "everybody lies about sex." The distinguished sex researcher, Alfred Kinsey accounted for the lie factor when he claimed that 50 percent of American women had engaged in premarital sexual activity. Only 35 percent of his female sample admitted to premarital sexual experiences and he added 15 percent for the "lie factor."[14]

One TV news report claimed that female virgins at a Baltimore high school were claiming to have sexual experience when they had none. A common discrepancy is the number of lifetime sexual partners for men and women. Often the men will claim nine sexual partners, the women five. Assuming that most of them were heterosexual, the number should be equal. There are a few statistical flukes that might account for some of the differentials. When I mentioned this to my female students at Howard in 1995, they claimed that women used strange accounting methods in determining the number of sexual partners, to reduce the number. Thus, they eliminated from the total men who did not spend the night, who used a condom, etc. However, one researcher went back to the original subjects and found that the males overstated the number of sexual partners.

I have selected the chapter topics that seem to be the most important in understanding Black sexuality. The section on sexual deviations is fairly brief because there is not much literature on the subject. One reason for the paucity of literature is the low rate of Black participation in sexual deviations. With America's propensity for doing research, and making racial comparisons, there is little that has not been uncovered. I had the advantage of collecting papers on Black sexuality over the years and access to materials, journals, and books at the Institute for the Advanced Study of Human Sexuality, a place within walking distance of my residence in San Francisco. I can only hope this book will be a standard-bearer for many years.

Notes

1. Anthony Elliott, *Psychoanalytic Theory: An Introduction*. Cambridge, Massachusetts: Blackwell, 1994.

2. Friedrich Engels, *The Origin of the Family, Private Property and the State*. Chicago: C. H. Kerr, 1902.

3. Alfred C. Kinsey, et al., "Sexual Behavior in the Human Female." Philadelphia: W. B. Saunders, 1953.

4. Tamara Thiessen, "Sex and Shopping—It's a French Thing." *The Age*, March 6, 2004, p. 21.

5. *Ibid.*

6. Ellen Hale, "EU Funding Goes to What Some Critics Call 'Bimbo School.'" *USA Today*, March 10, 2004, p. 2-A.

7. Jon Swartz, "Carnal, Tech-knowledge Team up." *USA Today*, March 18, 2004, p. 6A.

8. Rick Hampson, "The State of Our Unions: Divorce, Cohabitation, and Adultery Have Hurt Institution of Marriage." *USA Today*, February 26, 2004, p. A-1.

9. "Young Adults Voice Concerns." *USA Today*, February 13, 2004, p. 9-B.

10. "Chastity Pledge does not reduce STD Rate." *USA Today*, March 11, 2004.

11. Hampson, *loc. cit.*

12. Reay Tannahill, *Sex in History*. New York: Scarborough House, 1992, pp. 21–22.

13. "Fertile Ground for Real Catty Pursuits." *MX News*, February 18, 2004, p. 4.

14. A. Kinsey, et al., *op. cit.*

CHAPTER ONE

~

Sexuality on the Dark Continent

Anybody who has seen pictures of nude African women in magazines, read the statistics estimating that as many as a quarter of the adult African population is infected with HIV and is aware that polygamy is still practiced in much of the dark continent might reasonably believe that its peoples are not subjected to any restraints on the sexual impulse, that they represent the id in its most basic form. While there have been numerous changes in Africa, south of the Sahara, many of them brought about by the exposure to and domination by Europeans, the sexual norms and practices of pre-slavery Africa were very different. A variety of sexual behavior existed among pre-European contact civilizations of the African continent. Among these widely differing African societies, a common strand was the strict regulation of sexual practices by the rules of the different tribal groupings. Unlike contemporary America, the individual in Africa did not have the discretion to decide which rules to obey and those to be ignored. The group was paramount and violation of its rules could be punished as harshly by castration and death.

If, as we will later discover, there is much to question about the findings of current sex research, how valid is our knowledge of sixteenth-century African norms and practices regarding sexual matters. Not only was all of the research carried out by Europeans or their American descendents, many of these researchers openly acknowledge their purpose as serving the colonial administration. There is no shortage of obvious distortions about African sexuality to cite as examples with almost all pre-1950 Africanist writings depicting the dark-skinned denizens of Africa as savages, with animal-like sexual behavior, massive sex organs, and even intercourse between African females and gorillas. Fortunately, post-colonial sex research has corrected many of these myths. Yet, they were often seeing the effects of a different Africa, one forever changed by its colonial domination and exposure to Western culture. Thus, we must sort through much of the colonials' research into African sexuality to determine what sort of sexual value system they brought as bondsman to the new world.

Before using our own frame of reference for dealing with African sexuality, we must view it in the political context in which the behavior was shaped. European expansionism and exploitation of Africa, its wealth and peoples was intimately linked to its sexuality as well as its racial traits. The early colonialists looked upon the Africans' different sexual norms and behavior not as cultural relativism but an indisputable sign of bestiality and savagery. The men were described as lustful and the women as promiscuous. Their real motives were described by Nagel:

> There were, of course, good reasons for these fantasies of African sexual exoticism and masculine sexual excess. The most obvious, of course, was to justify the Europeans' brutal treatment of both African men and women, especially their sexual violations of African women. The emphasis on African sexuality and savagery in the reports of almost exclusively male Christian European travelers and explorers contributed to a growing and ingrained sexual ethnocentrism among Europeans. Besides serving to develop a sense of European cultural and technological superiority and to excuse atrocities, there were also clear material motives for depicting Africans as sexually savage and promiscuous. These motives were linked to colonialism and the slave trade.[1]

It was simply an ideological device to rationalize the appropriation of the lands and assets of savages and using them as free labor instead of justifying otherwise morally and politically indefensible practices. Only in the context of a puritanical Europe and America in the sixteenth century could the sex lives of a native people be a defense against their rape and pillage. Given current beliefs in twenty-first-century America, we may not be that far removed from their European ancestors.

What about the sexuality of Africans prior to European contact, domination, and enslavement? Other than the records of European travelers, a particularly subjective source, there is almost no quantitative assessment of African sexual practices. Beset by an AIDS pandemic, grinding poverty, a draught, military and corrupt governments, and civil wars, African nations cannot expend their scarce resources on the sex lives of its people. Some

African governments have come under foreign criticism for not forthrightly dealing with the AIDS crisis and its concomitant sexual practices. That leaves us with the ethnographic data, most of it collected by foreigners.

During the 1960s, there were fewer than twenty Black American anthropologists, almost no Black Africans trained in that subject. The anthropologist carrying out the research had to rely on the reports of native peoples, many who told them of ideal behavior—not informal or covert sexual practices that violated Tribal regulations. We are struck by inconsistencies in the interpretation of African sexuality, which in large part is consistent with our knowledge base of current American sexual behavior. Consequently, we cannot, with any confidence, make any generalizations about the prevalence, frequency, or proportion of any sexual activity. In a continent populated by more than five hundred linguistic and cultural groupings, we can barely scratch the surface of its structure of sexuality.

In describing what is known, we are largely staying away from recent ethnographic accounts to avoid the contamination of Western influences and exposure. By using some of the research conducted during the colonial era, we may find that many tribal groupings had retained centuries old sexual patterns before many residual effects of colonialism kicked in. Writing in the 1960s, the Black sociologist E. Franklin Frazier claimed that the most important thing to know about the sexuality of Africans is that it is an expression of their religious values, largely associated with reproduction.[2] What we need to understand is that the religious values are not linked to sex itself, only to the reproductive process. Unlike the ancestors of Euro-Americans, God did not speak to the conduct of Africans in the sexual realm. It was purely a secular matter governed by the rules of each tribe or clan. In most cases, sexual intercourse was seen as a natural function, to the extent that pregnancy before marriage was occasionally encouraged in order to prove fertility.

Another important distinction between European and African sexual structures was the interface between gender roles and biological sex. Whereas the social roles prescribed by gender overlap biological sex in European societies, in the sense there are men's roles and there are women's roles, in some African societies, men's and women's gender roles are reversed. On occasion, the daughter assumes the role of a son or a wife assumes the role of a husband,[3] for example in matrilineal societies a woman who takes another woman as her spouse for certain purposes. We cannot delineate the complex social structure of hundreds of tribal groupings in this work. What we need to understand is that Africans did have a social structure, as did Europeans, that was used to carry out its social imperatives. It did not mirror European societies because Africans did not have the same cultural imperatives, given their different territory and needs as a sovereign people.

One of the reasons early European travelers to Africa labeled it an immoral continent was the fact that complete nudity prevailed among its peoples, particularly in tropical and subtropical areas. However, there were exceptions, such as the Bala society,[4] where nakedness in mixed company was not practiced. In other societies, some clothing was worn to cover the genitals, although they were not unexposed for sexual reasons. A woman, for example, had to take care that evil spirits did not enter her body through her vagina. One of the oldest penis-sheaths was designed to protect the penis from harm in war and from the spirits of animals killed in hunting. Only married women, of the Ibo tribe, wore clothes. To Europeans who saw the nude body as a sexual provocation, whose married women retained some clothing before their husbands during sex, it was a public exposure of their moral degradation. To the African natives, it was a logical adaptation to a hot, humid climate that made clothing of any kind uncomfortable.[5]

As any resident of a nudist colony could have advised those Europeans, the naked body seen on a regular basis by members of the opposite sex fails to titillate, to stimulate the most primal sexual urges. With the multi-billion dollar clothing industry of the United States reaping major profits off of the sexually provocative clothing they sell in the United States, any trend toward nudism would be highly unwelcome. Because nudity is so rarely seen outside of the eyes of sexual partners and other limited settings, it stirs up ideas, anxieties, and notions of morality itself throughout the centuries in the Western world. The sexual revolution in the twentieth century brought about some relaxation of the human body's, mostly female, exposure outside the marital bed. It can be seen on the Internet, films, art exhibits, and nude beaches. Meanwhile, under the influence of Islam, Christianity and colonization, nudity can rarely be seen in the urban areas of Africa. Ironically, as they covered up their bodies, Africans strayed even further away from their cultural traditions regarding appropriate sexual activity.

Probably the greatest distinction, before and after colonization between Europe and Africa has been the practice of polygamy, the legitimacy of plural spouses cohabiting with a man (mostly) at the same time. It is still widely practiced in Africa, mostly among the elite, despite falling from favor among younger Africans, particularly women. This practice has little to do with sexuality although it can be used to double a man's pleasure. We might note that it continues to exist in a majority of the world's societies albeit illegal everywhere in the developed world. The demographics of a nation do not permit a majority of men to have more than one wife at a time. Hence, it is confined to a small minority of men whose family, or themselves, can afford the bride price for a second wife. In today's African cities, that bride price must increasingly be paid in hard cash. Often the second wife is acquired after the man has been married for some time and, to avoid marital conflict, is done with the approval and assistance of the first wife. In some cases, it is facilitated by marrying the wife's sister.[6]

Not only does the man need the means to pay a bride price, he must also provide a second house in which the new wife and her children can live. The ostensible purpose of plural wives is to have some help with all the work at the family farm. It also confers status on wife number one when her husband can afford a second wife. She retains seniority and all the perks of being the first wife. Observers of these multiple wives arrangement have noticed they often do not live up to the cultural ideal. Despite, perhaps because of, the first wife's older age and seniority, the second wife is younger, thus seen as more attractive and more exciting. Instead of the senior wife sharing her husband's bed equally, she may find her younger counterpart enjoying the lion's share of her husband's sexual attention. Since women have little power in a male-dominated African world, his prerogatives go unchallenged.

This same powerlessness is why the plural spouses are almost always women. In only a few cases, where the number of women exceeds the number of men, wives are permitted to have official lovers. As for plural husbands, less than a handful of societies allow women to have more than one husband and, typically, under special conditions. It can be a lose-lose situation for women in those few cases where women are allowed to have more than one husband. Always, it occurs where there is a shortage of women for men to choose as wives. That shortage was most often caused by infanticide. Under circumstances where there is a severe shortage of food, the female children are killed. To mitigate the effects of this shortage, two men— typically brothers—will pool their resources to acquire a wife for both of them. She will be expected to do the female tasks around the farm and provide them with children. Sexual relations occur equally between the brothers and the first child belongs to the oldest brother.[7]

Although the existence of plural spouses is now largely a practice of the wealthy, it was not designed as an institution to enrich the sex lives of men in those societies. Men who have plural wives do not necessarily engage in more sexual activity than monogamous males. In our current society, where half of all marriages end in divorce, a type of serial monogamy, the African version might appear to be more stable. In terms of the twenty-first-century versions, some have asserted that in the context of the AIDS crisis in Africa, polygamy might be better than other arrangements preferred by many men:

a wife and one or more mistresses, perhaps resorting to a number of prostitutes. Others have insisted that plural wives facilitate the spread of AIDS since the more sexual partners a man has, the risk increases of the disease infecting others as some men acquire more than two wives and still engage in other affairs.[8]

Manifestations of African Sexuality

Whatever sexual pattern exists among African cultural groupings, it is often preceded by some ritual or rites of passage. Girls, in particular, are prepared for womanhood at a young age by initiation rites. In some tribes, initiation begins when a girl's breasts develop and she begins to menstruate. At the time, she will often be taken under the wing of female elders and be socialized into domestic and sexual matters. Her diet may be restricted and she may be required to observe a number of taboos. Boys are prepared for manhood by being required to carry out a number of tasks to prove their toughness, hunting skills, and other tests of manhood. Often they are grouped together with boys their own age in a separate environment and left alone to fulfill their tasks. Other times they will receive instruction from male elders in the tribe. His training is less specifically oriented toward sexual matters although he will learn tribal laws on when sex can occur and with what class of women.

As true of children of all cultures, all eras, unsupervised children may engage in sex play before puberty. Some tribes are very tolerant of it when they become aware of it. Others strongly discourage it. Students of African sexuality are not in agreement on whether premarital sexual relations were allowed by the majority of tribes. In the pre-European contact era, there may be no authentic assessment of actual behavior. The early European travelers made the spurious association between nudity and sexual morality when that was not true. Whatever premarital sexual activity that transpired did not last long since women married at very young ages in that era, ranging from thirteen to twenty years of age. All we can reliably say is that premarital chastity was required—even demanded—by some tribes and not by others. Generally, conception was followed by marriage to an appropriate partner.[9]

What we do know is that some tribes that required virginity in its brides had harsh methods for ensuring its moral code was followed and equally serious consequences if it was not. Among such tribes, a girl may be subjected to a brutal inspection by her father or other tribal members. If her hymen is not intact, she may pay with her life because of the shame she has brought on her family. Another test of virginity might occur on the wedding night. After the marriage is consummated, the bloodstains of virginity are exposed on the stained sheet for all to see. If no blood is shown, the bride's family is required to return the bride price and accept the daughter back into their family. Such instances are rare since the premarital examination already tests the existence of the bride's virginity.[10]

Where virginity in females is required, some tribes do not leave it to chance. The process of circumcision is used by tribes that have come under Semitic influence. It is applied to girls as young as three years old. This very painful operation involves sewing up the vagina, except for an opening for urination and menstruation. Prior to marriage, in another painful operation, certain tribal members, typically female elders, will remove the suture while the prospective bride writhes in pain. Another operation, in current public condemnation because it continues among African expatriate families, is clitoridectomy, a form of female circumcision to tame female sexual desire by mutilating female genitalia. Generally accompanying a ceremony, it involves the removal of the clitoris and other parts of a woman's genitalia.[11]

Obviously, as true everywhere else, the harshest proscriptions are on female sexuality. Many of the aforementioned practices still exist in contemporary Africa although believed to be employed by only a minority of African tribes. It is a cultural throwback that cannot be defended under the rubric of tribal tradition. Some estimates are that as many as one hundred million girls and women in Africa are still subject to this painful rite of passage. Despite these misogynistic patterns, many African women enjoyed a sexual freedom denied their European sisters of the sixteenth century. They were not shackled by burdensome and uncomfortable clothing, some were allowed to take lovers before and after marriage, and they might express their fondness of sex. One observer claimed that Turu women, having experienced a clitoridectomy, were still sexually excited and could have orgasms.[12]

Do the men of Africa face any consequences for the violation of tribal law? The answer is in the affirmative. If a man deflowers an ineligible virgin, he may be forced to compensate any future husband. The crimes of rape, incest, and adultery may be punished mildly by having to indemnify her present or future husband. In the worst-case scenario he may be banished from the tribe, castrated, or put to death. While certainly not in the above category, men must often undergo a three-year period of sexual abstinence, albeit married, from the time of his wife's pregnancy to the time of weaning, a time frame of three years after parturition. Sometimes the punishment depends on whom the offense was committed against. Adultery with one of the wives of a chief may be punished by mutilation, death, or castration. We know of no such punishment for men in contemporary Africa. Yet, there is the celebrated case of a woman sentenced to death for adultery in northern Nigeria at the time of this writing.[13]

Taboos, Practices, and Deviations

Africa is a repository of unique sexual customs, although some can be found in other parts of the underdeveloped world and among indigenous peoples in the developed world. Kissing, for example, does not seem to have been of much importance in pre-colonial Africa. Some men said they seldom kiss their wives while others mention it as a normal part of foreplay. Men may kiss a women's breast but never her vagina, while women may never touch the man's penis. In general, the touching of a spouse's genitals is frowned upon. Among the more interesting customs is wife lending, in which a husband consents to another man having sex with one or more of his wives. The man availing himself of such hospitality may be one of the husbands' brothers or from his age group. Death of a spouse imposes sexual restrictions in some cultures. In some cases, a woman is not allowed to have sex for a year following the death of her husband. A brother must marry the widow of his deceased brother and any children born of such a union will belong to the dead brother.[14]

Sexual problems were not unknown in pre-European contact Africa. Impotency and sterility are two of them and the most shameful things that can happen to a man. In the case of impotence, a wife may shout out, "My husband's penis has died"! By its public exposure, he is subject to great embarrassment and ridicule. The typical image of such a man is that he is doomed to be uneasy and unhappy. Among some groups, the wife may be allowed to leave him or take a lover. If the man is shown to be sterile, it automatically meant divorce in ancient Egypt. A woman did not bear as heavy a burden of sexually pleasing her husband. However, if she was infertile, many tribes permitted the husband to return her to her family and retrieve his bride price. Such a woman was often scorned and forced to do heavy labor.[15]

Until the invasion of Europeans, it seems that few tribes opposed masturbation in boys, although they discouraged it in adult males. Young girls may also engage in autoeroticism using their finger or a dildo. During the time when young boys are isolated in small groups during the rites of passage, they may individually or collectively masturbate. A common folk belief is that adult males who masturbate will lose interest in women. Some students of African sexuality believe that group masturbation was a form of homosexuality. Black Africans deny that homosexuality ever existed in historic African society or that it has much of a presence in its current structure. Women were also known to engage in mutual masturbation. It is a sign of the massive homophobia in darkest Africa that there are few visible signs of gay and lesbian life in African cities. That is also a reason that AIDS in Africa is regarded as a heterosexual disease because few men and women are brave enough to admit to engaging in same-sex practices. Homosexuality is still illegal in many African nations.[16]

Among native peoples, children are regarded as sexually unimportant since their activities do not involve reproduction, thus without effect either magically or socially. Once a woman begins to menstruate, a number of practices and taboos come into being. Many precautions are taken during this time, a common one being isolation of the menstruating female. Even married couples are subject to restrictions during this time of the month. The husband cannot have sexual relations with his wife; she may not cook or serve meals for him nor eat food with him. These various taboos are designed to ward off evil spirits. During the first menstrual cycle, a woman is deemed capable of great harm to other individuals and the tribe, ranging from male sterility to destruction of the group's crops.[17] Among boys, the practice of circumcision existed among some tribes. It was typically carried out around ages seven to twelve, the cutting instrument was a knife and a special ceremony marked the process. If all went well, the healing process was completed from two weeks to a month. Sometimes a boy was isolated during this period, restrictions were placed on his diet, and he could not eat or drink with adults.[18]

During their youthful period, which ended as early as age thirteen, a number of sexual practices were condoned that might be severely punished in adulthood. Among them was sex with animals, individual and group masturbation, and sex play. While bestiality will occur with cows, donkeys, goats, etc., there are tribes that punish boys if caught in the act. While there is folklore about women copulating with monkeys, actual behavior of female bestiality is not recorded by students of African sexuality. Once males and females have undergone initiation rites, these sexual practices occur in a covert manner and may incur fines if discovered.[19]

While there is no certainty about premarital sexuality in pre-colonial Africa, it did exist among some tribes. What made these sexual patterns unique to Europeans is that tribes often had prescribed rituals and roles in which premarital sexual relations took place. Sometimes designated female members of a tribe would serve as the sexual partners of young males after rites of passage, circumcision, and military service. While premarital sexual activity occurred in a random and chaotic manner, the norm was that it was condoned only when it transpired within the context of tribal laws. Some tribes actually required virginity in most of its female members but excluded some women, who were allowed to take on males prior to marriage because they were infertile or their husbands were impotent or sterile. Some tribes had laws that permitted couples committed to marriage to engage in sexual activity, with each other or different partners prior to the nuptial ceremonies. Whereas both young males and females were allowed to engage in premarital coitus, a woman who had too many lovers would be denied any opportunity for a marriage in the future.[20]

Courtship, which included prenuptial sex, did occur among some tribal groups. Young people were allowed to select a future spouse but marriages were generally arranged between families and tribes. Even if a couple wished to marry, it could only happen if the individuals selected were eligible marriage partners. Marriages could only take place with groups that had trading or military alliances with one's tribe. Sometimes one had to marry outside a particular lineage, at other times they were required to marry within certain groups. Therefore, marriages were rarely arranged directly between individuals. In most of sub-Saharan Africa, a bride price had to be paid by the groom's family to the family of the bride to compensate that family for the loss of her services. The bride price, in pre-colonial Africa was never in the form of currency but rather in the nature of livestock, agricultural commodities, even in the form of work provided by the groom. This bride price was also designed to ensure good treatment of the bride and to provide for the surety of marital expectations. In some cases, an impotent, sterile, or unfaithful husband could lose his wife—and his bride price upon discovery.[21]

Sexual Deviations

Abnormal sexual practices could be the very esoteric definition of an African tribe. For example, incest could diverge widely from the American definition of this practice. Whereas many American states define marriages between first cousins as incest, thereby nullifying the legitimacy of such a marriage, an African tribe might actually require such a marriage. Most African tribes, today and centuries ago, traced ancestry only through one side of a person's parentage. If descent was traced only through the father's side of the family, a son or daughter was not related to the mother's family members. Therefore, individuals classified as cousins in Western society were unrelated in many African cultures. Marriages or carnal relations were typically prohibited between parents and children, brother and sister. There has been speculation about brother-sister marriages in ancient Egypt. The penalties for violation of the incest taboo, however it is defined, was severe and included expulsion from the tribe, enslavement, and death.[22]

Prostitution, while widespread in contemporary Africa, is regarded as rare in the sixteenth century. Being a prostitute is one of the world's oldest professions and may have existed among some of the nomadic tribes. Because tribes provided for the sexual relief of its members, prostitution rarely existed because it was not necessary. Where prostitution was practiced, it was generally sacred or ritual prostitution where women offered themselves up for sexual services as part of a ceremony. These "sacred" prostitutes were frequently part of fertility rites, which had the power to make women fertile.[23]

Adultery can elicit the harshest penalty when prohibited by tribal law. Yet, it takes on the character of a legalized institution among some tribes. We have already mentioned wife lending in some of them. How married women can take lovers if their husbands are impotent or sterile. In some tribes, men make presents to the husband—or work for him—in exchange for his wife's sexual favors. Where the wife engages in overt sexual activity with the knowledge of her husband, the resulting children are considered his. Where adultery is not sanctioned, it is often punished more harshly if the woman is of a higher status or the wife of a chief. Whereas punishment, in the form of banishment, castration, enslavement, and death, was meted out to both men and women, the harshest punishment was reserved for women. Among the punishments was being exhibited completely naked to public view while a vaginal washing was performed. Another example was the mutilation of the female sexual organs. One tribe punished an adulteress by cutting her skin in parallel strips with a knife, then rubbing pepper into the wounds. For men the punishment was as mild as compensating the husband by providing him with a gift or paying a fine.[24]

The act of rape was regarded as very rare in African society. It was widely viewed as a serious offense because it is a crime against property. Since most women were married, the husband had to be compensated in some way. When rape did occur, a typical punishment was castration of the offender. When slavery still existed, as it did in pre-colonial Africa, the punishment might be enslavement without a chance of ever regaining one's freedom. It must be noted that these harsh penalties were reserved for the rape of women in their tribe. Group rape often occurred in an institutionalized way when tribes made raids of their enemies and made away with the female members. After being raped, it was typical to sell them into slavery.[25]

Another form of rape was between that of Englishmen and African women. The early reports of European travelers were of the sexual aggressiveness of African women. There are descriptions of "hot constitution" ladies possessed of a "temper hot and lascivious, making no scruple to prostitute themselves to the Europeans for a very slender profit, so great is their inclination to white men."[26] Such descriptions of self-importance and reverence masked the fact that African women were wantonly raped by European travelers and their colonial descendents.[27] Granted, in pre-colonial Africa, they were greatly outnumbered by Black Africans. Yet, they had access to women captured by raiding parties. Once they colonized the Africans, many women were raped or forced to become concubines. As we now know, the mantle of a religious façade has not prevented men from giving into their sexual impulses. Under colonial administrations, the Europeans controlled the dispensation of justice. Certainly, we realize that English slave traders and slave owners sexually exploited female slaves on the passage to the new world and afterwards.

Just how much sexual deviation existed among Africans is unknown. The penalties for violation of a tribe's moral code were so severe as to discourage all but a few from engaging in forbidden sexual behavior. Sometimes the worst penalty was not death, castration, or enslavement. It was ostracism. Offenders had to publicly acknowledge their sin and were often scorned by other tribal members. Banishment from the tribe was also to be avoided since it left the individual on his own since other tribes would not accept into their fold unrelated individuals. Of course, one tribe's sin could be sanctioned behavior in another tribe. While the punishments were severe, the sex drive is so powerful that there will always be individuals who will violate a society's code of behavior.

As for the differences between African and European sexual behavior, it was mostly a matter of time and place. Other than the nudity they adopted in response to the tropical climate in which they lived, Europeans had engaged in similar behavior in the past and were to indulge in it in the future.[28] Even such practices as wife lending were confined to only a few tribes and restricted to age grade men or brothers. Chances are that it was less prevalent than our current practice of group sex since it was under the control of their community. One might easily defend the nudity found among African peoples as a rational adaptation to their physical environment. Breasts were not a sex symbol to them and massive nudity meant little when sexual activity was under community control. Africans saw no reason to see sex as a sin shrouded in secrecy. That view has led to hypocrisy and mental aberrations where it still exists. Where a people has been allowed personal and political freedom, as in twenty-first-century America, few have elected to suppress their sexual instincts for long.

Into Africa

From the sixteenth century to the present date, African sexuality was shaped by outside forces. Islam was one of them as their mission to proselytize impacted on traditional sexual values. It was more successful than Christianity since its religious values accepted polygamy while Christianity did not. Still, it was a conservative force especially with its doctrine on the role of women. Despite being in a very male dominated society, African women had more sexual freedom than did their European counterparts in the early part of Islamic and Christian influence. The Christian missionaries attempted to suppress existing beliefs and practices while overturning traditional values of morality. Their puritanical values would be deemed unhealthy by today's American standards, even among mainstream religious institutions. In most cases, the Africans had more healthy sexual codes and practices while European religions did everything they could to suppress natural sexual impulses that had been functional for centuries.

The impact of European colonialism was mixed in the area of sexuality. The Europeans subverted African institutions and robbed the continent of its vast natural resources. However, some of its harsh punishment for violations of its moral code, by the Africans, needed legal correction. Punishment of death, castration, and enslavement were way out of line with current legal prescriptions. We might note that equally harsh penalties existed during the earlier period of American history. Some have complained that, in some cultures, the punishment is too lenient. For example, the crime of rape incurred a fine of ten dollars, paid to the husband of the victim in some tribes. Despite the healthy attitudes Africans had toward the human body, one is not likely to see any nudity among African natives in urban centers today.[29]

In twenty-first-century Africa, the commonality of diverse African societies regulating sexual behavior by the customs of the various tribal groupings no longer exists. According to one native scholar:

> This belief might have been true once for Nigeria. Cultural taboo, strict regulation of sexual behavior and social disapproval can be said to have very little or no influence on the sexual behavior pattern, particularly in western and eastern Nigeria. There is very little sex regulation despite taboos in these areas of Nigeria. There might still be in some isolated areas, or among some sub cultural groups a restraining factor such as "importance of purity" before marriage. However, this is fast dying out, especially as a criterion for wedlock.[30]

The reasons for this change are the same for other parts of the world undergoing significant social change. Poverty, a desire for more individual freedom, greater cultural and social amenities and a long draught have driven millions from the rural areas into the cities, where tribal groupings have no means to enforce their regulations and customs. Military dictatorship and civil wars have weakened the power of government to enforce what laws that do exist.

Many of these problems are a residual effect of European colonialism. Europeans divided up the parts of Africa without regard to tribal identity and placed different, often hostile, tribes in the same nation state. For decades, perhaps centuries, Africans will be paying the price for the intervention and plunder of their continent by these fair-skinned foreigners.

When an African scholar surveyed the sex habits of Nigerian university students, he discovered 66 percent of them had engaged in premarital sexual activity. Only 18 percent of them had their first premarital sexual experience by the age of sixteen and 66 percent when they were between twenty-two and twenty-seven years of age. Moreover, his percentage included married respondents. Only 15 percent had more than two sexual partners in the last six months, with younger students and males more likely to fall into that category. It was discovered that very religious students did not differ in their premarital sexual experience than less religious students. While the differences in his sampling methods make comparisons with similar Americans difficult, on the surface it renders African university students as more conservative.[31]

Given the current United Nations estimate, that as many as twenty-eight million adult Africans are infected with HIV, the virus that causes AIDS, are Africans now that sexually permissive?[32] First, estimates are often nothing more than guesses, educated and uneducated. We only know that a large number of AIDS cases have been diagnosed on that continent. Although labeled as caused by heterosexual intercourse, the stigma attached to being gay in Africa leads to few men willing to admit to their homosexuality. Unsanitary medical instruments and techniques may be the cause of a number of cases. Others may be caused by men having sex with prostitutes, women who sell their body due to poverty. A low percentage of men using condoms may account for the rest. Overall, it is likely that poverty is more of a factor in the number of AIDS cases than the sexual promiscuity of Africans.

For our purpose, we were interested in the sexual values and practices that African natives had when enslaved and brought to the United States in the sixteenth century. We know that Africa had a diverse spectrum of sexual behavior, ranging from the very restrictive to the permissive. Whatever their sexual pattern extant, it was under strict tribal and community control. That was one common strand for all African peoples. Sexuality was not, in general, regarded as a sin or as something to be determined by a supreme being. In contrast to the Puritans of America, who felt the ideal state for humankind was celibacy, in retrospect the Africans were trailblazers for a sexual freedom that most Americans today embrace. That was to change when they were brought in chains to the shores of America.

Notes

1. Joane Nagel, *Race, Ethnicity, and Sexuality: Intimate Intersections, Forbidden Frontiers*. New York: Oxford University Press, 2003, p. 96.

2. E. Franklin Frazier, "Negro, Sex Life of the African and American" in *The Encyclopaedia of Sexual Behavior*, ed. Albert Ellis and Albert Arbanel. New York: Hawthorn Books, 1967, p. 769.

3. Benjamin Bowser, "African American Culture and Sexuality: Historic Background." Unpublished paper, 1992.

4. Alan P. Merriam, "Aspects of Sexual Behavior among the Bala" (Basongye) in *Human Sexual Behavior*, ed. Donald S. Marshall and Robert C. Suggs. New York: Basic Books, 1971, pp. 71–102.

5. Boris De Rachewiltz, *Black Eros: Sexual Customs of Africa from Prehistory to the Present Day*. New York: Lyle Stuart, 1964, pp. 137–138. An excellent source since its purpose was to describe behavior uninfluenced by outside sources.

6. Marc Lacey, "Kenyans Get the Scoop on President's Polygamy." *San Francisco Chronicle*, December 18, 2003, p. D6.

7. Rachewiltz, *op. cit.* pp. 240–246.

8. Lacey, *loc. cit.*

9. Bowser.

10. Rachewiltz, *op. cit.* pp. 251–266.

11. Nancy Ramsey, "In Africa, Girls Fight a Painful Tradition." *New York Times*, January 3, 2004, p. A29.

12. Harold K. Schneider, "Romantic Love among the Turu" in *Human Sexual Behavior, Variations in the Ethnographic Spectrum. Op. cit.* p. 62.

13. "Appeals Court Acquits Nigerian Mother Sentenced to Death by Stoning." *Jet Magazine*, December 13, 2003. pp. 46–47.

14. Rachewiltz, *op. cit.* pp. 266.

15. *Ibid.* pp. 267–269.

16. Elizabeth Bryant, "No Gay Tolerance in Africa's Anglican Church: Growing Rebellion against Liberal Doctrines of U.S." *San Francisco Chronicle*, January 14, 2004, p. PA-12.

17. Rachewiltz, *op. cit.* pp. 152–162.

18. *Ibid.* pp. 162–170.

19. *Ibid.* pp. 280–283.

20. Merriam, *op. cit.* pp. 84–85.

21. Rachewiltz, *op. cit.* pp. 240–251.

22. *Ibid.* pp. 21–33, 244–245.

23. *Ibid.* pp. 279–280.

24. Merriam, *op. cit.* pp. 88–89, Rachewiltz, pp. 266–269.

25. Merriam, *op. cit.* p. 98.

26. Winthrop D. Jordan, *White over Black: American Attitudes toward the Negro; 1550–1812*. Baltimore: Pelican Books, 1969, p. 35.

27. *Ibid. Loc. cit.*

28. G. Rattray Taylor, *Sex in History: Society's Changing Attitudes to Sex throughout the Ages.* New York: Ballantine Books, 1954.

29. Merriam, *op. cit.* p. 98.

30. Femi Soyinka, "Sexual Behavior among University Students in Nigeria," *Archives of Sex Behavior.* January 1979, Vol. 8 p. 15–26.

31. *Ibid.*

32. Edward Epstein, "Groups Fighting AIDS in Africa Call for Funding Increase." *San Francisco Chronicle*, January 14, 2004, p. A-7.

~

CHAPTER TWO

The Myth of Black Sexual Superiority

Basic to any adequate understanding of Black sexuality is an understanding of the historical development of Black life in this country. Before Blacks were enslaved in North America, their sexual behavior was under strict family and community control, although Africa is too large a continent to permit the making of sweeping generalizations about sexual behavior there. In some cultures, the restraint was so great that it was the custom to tie up the female vagina until marriage, a kind of modified form of chastity belt. In other African societies, some institutionalized forms of premarital sex relations were permitted. Thus, it is not possible to judge whether the African experience provided a strict or a permissive culture, but only that there were many variations in sexual values and behavior, and that all sexual practices were under the control of the kinship group or the community.[1]

When Blacks were brought to this country, one of the first things that happened was the breakdown of that community and family control. For instance, while there were over six hundred tribal groupings in Africa, their members were put aboard slave ships without regard to tribal distinctions. Because they came from different and sometimes antagonistic tribal groups, there was no particular respect shown by members of one group for the sexual values of another tribal group. The consequence was the incipient breakdown of all sexual controls. The moral basis for restraint on sexual behavior began to change because of the constant infusion of groups from different tribes that did not respect the sexual values of other tribes.

While the African's sexual behavior was permissive vis-à-vis European sexual patterns, it was at least under group control. But under slavery that control was eliminated and the only restraint was lack of desire. In the beginning of the slavery era, however, the shortage of Black women imposed some restraints on the Afro-American's sexual impulse. After 1840, when the sex ratio of the slave population grew more equal, there were few if any restraints on the satisfaction of the slave's sexual desires. There are reports of male slaves seizing the closest female slave and satisfying their sexual appetites.[2]

Sexual promiscuity and exploitation were strongly encouraged by some slave masters. The practice of using virile Black males to sire children by a number of female slaves indicates that many slaveholders were more interested in the fertility of their slaves than in their moral conduct. In fact, the function of female slaves was to breed additional slaves, who would become organic property for the slave-owning class.

Predictably, the slave woman was also subject to the carnal desires of the slave master and his overseers. She was used and abused, sexually, by many white males on the plantation. Where there may have been some slave women who submitted voluntarily to the slave master's sexual advances, there is sufficient historical evidence to show that many of them were compelled to enter into various sexual associations with white males because of their captive status. The American slaveholder's sexual domination never lost its openly terrorist character.

There is little substance to the theory that the Black woman was the aggressor in her sexual relations with the slave master. Such a supposition ignores the type of existence the female slave led. As a slave, she had no protection from the sexual aggressions of salacious white men. She realized that the only recourse available to her was a violent death. As one historian has noted, if the slave woman submitted it was only under coercion. Indeed, some miscegenation was little more than rape, though no such offense against a slave woman was recognized in law.[3]

Slave women were deprived of any protection against the sexual assaults of white males. Under slavery, Blacks were not permitted to be witnesses against whites in a court of law. There were no laws to protect the Black woman from assaults upon her body. For example, the North Carolina Supreme Court ruled in the nineteenth century that no white male could be convicted for fornication with a slave woman. The North Carolina Constitutional Convention of 1835 declared that any white man might go to the house of a *free* Black, mistreat and abuse him, and commit any outrage upon his family. If a white person did not witness the act, no legal remedies were available.[4]

The cultural belief about the Black female's sexuality emerged out of the experience of slavery. The sexual availability of slave women allowed white men to put white women on a pedestal, to be seen as the goddesses of virtue. In a way, this became a self-fulfilling prophecy. White women were held aloof from the world of lust and passion and in many cases became more inhibited emotionally, sexually, and intellectually because of the oppressive presence of slavery. Consequently, while the white woman's experiences and status inhibited sexual expression, the Black woman's encouraged it.

While the Euro-American concept of Black female sexuality developed out of the peculiar conditions of slavery, the Black female's sexual morality was also shaped by this experience. Once she accepted the fact that she did not have control over her body, the importance of virginity to her was considerably reduced. The Black woman came to look upon herself as the South viewed and treated her. In fact, she had no other morality by which to shape her womanhood.

The end of slavery did not give the Black woman any greater right to sexual integrity. What slavery began, racism and economic exploitation continued. In the post-bellum South, Black women were still at the mercy of the carnal desires of white men. According to W. J. Cash, Black women were forced to give up their bodies like animals to white men at random.[5] Others have noted that many Southern white men had their first sexual experience with Black women. In some cases, the use of Black women as sexual objects served to maintain the double standard of sexual conduct in the white South. Many white men did not have sexual relations with white women until they married. Some Southern white men were known to jokingly remark that until they married they did not know that *white* women were capable of sexual intercourse.[6]

It was protection of the sexual purity of white women that partially justified the erection of racially segregated institutions in the South. The Southern white man assumed that Black men have a strong desire for intermarriage and that white women would be open to proposals from Black males if they were not guarded from meeting with them on an equal level. As Jessie Bernard writes, "The white world's insistence on keeping Negro men walled up in the concentration camp (of the ghetto) was motivated in large part by its fear of their sexuality."[7]

Meanwhile, the Black woman in the South was left without any protection against the sexual assaults of white men. The Black man could not protect her unless he was prepared to lose his life in her defense. This does not mean that he did not try. After emancipation when the marriages of Black women were legally recognized, Black men began to demand that Black women be treated with respect and courtesy and that white men cease their seduction and rape of Black womanhood. In 1874 one Black congressman declared, "We want more protection from the whites invading our homes and destroying the virtue of our women than they from us."[8]

The sexual exploitation of Black women was not always accompanied by violence. White men were able to use the economic deprivation of Black women to their sexual advantage. The sexual exploitation of Black women who worked as domestic servants is legendary. Throughout the South, white men were able to sexually use Black women in the course of the woman's employment, or in the course of their seeking employment. One such example of the white male's economic advantage serving sexual ends is reported by John Howard Griffin. He quoted the following revelations of a white employer:

> He told me how all of the white men in the region crave colored girls. He said he hired a lot of them both for housework and his business. And I guarantee you, I've had it in every one of them before they get on the payroll.
> "Surely some refuse," I suggested cautiously. "Not if they want to eat-feed their kids," he snorted. "If they don't put out, they don't get the job."[9]

It is easy to understand why there failed to emerge in the Black culture the rigid sexual regulations so prevalent in the dominant American society. As the violation of her body became routine, the Black woman could not value that which was not available to her—virginity. She has been sexually used by men of both races. It has been noted that after emancipation, many Black men had a casual sexual life. Many of them wandered from town to town, seeking employment. Frequently, they were taken in by lonely women engaged in domestic service who were sympathetic to their hard luck stories of life on the road. Once their sexual hunger was satisfied, these Black men took to the road again.[10]

Only among the middle-class group did Black women have much protection against the unwelcomed sexual advances of white men. Middle-class Black males preferred that their wives stay at home. This middle-class element in the Black population was very conscious of its unique position in relation to the masses of Black folk. Contrary to their lower-class brethren, they placed an exaggerated emphasis upon moral conduct and developed a puritanical restraint in contrast to the free and more liberated sexual behavior of the dominant Black population. While the legacy of slavery and the effect of white racism strongly influence the sexual practices of Black women, there are many other social forces that impinge on the sexuality of Black women. Among these forces is religion.[11]

Again, while it is difficult to generalize about African religions, it was generally the case that, unlike American society where religious values influence sexual values, in Africa violations of a group's sexual mores were considered to be against individuals and not against God, consequently the influence of religious values on the sexual behavior of Blacks was minimal. In the United States, however, the role of Black religion has often been more expressive than instrumental, the Black churches being more oriented toward allowing members to release tensions from the effects of oppression, racial discrimination, and so on, than toward setting moral standards for their constituencies. This does not mean that Black churches have not emphasized moral restraint and encouraged chastity, at least for women, before marriage. It simply means that not much emphasis has been placed on this as in white churches, and of course Blacks have not grown up with the puritanical background of most whites in this country. There are some exceptions in the Black community, especially among middle-class religions, where there is more stress on moral purity before marriage. There are also exceptions in certain fundamentalist sects such as the Seventh-Day Adventists, Jehovah's Witnesses, and the Nation of Islam. But, all in all, it can be said that the Black churches have not played as much of a prohibitory role in the premarital and extramarital sexual relations among the Black population as have the white churches among whites.[12]

However, the Church served as a guiding force on the morals of many families and their members. For example, many Black churches (after slavery) punished women for illegitimacy (by expulsion) and made every effort to elevate the position of the families. In communities where the Church was supported by the families with traditions of regular family life, the Church reflected the character of its constituents, and in turn controlled to some extent their behavior. But among impoverished peasants scattered over Southern plantations, the Church was only a poorly organized expression of weak community conscience. If the family unit was strong, the Church was an important controlling and directive moral force.[13]

Slavery and Black Male Sexuality

Sexual Abuse was not confined to Black female slaves. The males were treated as studs, shuffled from plantation to plantation to mate with slave women and produce children who would also be legally defined as slaves. The first African males had come to the Americas as indentured servants, a period of servitude also incurred by White men and women in the early colonial period. Since almost all the Africans were males, their only source of companionship was Euro-American female servants and Indian women. Many of these liaisons ended in marriage and produced children. The practice became widespread enough, in a region with a shortage of Euro-American women, that laws were passed to prevent it and indentured servitude was ended. Instead, slavery was installed and soon became exclusively associated with the dark-skinned Africans.[14]

In order to avoid miscegenation between African men and Euro-American women, more women were imported from Africa in order to prevent it and discourage male slave rebellions and runaways. Despite numerous stories of slave families torn asunder by insensitive or bankrupt slaveholders, advocates of an efficient system of slavery assumed slaves embedded in intact families made for a more docile male slave. For Euro-American women who continued a sexual association with African males, the stakes were raised higher. The State of Maryland passed a law subjecting Euro-American women themselves to a slave status for sexual transgressions with a male slave. Some particularly greedy slave owners actually encouraged their male slaves to rape English servant women in order to force them into slavery.[15]

The use of male slaves as studs was not a position of privilege. It meant not knowing their children in many cases and having no rights in them. Since slaves were defined as property, they were denied the right to a legal marriage. However, many slave owners recognized stable relationships among slave couples because it was to their advantage to do so. Still the male slave, coming from a male dominated society, was denied the essential elements of manhood. Rations were often in the mother's name and most means of subsistence were supplied the slaves by their owners. Even the children were under the control of their mother or owner.[16]

Many historians today believe, based on a variety of records and slave narratives, that the slaves constructed their own form of marriage, that a moral code existed in slave society, and that stability and faithfulness characterized those marriages. Some slave marriages could be terminated by one partner because of the adulterous behavior by the other partner suggests that African morality was transplanted to the Americas. Churches for Black slaves existed in many of the slave states, in towns, and on plantations. These churches served to reinforce morality among the slaves and members could be expelled for sins such as dancing. Many male slaves demonstrated their commitments to their families by remaining on their plantations the length of their slave marriages and their desire to legalize those marriages when slavery ended.[17]

Wherever men have power over women, who are not members of their own group, sexual abuse has been massive. The male slave was also a victim of the wanton rape of his wife and daughter by Euro-American men in the

South. Those rapes served to humiliate the men of slave society. He was sym-bolically castrated and humbled when he could not do anything to defend his wife and daughter from the sexual abuse of Euro-American men. It placed the male slave at a distinct disadvantage, as anything involving sex can do, as the female slaves were placed in a preferred position for prestige and train-ing. Some have suggested that many slave women used their position in or-der to protect their children and the Afro-American men they were com-mitted to.[18]

For years, the speculation by Frazier and others that Black male slaves failed to develop the institutional roles of husband and father dominated the literature. This supposition was based on the fact that the conventional en-actment of those roles was not available to him.[19] This argument was ex-tended to the twentieth century to explain the higher rates of out-of-wedlock births and single parent households amongst Black Americans.[20] However, it was never conclusively "proven" that his role in the slave family was biolog-ical instead of sociological. Historians were divided over the matter and no absolute evidence exists to document either point of view. What quantitative data uncovered did reveal is that between 1880 and 1925 the majority of Blacks of all social classes belonged to nuclear families. Most births were in wedlock and an overwhelming majority of Black women was reported as ever married around the turn of the twentieth century.[21]

The view that Blacks were sexually promiscuous after slavery ended pre-vailed in American literature and folklore. The historian, Arthur W. Cal-houn asserted, "At the opening of the twentieth century, the point where the Negro American was furthest behind modern civilization was in his sexual mores. Immodesty, unbridled sexuality, obscenity, social indifference to pu-rity were prevalent characteristics."[22] Whereas Calhoun can be faulted for al-lowing his Caucasian membership to blind him to the variety of sexual pat-terns extant among Black Americans, seeing them as a monolithic group, W. E. B. Du Bois could not claim the same exemption. While repeating the same allegation as Calhoun, he did write, "this is what slavery meant, and no amount of kindliness in individual owners could save the system from its deadly work of disintegrating the ancient Negro home and putting but a poor substitute in its place."[23]

Whereas both men were alive to observe behavior, at least on the surface, around the turn of the twentieth century and I was not. It does strike me as strange that the racial group of males who removed people from their land, forced them to work without pay, tore asunder their families, raped their women, sold their Mulatto daughters to others and lynched any Black male who dare fancy a Euro-American woman, should be considered the standard of civilization as we know it.[24] Does the label of clueless on the meaning of "civilization" apply here? Do those who have sex outside wedlock, produced offspring without a marriage certificate, have more than one sexual partner deserve to be categorized as uncivilized whereas the ones committing and condoning the most barbaric practices be honored and revered. How many Americans of Generation Y will meet the standards of civilization in their lifetime? And, will future generations condemn them as a nation of barbarians?

There is a body of literature questioning the motives of Euro-American males who participated in the character assassination of Afro-Americans and their sexual habits. Speculation is rampant about the Black mammy or nursemaid for the sexual preferences and erotic dreams of Euro-American males. Some have claimed he has shown an almost unnatural interest in Black males and their genitals. Male slaves were often shown naked at auction and their genitals examined before purchase. When the thousands of Blacks were lynched for alleged sexual oppression against Euro-American women in the early twentieth century, their genitals were severed from their body. This preoccupation with Black male genitalia is seen as a manifestation of the Euro-American males' sexual jealousy of the Black male.[25] In his liberated sexuality, he represents the savage instinct to many, the animal that must be controlled lest he introduce the European female to a world the Euro-American male cannot compete with under fair conditions.

Racism and Sexuality

One needs a deep understanding of the importance of sex in the United States in order to see the interrelationship of sex and racism in American society. In a society where white sexuality had been repressed, the imagined sexual power of the Black male poses a serious threat. According to Hernton:

> There is in the psyche of the racist an inordinate disposition for sexual atrocity. He sees in the Negro the essence of his own sexuality, that is, those qualities that he wishes for but fears he does not possess. Symbolically, the Negro at once affirms and negates the white man's sense of sexual security. . . . Contrary to what is claimed, it is not the white woman who is dear to the racist. It is not even the Black woman toward whom his real sexual rage is directed. It is the Black man who is sacred to the racist. And this is why he must castrate him.[26]

The May 1974 issue of the SIECUS Report included ten important position statements adopted by the SIECUS Board of Directors. This statement concerning sex and racism, reads as follows:

It is the position of SIECUS that:

In any efforts aimed at identifying and improving a society's attitudes and understanding about racism, distortions of facts which are sexual in nature must be recognized and combated as such.

Racism is frequently manifested by distorted views of the sexuality of other ethnic groups, creating barriers to interpersonal relationships. Members of the stereotyped groups may themselves come to believe these racist sexual myths, so that the sexual self-concepts of both racist and victim are distorted, and they are denied the opportunity to understand, appreciate, and enjoy the sexuality to which all human beings are entitled.[27]

Some years ago, Calvin Hernton wrote that the race problem is inextricably connected with sex.[28] He cited the finding by Gunnar Myrdal that white Southerners thought that what Blacks wanted most was intermarriage and sexual intercourse with whites.[29] Hernton may have overstated his case since racism had a strong economic and psychological base that has kept the specter of racism alive long after the barriers to interracial sex and marriage were dropped. Yet, the relationship between sex and racism is not a spurious or insignificant one. Even among the most enlightened whites, the association of Blacks with an organic hypersexuality and hence, immorality lingers on in their collective consciousness. As with many cultural images of a group there is some validity to the stereotype of Black sexual potency, if for no other reason than the self-fulfilling prophecy: that if a group be repetitively treated or regarded in a certain way, its members eventually come to see themselves as others view them.

The image of Blacks as hypersexual beings is deeply rooted in American history, culture, and religion and is too complex to delineate here. In the early part of the twentieth century, respected scholars imputed a genetic basis to the alleged hotter sexual passions and richer fertility of the Black population. Subsequent research has done little to invalidate the earlier generalizations about Black sexual drives or to illuminate the sociocultural forces that differentiate between Black and white sexual behaviors. The result has served to foster and reinforce white stereotypes about Black immorality and hypersexuality. Such false images serve to fuel the fears of those whites who remain psychologically wedded to America's puritanical view of sexuality, and to galvanize their resistance to Black demands for equal opportunity in American life.

It can be stated with certainty that the past and present attitudes about Black sexual behavior, held by Euro-Americans is that they are morally loose people. Originating among the Europeans who observed the sexual codes of

Africans, it was an attitude perpetuated by their own actions in denying slaves the right to marry and mating them as they would their livestock. Wherever Black sexuality was discussed in the academic literature, the notion of them as a permissive, immoral group was reinforced. As recently as the 1990s, a scholar named J. Philippe Rushton was allowed a forum to promote his views of Afro-American sexual promiscuity as caused by genetic traits.[30] Some years ago, the leading Black sexologist collected sexual stereotypes from a diverse group of Black and white women, lay and professional groups represented. In the areas of sexual anatomy attitudes and values, she identified 27 Black sexual stereotypes. In general, she found that Blacks were viewed as having the most undesirable traits involved in these stereotypes.[31]

Stereotypes, by their very nature, are generalizations about a category of people that ignore individual variations within the group. Thus, all Black women are perceived as sensuous, permissive, and promiscuous. The men are animalistic, lust after white women, frequently desire sex, are unfaithful in their marriages, and do not believe in the institution of marriage. Given that the racial differences in sexual attitudes and behavior have really narrowed by the twenty-first century makes the persistence of these sexual stereotypes all the more puzzling. What remains are differences of degree not of kind. Some of them can be refuted by available statistical data; the few significant differences that remain may be largely of interest to prurient minds. Perhaps their greatest consequence is to present a rationalization for the persistence of racial inequities in the United States.

An Examination of Sexual Superiority

Three decades ago, this writer raised the question: Are Blacks sexually superior? My answer at that time was "if sexual superiority means to enjoy the pleasures of sexual congress without feelings of guilt and fear, freed from the restraints of white Puritanism, the answer must be in the affirmative."[32] In the intervening years, there has been a dramatic increase in the frequency with which most white Americans engage in various sexual activities and in the number of persons who include formerly rare or forbidden techniques in their sexual repertoires. These changes have given rise to the need to reexamine the question of Black sexual superiority in light of what is regarded as the white sexual revolution.

A review of the past record of white beliefs about Black sexuality casts in bold belief the view that "for the majority of white men, the Negro represents the sexual instinct (in its raw state)." As long ago as the sixteenth-century, Englishmen were imputing to Africans an unrestrained lustfulness. Certainly, in comparison to European dictums about chastity being the best state for men and their *norms*, that women should not enjoy sex under any circumstances, Africans represented the sexuality of beasts and the bestiality of sex. History, however, tells us that Europeans were not always a puritanical culture.[33] Some claim that the beginning of human society (i.e., white society) was characterized by unrestrained sexual relations between man and woman, father and daughter, mother and son. Only with the development of private property, when men needed proof of paternity in order to will their resources to the right heir, was sexual exclusivity for women only brought into existence and mostly among the propertied classes.[34]

Within the African continent, at least south of the Sahara, their view, in general, of sex was directed toward both physiological and psychological adjustment. Tribal values on sexual behavior were strongly woven into their social structure and the first instinctive manifestations of sexuality were conditioned by their mores and environment. Public rituals often existed to confirm the appropriate sexual elements and remove the improper ones. Whereas Europeans saw sex as inherently sinful, the African ethos was that breaches of Tribal sexual law are offenses against individuals and social groups, not against God. The African was concerned with crime and not with sin. Conversely, it is impossible to generalize about African sexual permissiveness since there were large numbers of them who imposed harsh penalties on women who did not enter the conjugal state as virgins as well as many who allowed youth to satisfy sexual desires before marriage.[35]

It was with these diverse sexual values that Africans were brought to this country as slaves. There is sufficient evidence in the form of slave narratives, the slaveholders' own records, and the considerably lighter hue of Afro-Americans that those tribal norms were contravened on a massive scale, whenever possible and by bondsmen, overseer, and slave master alike. However, within the slave quarters, there were boundaries imposed on sexual activity among its inhabitants. A relationship between one man and a woman was respected and whenever possible, they confined their sexual relationships to each other.[36]

After slavery ended, Afro-Americans probably did have a more permissive sexual code than many Euro-Americans, but that fact has to be placed in the proper historical context. In accordance with Freudian theory, we can assume that the sexual drive exists in all individuals and has to be expressed in some form.[37] Historically, males in this culture have been allowed unrestrained libidinal expression. It is women on whom the greatest restraints have been placed, and bourgeois women at that. Even among working-class white women, the norm of chastity has been honored more in the breach than in its observance. A major reason for the class difference is the greater use of economic resources by the bourgeois male to exact sexual chastity from the women in his class. Where there is no exchange value of sex for material reward, the libido thrives in a more liberated way.

Thus, because the Black masses enjoyed a more healthy sexual equality than was possible for whites in the post-bellum era, a more permissive sexual code developed. Moreover, some of the controls on Euro-American sexuality did not exist in the same degree among Afro-Americans. The puritanical exhortations of organized religion served to effectively check much of the Euro-American's sexuality while the Black church functioned more as a tension reducing institution and eschewed monitoring the moral standards of its parishioners. Black males did not classify women into bad and good groups on that basis of their virginal status. White men did make these distinctions and women were eligible for the respectability of marriage according to their classification in our group or the other. During an epoch in which the majority of white women were economically dependent on their men, this was an effective censor of their sexuality. Black women, in the main, were more economically and psychologically independent.

What we will discover is that Blacks are more liberal in some sexual areas and more conservative in others, not enough to make any moral distinction. The percentage of Black women who have children out of wedlock is not a function of their sexual morality as much as it can be attributed to a complex of demographic, economic, and social forces. As for the sexual superiority question, no person has the answer. There is neither definitive measurement of what constitutes sexual superiority nor any consensus if one were attempted. It is assumed that most men achieve some type of physical relief from their sexual activity. In the case of women, their satisfaction with their sex lives can be as much mental as physical, or a combination of both. Certainly, orgasms cannot be the sole measurement of sexual satisfaction for women. Using their electronic hookups, Masters and Johnson found that some women in their research were not even aware that they had an orgasm.[38]

The general rule is that female sexual satisfaction is a function of male sexual abilities. However, sexual satisfaction studies are probably no more reliable than marital satisfaction research. The response may depend on when she is asked and what social class she belongs to, in turn impacting her life satisfaction based on her access to money and status. Given these reservations, we can note that the earlier studies revealed Black women to rate sex as important to their marriage and it was in the area of "love" and sex that Black wives rated their husbands the highest. Those studies were largely conducted in the 1960s and subsequent research shows a large number of Black women not that satisfied with their sex lives.[39]

One researcher who extensively investigated all aspects of Black female sexuality was Gail Wyatt, the nation's foremost Black sex researcher. She found that sexual communication is critical to sexual satisfaction for Afro-American women. By communication, she means a woman and her partner conveying their sexual needs verbally and nonverbally. She found that communication was maximized when the woman actively initiated sex. Another essential element in their sexual satisfaction was their attitudes about sex. Women who perceived sex as unpleasant/painful, unsure if sex was right or wrong, who felt guilty about it, or were fearful of the consequences of sexual activity were less satisfied with their sexual relationships. In general, her sample's respondents were satisfied, had positive feelings, were highly orgasmic, and expressed their sexual needs.[40]

In what is likely the most extensive sexual survey since the Kinsey report, which includes Blacks, a slightly different picture emerges. Overall, most women were satisfied with their sexual partners and achieved orgasms most of the time. However, compared to Euro-American (31 percent) women, almost a majority of Black women (45 percent) lacked interest in sex and a third of Black women were unable to achieve an orgasm in contrast to one-fourth of Euro-American women. About a third of Afro-American women did not find sex pleasurable whereas only a fifth of Euro-Americans did not like it. Perhaps their distaste for sexual interaction is the reason that Afro-American women, of the four major race/gender groups were most likely to have had no sexual partner in the year prior to the survey being taken. Still, it is incumbent of us to acknowledge they face a shortage of available Black men and seldom engage in sexual activity with non-Black males.[41]

Not only do Black women face a shortage of available men, of all race/sex groups, they are the most likely to have all their sexual experiences within their own race. Almost 20 percent of Black males have non-Black sexual partners, contributing further to the shortage of sexual partners for them, while only 3 percent of Black women have sexual partners who are not Black.[42] As for the high percentage of them expressing no interest in sex, that may be a function of their unhappiness with their partners in areas other than sex. Studies that have looked at marital happiness always find Black wives less satisfied with their spouses than white wives. A big reason is they do not have the same resources, have to work outside the home, and are forced to marry men with more undesirable traits than comparable white women.[43] Orlando Patterson, a sociologist at Harvard University claims that Black male-female relations are in a chronic state of crisis, a major source of instability in their union is the huge number of Black men who engage in extramarital sexual relations.[44]

One question that must be posed: What is the empirical basis of Black male sexual superiority? Contrary to prevailing folklore, it is not the size of his penis. According to research carried out by the Alfred Kinsey Institute at Indiana University, the majority of both white and Black penises measured in their sample were less than or equal to four and a half inches in the flaccid state and less than or equal to seven inches in their erect state. However, three times as many Black males had penises larger than seven inches in length in the erect state.[45] We might note that these measurements are based on self-reports of Black and white males. Furthermore, the Masters and Johnson report indicated no particular relationship between penis size and female sexual satisfaction except that induced by the psychological state of the female sexual partner.[46]

Perhaps we should look closer at male sexual performance as a factor in Black female dissatisfaction with their pleasure from sex. Ted McIlvenna, president of the Institute for Advanced Study of Human Sexuality, reports that he served on a government commission in the 1970s that looked at Black sexual behavior. What the commission found were a number of sexual problems arising from the substance abuse of Black men.[47] As we now know, the use of alcohol and drugs can retard sexual performance while releasing inhibitions. It can produce physiological side effects, particularly for men, that bring about reduced sexual capacities. Almost half the Black men in the extensive sex survey used alcohol before or during sex.[48]

As the Black population has aged, the men have developed numerous health problems that can impact sexual performance. When we speak of male sexual dysfunction, of a physical nature, it typically refers to premature ejaculation and erectile dysfunction. In the sex survey, Black men report that they were slightly more likely to experience such problems than Euro-American men were. When it comes to climaxing too early, that can be a matter of expectation or definition. If a man expects to last as long as thirty minutes, any time of ejaculation before that goal might be premature. Still the fact that Black males have considerably higher rates of hypertension, stroke, heart disease, prostate cancer, and diabetes than Euro-American males can have serious consequences for their sexual performance. At least the sex survey found men who were in poor health also reported those same sexual problems.[49]

Of course, male impotency and premature ejaculation can have as its basic cause sources that are more psychological. Anxiety about one's performance can be caused by a very aggressive female who often initiates sexual activity and is the more excited partner, establishing expectations that he fears cannot be met. One group of researchers found that Afro-American women were more likely to make independent decisions about the timing and type of sex.[50] Because he did not participate in the decision, he may feel powerless about his ability to perform under those conditions. One factor that contributed to her independent decision making was the greater likelihood that she did not live with her main sexual partner and the lower level of commitment produced decisions that are more independent.

Low self-esteem can be another contributing factor. A man who is married to a wife that earns more money or has a higher educational level can be rendered sexually impotent by feelings of inadequacy. Men can be turned off by their sexual partner due to her physical appearance, obesity, if she is cold and unresponsive, too demanding, etc. A major set of factors are physical fatigue and emotional stress for males. This is particularly true in an ongoing sexual relationship where the initial thrill of sex is gone.[51] Men, more than women, often prefer the newer and younger women to spark his interest. After all, compared to Euro-American males in the sex survey, a larger percentage of Black males claimed a nonpleasurable sexual experience, an inability to ejaculate, or a lack of interest in sex.[52]

Despite the various health problems and lack of sex interest among Blacks, there were only minor variations in the frequency of sexual activity by racial membership. Overall, young people who do not live together are more inclined to spend much time on sexual matters. In terms of frequency, married couples are more likely to have sex on a regular basis than unattached individuals are. They do not need to find a sexual partner since one is easily accessible in the same household. A free-floating single, particularly a man, must find a sexual partner in a physical environment with varying degrees of difficulty. Since a majority of adult Blacks are not married and living with a spouse, the single life is the context in which sex is played out. Not only are they unmarried but, compared to other racial groups, they are less likely to cohabit with anyone.[53]

One advantage of marriage/cohabitation is the greater ability to communicate about sexual problems or seek professional help. Free-floating singles typically abandon the relationship in the case of sexual incompatibility. In recent years, Black couples have sought therapy for a variety of sexual problems. A major problem is there are very few trained Black therapists and the Euro-American therapist may lack a proper cultural sensitivity that may be a factor in their sexual dysfunction. However, there are risks in an exclusively racial interpretation of a couple's sexual difficulties when they may be caused by the same psychological and physiological causes as occurs in couples of other races.[54]

As we have already noted, health problems are a big factor in Black male sexual dysfunction. This is particularly relevant to older Black men due to the greater preponderance of health issues for men over the age of fifty. Black women face their own problems associated with the aging process. One of the biggest will be menopause. As they age, their natural hormones erode and the sex drive diminishes for many of them. The lack of vaginal lubrication can make sexual intercourse very painful and the menopausal time of life can create problems of psychological adjustment for Black women during this sexual cycle of their life. In her best-selling book, "The Silent Passage," Gail Sheehy investigated menopause among Afro-American women and proclaimed that, compared to Euro-American women, they stand a greater chance of passing through menopause with no psychological problems. Sheehy's explanation was that Black women do not link their self-worth to their age or to how young they appear. Their sexuality, she felt, came from their spiritual strength that derived from the historical situation they previously faced.[55]

These same Black women continued to define themselves as sexually desirable no matter what their age. Since they were not put on a pedestal or pampered when they were younger, their prestige and self-esteem increased as they grew older. Observers point to the fact that anorexia is almost unknown among them, as evidenced by the categorization of 60 percent of Black females as overweight in the 1990s. Whether Afro-American males share their view of the middle-aged overweight women of his race as sexually desirable is unclear. Does it have any bearing on their interracial entanglements or the fact that a majority of Black women are not married or cohabiting with a man?

None of this critical analysis of Black sexuality should be allowed to overshadow the positive aspects of their sexual life. In the main Blacks continue to engage in and enjoy their sexual encounters. Part of the problem arises from the conflict of traditional values with new realities. And, for the bourgeoisie, they were not Black values. This does not mean that the Black sexual experience has been a bleak or negative one. For the most part sex has been the one haven they have had from the daily oppression of racial problems. With all its intrusions, the racial order did not enter their bedrooms.

It is not the sexual revolution but the new Black reality that commands our attention. For the first time in their history the majority of Black women, and large numbers of men, are and will remain unmarried. Perforce, their sexuality must be harnessed in such a way as to promote the meeting of this universal human need. Sex should be used as a means of communicating, not as an instrument of domination and control. Both men and women must cultivate modalities of healthy sexual expressions that will preserve their basic integrity and humanity. As for the question of Black sexual superiority, they do not need the label of sexually superior any more than they have heretofore needed the appellation of mentally inferior. Above all, they need a sexual ethos that will contribute to their unity as a people and that value system must serve all of the Black community.

Notes

1. Wilfred D. Hambly, "Africans, The Sex Life of" in *The Encyclopedia of Sexual Behavior* ed. Albert Ellis and Albert Arbanel. New York: Hawthorn, 1967, pp. 69–74.

2. E. Franklin Frazier, *The Negro Family in the United States*. Chicago: University of Chicago Press, 1966 p. 17.

3. Angela Y. Davis, "Rape, Racism, and the Myth of the Black Rapist" in *Women, Race, and Class*. New York: Vintage Books, 1981, pp. 172–200.

4. Joane Nagel, *Race, Ethnicity, and Sexuality: Intimate Intersections, Forbidden Frontiers*. New York: Oxford University Press, 2003, pp. 106–107.

5. W. J. Cash, *The Mind of the South*. New York: Vintage Books, 1960, p. 84.

6. John Dollard, *Caste & Class in a Southern Town*. Garden City, New York: Doubleday Anchor, 1957, p. 139.

7. Jessie Bernard, *Marriage and Family among Negroes*. Englewood Cliffs, New Jersey: Prentice-Hall, 1966, p. 175.

8. Maude Katz, "The Negro Woman and the Law." *Freedomways*, 1966, 22, No. 3, p. 283.

9. John Howard Griffin, *Black like Me*. New York: Signet, 1963, p. 100.

10. Frazier, *op. cit.* p. 214.

11. Dollard, *op. cit.* p. 147.

12. Orlando Patterson, *Rituals of Blood: Consequences of Slavery in Two American Centuries*. Washington, D.C.: C. vitas/Counterpoint 1998, pp. 118–119.

13. Frazier, *op. cit.*

14. David Eltis, *The Rise of African Slavery in the Americas*. New York: Cambridge University Press, 2000.

15. Kathy Russell, Midge Wilson, and Ronald Hall, *The Color Complex: The Politics of Skin Color Among African Americans*. New York: Doubleday Anchor, 1992, p. 13.

16. Eltis, *op. cit.*

17. Sterling Stuckey, *Slave Culture: Nationalist Theory and the Foundations of Black America*. New York, 1987.

18. Gerda Lerner, *The Majority Finds its Past*. New York: Oxford University Press, 1979, p. 72.

19. Frazier, *op. cit.*

20. Daniel P. Moynihan, *The Negro Family: The Case for National Action*. Washington D.C.: U.S. Government Printing Office, 1965.

21. Herbert Gutman, *The Black Family in Slavery and Freedom 1750–1925*. New York: Pantheon, 1976.

22. Arthur W. Calhoun, *A Social History of the American Family From Colonial Times to the Present*, Volume 3. Cleveland: Arthur H. Clark Company, 1919, p. 43.

23. W. E. B. Dubois, *The Negro American Family*. New York: The Negro University Press, 1969, p. 37.

24. Martha Hodes, *White Women, Black Men: Illicit Sex in the Nineteenth Century South*. New Haven: Yale University Press, 1997.

25. Sandra Gunning, *Race, Rape and Lynching: The Red Record of American Literature 1890–1913*. New York: Oxford University Press, 1996.

26. Calvin Hernton, *Sex and Racism in America*. New York: Doubleday, 1965.

27. Sex Information and Education Council of the U.S., *Siecus Report*. May 1974, Vol. 3, No. 5, p. 1.

28. Hernton, *op. cit.*

29. Gunnar Myrdal, *An American Dilemma*. New York: Harper and Bros., 1944, pp. 60–61.

30. J. Philippe Rushton, "Race Differences in Behavior: A Review and Evolutionary Analysis." *Personality and Individual Differences*, 1988, 9, pp. 1009–1024.

31. Gail E. Wyatt, "Identifying Stereotypes of Afro-American Sexuality and Their Impact upon Sexual Behavior," in *The Afro-American Family: Assessment, Treatment and Research Issues*, ed. Barbara Bass, Gail E. Wyatt, and Gloria Johnson Powell. New York: Grune and Stratton, 1982, pp. 333–346.

32. Robert Staples, "The Mystique of Black Sexuality." *Liberator* 7, March 1967, p. 10.

33. G. Rattray Taylor, *Sex in History: Society's Changing Attitudes to Sex throughout the Ages*. New York: Ballantine Books, 1954.

34. Friedrich Engels, *The Origin of the Family, Private Property, and the State*. Chicago: Charles H. Kerr, 1902.

35. Hambly, *op. cit.*

36. John Blassingame, *The Slave Community*. New York: Oxford University Press, 1972.

37. Sigmund Freud, *The Basic Writings of Sigmund Freud*, translated by A. A. Brill. New York: Modern Library, 1938.

38. Nat Lehrman, *Masters and Johnson Explained*. Chicago: Playboy Press, 1970.

39. Robert Blood and Donald Wolfe, *Husbands and Wives*. New York: The Free Press, 1960. Robert Bell, "Comparative Attitudes about Marital Sex among Negro Women in United States, Great Britain, and Trinidad." *Journal of Comparative Family Studies*, Autumn 1970, pp. 71–81.

40. Gail E. Wyatt and Sandra Lyons-Rowe, "African American Women's Sexual Satisfaction as a Dimension of Their Sex Roles." *Sex Roles*, 1990, 22, Nos. 7/8, pp. 509–524.

41. Edward O. Laumann, John H. Gagnon, Robert T. Michael, and Stuart Michaels, *The Social Organization of Sexuality: Sexual Practices in the United States*. Chicago: University of Chicago Press, 1994, pp. 116–121, 370–375.

42. *Ibid.* pp. 264–265.

43. Vonnie C. McLoyd, A. M. Cauce, D. Takeuchi, and L. Wilson, "Marital Processes & Parental Socialization in Families: A Decade Review of Research." *Journal of Marriage & the Family*, November 2000, 62, pp. 1070–1093.

44. Orlando Patterson, *Rituals of Blood. Op. cit.* pp. 126–132.

45. Alan P. Bell, "Black Sexuality: Fact and Fancy" in *The Black Family: Essays and Studies*, 2nd Edition, ed. Robert Staples. Belmont, California: Wadsworth, 1978, p. 79.

46. William Masters and Virginia Johnson, *Human Sexual Response.* Boston: Little, Brown, and Company, 1966.

47. Personal communication, August 2003. The results were never publicly released.

48. Laumann, et al. p. 124.

49. *Ibid.* pp. 372–375.

50. David Quadagno, D. F. Sly, D. F. Harrison, I. W. Eberstein, and H. R. Soler, "Ethnic Differences in Sexual Decisions and Sexual Behavior." *Archives of Sexual Behavior*, February 1998, 27, pp. 57–77.

51. Edward McNair, "Changing Sex Roles and Masculine Role Strain." A Doctoral Dissertation presented to the University of California at Berkeley, June 1983.

52. Laumann, et al., *op. cit.* p. 370.

53. Quadagno, et al., *op. cit.* p. 72.

54. Gaile E. Wyatt, Richard G. Strayer, and W. Charles Lobitz, "Issues in the Treatment of Sexually Dysfunctioning Couples of Afro-American Descent." *Psychotherapy, Theory, Research, and Practice* 1976, Vol. 13, pp. 44–50.

55. Gail Sheehy, *The Silent Passage: Menopause.* New York: Pocketbooks, 1993, pp. 94–95.

CHAPTER THREE

~

Images and Beliefs in Popular Culture

In twenty-first-century America, much of what passes for popular culture is derived from other nations or had its origin in Black popular culture. Because sexuality has always been an important aspect of Black life, its cultural forms have typically mirrored its sexual values and lifestyles. When Euro-Americans have appropriated components of Black culture, it often deleted or weakened the sexual element to more accurately match its prudish tastes. Black popular culture developed because the nation remains a physically and socially segregated society, each with its own values and aesthetics. The sexual liberalism of Blacks was an integral part of its music forms, comedy, films, and literature. When Blacks became part of the mainstream version of their cultural form, it was the desexualized one with one exception—rap music.

Afro-American culture has long been an oral one. It began with storytelling passed on from generation to generation. Although English had not been their native tongue, they used the power of its words to construct its cultural structure. So much of their culture was their adaptation to the environment in which they found themselves. One of the earliest verbal traditions was "playing the dozens." It is a verbal contest played by young males and contains its own rhythms, innuendo, slang, and grammar. Many would think of it as the forerunner to rap music with its rhyming patterns and using women as targets. The dozens might be seen as a game in which the performers try to outdo each other with insults. It is a test of the opponent's ability to tolerate insults hurled at his family, particularly his mother.[1]

The dozens game is centered on sexual and pornographic material. Almost every sexual act is integrated into the verbal contest. Students of this verbal game insist it is designed to test the sexual knowledge and skills of the verbal combatants. More importantly, it is a reflection of sexual attitudes among young Black males. At a young age, they demonstrate how knowledgeable they are about sexuality. In the past, it was used as a game that could release the sexual energy of pubescent and adolescent males. Nowadays they may be releasing that sexual energy onto their teenage female partner. Even females can, and do play the dozens as well as young white males. It has even been used in a beer commercial.[2]

Anyone reading examples of the rhymes in the dozens would think it vulgar and obscene. Yet, to the residents of America's inner cities, it is a cheap form of entertainment. The opponents, in the company of their peers, subject each other to vile sexual terms such as queer or syphilitic, while their sisters will be called whores and their brothers will be called defective. Because the targets are commonly women, Euro-Americans might regard it as the antecedent of male sexism. However, these are cultural expressions in a group that has more female equality than any other racial group and need to be understood in the particular context of Afro-American life. Black males, for all the outward show of misogyny, express the greatest amount of devotion to their mothers. That is one reason she is a target of the dozens—to test the internal fortitude of her son's ability to withstand the verbal assault on her.

Another cheap form of Black entertainment is comedy. Some of the original Black comedians played buffoons before Euro-American audiences, often in white face. Those who performed before exclusively Black audiences were comedians skilled at sexual humor. In America's largest cities, Chicago, Los Angeles, Detroit, New York, etc. a number of small clubs were devoted to Black entertainment. Those Blacks that did not live in one of those cities could avail themselves of the sexual humor of Black comedians in the form of party records, so called because they were often played at Black house parties. Two of the biggest names that emerged out of Black comedy in the 1940s and 1950s were Red Foxx and Moms Mabley. Both became mainstream attractions before their deaths but continued their sexual humor in live performances.

When a young crop of "clean" Black comedians was allowed to appear on national television in the 1960s, Foxx was excluded for a long time. Based in Los Angeles, where he performed regularly at nightclubs in the area, he was "discovered" and given a starring role in a television situation comedy *Sanford and Son* where he was sanitized and presented as an asexual owner of a junkyard. The show was the number one television program for a number of years but Foxx refused to live up to the clean image in his live appearances and audiences were so warned in advertisements for his comedy concerts. Moms Mabley never achieved much mainstream success but was the best-known Black female comedian of her era. Unlike the few Euro-American female comics, Moms openly talked about her sexual needs and wanting a young man to satisfy them. Although Foxx's and Mabley's humor centered on sexual matters, they were as genuinely funny as any of the "clean" white comedians of their era. Both attained fame at advanced ages due to the sexual nature of their material.

In the 1960s, a new group of young comedians emerged on the national scene: Bill Cosby, Dick Gregory, and Flip Wilson. Among them was a clean cut young Black man from Peoria, Illinois named Richard Pryor. His material was nonracial and very clean. Suddenly, he dropped out of the mainstream comedy circuit, moved to Berkeley, California, and reinvented himself. In the late 1960s, he re-emerged with highly sensitive racial and sexual material laced with lots of profanity. Initially, he was discovered by the Black elite, sold millions of comedy albums, and went to Hollywood. In the 1970s, he became the biggest Black film star since Sidney Poitier. However, his movies rarely capitalized on his brilliant comedy talent and this most sexual of Black men was generally neutered in his movies. Still, his electrifying live performances shared with the late Elvis Presley an exhibition in three concert movies shown in movie theatres. Until his death, he retained the sensual aspect of his comedy performance but was never able to translate that to the silver screen except in his concert movies. Suffering from his personal demons, he could never have his material diluted enough to appear regularly on television.

Pryor became the model for all future Black comedians including a strong sexual content in all their material. One of his protégées, Eddy Murphy, started out as a stand-up comic in suburban New York comedy clubs. He made his name doing impressions on the television show *Saturday Night Live*, went to Hollywood and became the biggest Black movie star of all time. He acted in comedies where he rarely kissed a woman and tried to emulate his idol in live performances. While his material had a strong sexual content, it simply was not as hilarious as Pryor's and he is best known as a comedy actor. Television became the training ground for Black comedians and one program, *Def Comedy Jam*, devoted only to Black comedians became a sexual free-for-all in its graphic content. Appearing at midnight, on the cable network HBO, it had some of the most ribald humor ever seen on the small screen. It produced three Black comedians, Martin Lawrence, Chris Tucker, and Chris Rock, who went on to success in theatrical movies.

The success of Black comedians, with their sexually tinged material, also led to a series of Euro-American comics trying blue material. Profanity became a standard part of comedy routines. It must be noted, however, that none of the white comedians using sexual humor ever succeeded in establishing a movie career, as did the Black comedians. While men dominate the comedy field, the most successful female stand-up comic was a Black woman named Whoopi Goldberg. One of the few Black women to win an Oscar, she starred in a number of lackluster movies and did not achieve much success as a stand-up comedian. Those who attended her live performances may have been shocked by the strong sexual content of her material and the profanity she uses. Among those surprised were viewers of the Academy Awards ceremony at some of her subtle risqué remarks. Many think that Euro-Americans are more comfortable with Afro-Americans in comedy roles, particularly on television, where they do not have to be taken seriously and are rarely in charge.

The Sexualization of Music

While much of Black comedy originated in cities and had an urban sensibility, Black music began on the plantations of the rural South. It spread to cities of the south and the blues were dichotomized into the Mississippi delta blues and urban blues. The connection between sexuality and forms of Black music was very direct. Ragtime was first played by Black pianists in the brothels of New Orleans when they tried to imitate the sound of the city's brass bands by shifting the accent from the weak to the strong beat. The most famous ragtime musician, Scott Joplin, began playing in the brothels, sampled some of their women, and died of syphilis in 1917. Whereas we think of jazz as an urban music form, its roots lay in the rural peasants of the Southern states. The young Black men found employment in the brothels of New Orleans, particularly a district known as Storyville. In Storyville, you had the center of all vice in one of America's most vice-ridden cities. Among the saloons, clubs, and brothels were the men who gave us one of the world's most respected forms of music.[3]

Jazz and ragtime were instrumental music. It was in the blues that the naturalistic attitudes toward sexuality were expressed in words. Blues got their name from the pain and suffering of Afro-Americans on the plantations of the Deep South. It was during the 1920s that a label was attached to this music form and its early years were dominated by women. There are some scholars of this music form who believe the women were given a prominent place in blues history because Euro-Americans would tolerate orgiastic interplay between white men and Black women but could not abide Euro-American women being sexually enticed by Black men.[4] Some of the blues songs had very suggestive titles such as, "I'm a Mighty Tight Woman," "Anybody Here Want to Try My Cabbage," and "If It Don't Fit, Don't Force It," ragtime had even more explicit sexual titles like, "She's Got a Good Pussy" and "The Naked Dance."[5]

Many of the female blues singers lived the life they sang about. Many had been raped, were born out of wedlock, and grew up around brothels. They were aware of sexuality before reaching their teens and having a child was a sign of a woman's maturity.[6] Thus, some of the raunchiest blues were sung by women. Memphis Minnie was the most prominent female blues singer in a field that had become dominated by men. A number of her songs were openly sexual, such as "Dirty Mother for You" and "Butcher Man." Another female blues singer, Lucille Bogan sang "Shave 'Em Dry," a song that Bill Wyman calls "The dirtiest song ever recorded." Apparently, she recorded two versions of the song, one with double entendres and another that was more direct.[7]

The male blues singers were themselves far ahead of the sexual revolution. However, their songs were full of metaphors and double entendres. One example is this song by the Memphis Jug Band:

> Woke up this morning,
> Feelin sad and blue,
> Couldn't find my yo yo,
> Didn't know what to do,
> Come home daddy,
> Mama's got them yo yo blues[8]

Rarely have these songs been sung in mainstream media. Most of these blues singers played the chittlin circuit, consisting of small clubs and juke joints in the Black section of town. Euro-Americans kept them confined to that musical ghetto because it was seen as a threat to Western morals. In the Black community, sex was perceived as a natural force in life whereas the Euro-American still publicly declared it as a source of shame and guilt. While Blacks were not allowed to represent their music, it liberalized the sexual attitudes of white America when Elvis Presley brought Black music and style to the national stage.

Although many Blacks feel that it was only when a white male sang their music that it became acceptable, it was the only entry for rhythm and blues in the America of the 1950s. Any Black male employing the open sensuality of Elvis might have been lynched if he ventured into the southeastern part of the United States. As it was, Elvis was condemned for causing juvenile delinquency and moral decay all over America. Often he had to change the lyrics of songs written by the Black blues men with all their sexual innuendo. By the time he came along, the music form had evolved into rhythm and blues, sometimes called urban blues or race music. To distinguish the music sung by white artists like Elvis Presley, Buddy Holly, Jerry Lee Lewis, and others they called it rock and roll, later shortened to rock.

Whatever the name, the R & B music created by Blacks continued to contain sexual innuendo, metaphors like "Shake, Rattle and Roll," "Roll With Me Henry," "Sixty Minute Man," and others. Many of the songs of Little Richard had sexual overtones. One of the most sexualized songs was "Work with Me, Annie," by Hank Ballard and the Midnighters. In case you are wondering how Annie was doing this work, the sequel to that song was "Annie Had a Baby, Can't Work No More." The song was banned on many radio stations.

Traditional blues never really entered the mainstream as sung by Black artists. The white artists such as the Rolling Stones and Eric Clapton popularized much of the music and made a lot of money from it. Many younger Blacks do not listen to the music and it has been younger whites and some older Blacks that have kept the music alive. It is rarely played on urban radio stations and most of the classic bluesmen are now dead. What took its place was largely shorn of its sensuality. The soul music of Motown was more melodic and designed to appeal to Euro-American audiences. One exception was Marvin Gaye, who issued one of the most overtly sexual songs with his rendition of "Sexual Healing." In the 1980s, Prince pushed the envelope with songs about every sexual act imaginable. By that time, Euro-American singers and the Rolling Stones had started to record overtly sexual songs. One of the Stones' songs created some controversy when a song described Black women as loving to have sex all night long. Given his hundreds of sexual conquests, Mick Jagger certainly includes Black women among them. Still it is too small a number to make such a generalization.

Disco, as a music form, did not last very long or produce many stars. Its biggest star was a Black woman named Donna Summer. Her record company marketed her as a "sex goddess." The titles of her biggest hits were "Hot Stuff" and "Bad Girls." But her first big hit was the overtly sexual song, seventeen minutes long, "Love to Love You, Baby." She became the prototype for the sexual styles of Madonna, Britney Spears, and others. Some claimed she projected such a hedonistic sexual image that she became a poster girl for the excesses of sex and drugs in the 1970s. Ms. Summer claims that, in part, the creation of her sex goddess image led to a suicide attempt. She is now a born-again Christian.[9]

A Black feminist writer, bell hooks, has claimed that Black female singers have appropriated the sensual image of Black women in order to benefit from it. According to her, "many Black women singers, irrespective of the quality of their voices, have cultivated an image which suggests they are sexually available and licentious. Undesirable in the conventional sense, which defines beauty and sexuality as desirable only to the extent that it is idealized and unattainable, the Black female body gains attention only when it is synonymous with accessibility, availability, when it is sexually deviant." Her main target is Tina Turner, the epitome of the sexualized female singer. Others may see Ms. Turner as true to her Black heritage and nothing more. Who, among us, actually thinks she is accessible to any man? For years, she performed her erotic routine with her husband standing behind her. And she has never been associated with sexuality in the manner of Madonna and Britney Spears.

The case of Janet Jackson is not as clear-cut. We have no reason to think that anybody but Ms. Jackson is orchestrating her erotic image but her. Unlike the very talented Tina Turner, Ms. Jackson has attained her fame largely through family connections and well-choreographed dance steps. Now that her career is on the downside, she has resorted to flaunting her sexuality to jumpstart very slow record sales. Not only did she bare a portion of her breast during the Super Bowl halftime show, she has released an album replete with sexually graphic lyrics. Writing her own songs, she includes lyrics like "Boy you're about to make the rain come down" and "I'm wet for you." One music critic said she was writing from the perspective of a hooker.[10]

Her one redeeming virtue is that her private life does not begin to resemble that of her brother. Ironically, her "worst indiscretion" was lying about living with a man that she had actually married. Compare that to the deeds of one R. Kelly, who was accused of engaging in sex with a fourteen-year-old girl. It seems Mr. Kelly has also written a number of hit songs about his sexual promiscuity. His last three hits were "Ignition," "Snake," and "Thoia Thoing." They all have similar plot lines. R. Kelly is at a concert or a club, sees a girl dancing, seduces her, and takes her to one of the following places: an afterparty, the hotel lobby, or his room. His sexual metaphors are quite transparent and something more than innuendo. His response to the charge of sex with a minor is contained in another song he wrote, "Age Ain't Nothing but a Number." Although arrested and indicted for possessing and producing child pornography, the charges have been dropped due to a technicality.[11]

The performers in hip-hop are a breed apart. R. Kelly could use his arrest on child pornography to boost his street credibility in that genre. Many of the stars of this genre have been in jail, are facing jail, have been shot or murdered. There are too many sexual charges to list and, most importantly, it is the most popular form of music in twenty-first-century America. In the October 11, 2003 issue of Billboard's Hot 100, all top ten songs were by Black recording artists, a first in the fifty years it has been ranking music by sales. With the exception of the number one song by Beyonce, all the other nine songs were by rappers.[12] About 70 percent of the hip-hop records sold are purchased by whites.[13]

In the movie "About a Boy," a young white boy is asked what he is listening to. His response is "Its rap music, mostly by Black people. They are very angry—mostly, they want sex"! Indeed, they are laden with explicit demands for sex and do not bother with metaphors, innuendos, or double entendres. Ja Rule's song "Bitch Betta Have My Money" says, "game is the topic/what's between your leg is the product/use it properly/and you'll make dollars, bitch."[14] Obviously, it is a controversial music form and some even question the use of the term music since the songs do not have a melody. It is the constant references to females as bitches and ho's (short for whore) that have generated the most controversy. Attempts to censor this music have gotten no further than a labeling system that warns buyers about a record's content. A group of Black women started their own radio station and is playing only music that treats women with respect.[15]

Not only is hip-hop the best selling form of music but its stars are performing on television, starring in movies, and appearing in commercials. Not all of hip-hop is the gangster rap with sexist lyrics and it has not gained social acceptance. However, not all women seem offended by being called bitches and ho's and some of them are also using the term for each other. Moreover, there are a few female hip-hop artists who have joined the men with explicit messages of materialism and sex in their songs. It has brought them success and they are now appearing in movies and television shows. Little Kim and Foxy Brown are two of the most successful female rappers.[16]

Whatever one may think of hip-hop being given a public forum for its music emphasizing sex and violence, it is a realistic reflection of the lives of young Black men. They come from an environment in which violence is endemic and men are preoccupied with obtaining sexual access to females. How sexist it is depends on actual observed behavior. Many of the male rappers come from female-headed households and buy their mother a house with the money they receive from record royalties. The differential access to sexuality does shape their attitude toward females as ho's, demanding something in exchange for sexual access. Whatever its merit, it appears that hip-hop music will be with us in the future.[17]

Sassy Fat Mommas and Neutered Studs

When the first movie was made, *Birth of a Nation* by D. W. Griffith, it portrayed Black men as rapists who lusted after white women. A Black man named Oscar Micheaux financed and produced movies with all Black casts from 1919 to 1948. Since he had no distribution network, he often went from town to town showing his movies to Black audiences. Micheaux put on the screen all sorts of issues that had been taboo up to that time: rape, concubinage, and lynching. One of his movies, *Within Our Gates*, was a direct response to *Birth of a Nation*. Unfortunately, most of his films were lost to us and others are rarely seen. In mainstream cinema, Black women were often maids to white female stars, were typically fat and some were allowed to be sassy. The men were universally depicted as lazy, shiftless, and cowardly. The archetypes were Amos and Andy caricatures as portrayed by Mantan Moreland and Stephen Fetchett. All of those portrayals were far removed from the sexual image they had in real life.[18]

Mostly, Blacks were not seen on the silver screen. White Southerners did not want to see their image at all. Hollywood filmmakers got around their objections by using them in musical sequences that could be deleted when the movie was shown in Southern states. Because there was a number of Black movie theatres, films were produced that catered to Black audiences. The white Southerners were so irrational that they objected to the film, *Pinky*, about a Black woman who "passes" for White. What they objected to was the actress, Jeanne Crain, falling in love with a white man. The actress actually was white, putting them in the absurd position of objecting to a white woman falling in love with a white man because she was acting the role of a Black woman.

As race relations improved in the United States, the stereotypical roles played by Blacks gradually disappeared. In their place, during the late 1950s we got two "normal" Black men played by Sidney Poitier and Harry Belafonte. While Belafonte is seen as more of a calypso singer who starred in fewer than ten movies, he was one of the first Black sex symbols, rivaling Elvis Presley's record sales at the time. However, he was rarely seen singing on television with Euro-American women screaming in ecstasy. He did make one movie, *Island in the Sun*, with a white female love interest. Poitier, on the other hand, had a long career and once was ranked as the nation's number one box office attraction. Poitier played Black men with a quiet dignity they had been denied on the screen for decades. Despite his leading man status, films that included white actresses never showed him and them touching. Even in one of Hollywood's most daring films at the time, *Guess Who's*

Coming to Dinner, he was engaged to marry a white woman that he hardly touched.[19]

Poitier's roles placated older Blacks who had grown up watching the shuffling, shiftless Black men on the big screen. During the late 1960s, things begin to change. Jim Brown, a great football star, joined Poitier as a screen idol. However, he had little tolerance for the "look, don't touch" rule of Hollywood films. Soon he was seen bedding down a series of white women, including sex goddess Raquel Welch. The turbulent 1960s ignited a number of changes in America and it was engulfed in turmoil caused by the civil rights movement and an unpopular war in Vietnam. Movies changed in general and a dramatic change was underway in the sexual image of Black men in films. From the 1950s to the 1970s, Black women were quietly in the background. They still played maids to female stars but were less fat and sassy.[20]

The late 1960s through the 1970s witnessed the birth and explosion of cinema known as "Blaxploitation" films. They were dozens of movies, made on a low budget by Black and white producers, distributed by major studios, and intended for predominantly Black audiences. Most were simplistic plots organized around a generous dose of sex and violence. One of the first and most revolutionary of the movies was *Sweet Sweetback's Baad Assss Song*, directed and written by a respected Black filmmaker named Melvin Van Peebles, today better known as the father of Mario Van Peebles. *Sweetback* was the story of a Black man on the run after killing two police officers observed beating a fellow Black man. Much of the movie consists of his sexual escapades that he uses as a means to escape to safety across the Mexican border.[21]

Movie critics may debate the artistic merits of that movie forever. What white Hollywood noticed is that the movie made a bunch of money, about ten times its production costs. That led to similar themed movies, which had the benign effect of increasing Black pride. After watching a neutered Sidney Poitier, they were being given the opportunity to sock it to the man. Finally, they were having casual sex with white women on the big screen, defying white authority figures and watching "real life figures" from the hood. The problem for the Black middle class is that these realistic role models were mostly drug dealers and pimps, some of whom did not pay for their crimes.

Most of these movies were not very good by anybody's standards. That can be said about the majority of Hollywood films today. Many of the stars were ex-athletes, who could not act and the films might accurately be called a Black fantasy. A few of the movies are deemed worthy by knowledgeable movie critics. *Sweetback*, for reasons unclear to me, is one of them. The best of the lot is *Shaft*, directed by Gordon Parks, a respected Black photographer and esteemed movie director. John Shaft is the cool private detective described as a "Black private dick that's a sex machine with all the chicks."[22] The movie is embellished with the Oscar-winning song "Shaft" by Isaac Hayes. Looking back at *Shaft*, it was a huge success because it captured the backlash against the asexual Black men played on the screen heretofore. With *Shaft*, Blacks were seeing an explicit sexual being that had never been portrayed on the screen.

Although there was much interracial sex in these films, Black women did emerge as a force to be reckoned with. Some feel that Blaxploitation films treated women as sex objects. Certainly, these films were male dominated and women played passive roles. Rare for that time in Hollywood were the Supermmomas, played by Pam Grier and Tamara Dobson, called Foxy Brown and Cleopatra Jones. Wielding big afro hairdos and lethal weapons, these women used their femininity to blow away evil men in their movies. In one scene with a great deal of symbolism, Foxy Brown cuts off the penis of a villain. However bad they were in these movies there was generally the obligatory nude scene since the Black male audience expected that in these types of movies.

Despite their success, the criticism of Blaxploitation movies grew louder from organizations such as the NAACP, and Jesse Jackson against "these vulgar pictures." Eventually, Hollywood ceased to make them and many Black actors are bitter at the job opportunities they lost as a result of the Black middle class's disapproval. Actually, Hollywood found that they could make more money from big blockbusters such as *Jaws, Star Wars,* and *The Godfather*. Movies with predominantly Black casts continued to be made and were generally of a higher quality. A handful of Black directors made financially successful films that also received critical acclaim, such as *Boyz N the Hood, Menace to Society,* and *Dead Presidents*.

The Black director at the center of Hollywood admiration is a man named Spike Lee. He came from a middle-class background and attended the prestigious film school at New York University. The film that he made as his thesis is a cult classic. *She's Gotta Have It.* Directing and writing the script, he made a movie about a sexually liberated Black woman called Nola Darling. She is openly having sex with three different men and cannot decide between them. All three men encourage her to adopt monogamy and select one of them. At the end of the picture, she has not been able to decide and one of her lovers presses the issue by raping her and asking the question, "Whose pussy is this?" Her indecision indicates that it belongs only to her.[23]

Gradually, a new crop of Black male actors and a few females emerged that were able to star in major movies. A handful received Oscars and achieved financial success for their movies. However, Hollywood retreated to the neutered super stud syndrome with Black male actors. There are about ten of them and, with rare exception, most are stuck in sexless action roles. In action films, a love story is not central to the plot, since the main audience is young, white males. The most successful Black male actor Denzel Washington seems to think segments of the audience do not wish to see him in interracial sex/love scenes. He co-starred with the nation's number one female star, Julia Roberts, in the film *The Pelican Brief* and never touched her. In an interview, Julia Roberts complained, "that I've caught more grief over the lack of a love scene with Denzel. He didn't want to do it."[24] Washington's explanation this time was that Black women did not want to see him in love scenes with a Euro-American woman. Earlier, a white actress named Kelly Lynch claims she got down on her knees and begged Washington to have their characters kiss in the film. Then, he felt that young white males would not want him to kiss a white woman and refused.

Obviously, it is Euro-American women he wants to avoid since he has done love scenes with East Indian, Latino, and Afro-American women. At least, he had the opportunity for interracial sex scenes. Other Black male actors complain that Halle Berry, Whitney Houston, and Angela Basset have done sex scenes with white male stars whereas they can barely touch Euro-American female stars. Meg Ryan avoided the issue in her film with Denzel Washington by dying before he enters the picture. Even in interracial love stories such as *All That Heaven Allows*, the Black-white lovers are not allowed to touch. Meanwhile Halle Berry engages in one of the most graphic sex scenes ever with Billy Bob Thornton in *Monsters Ball* and wins an Academy Award.

Increasingly, Black male/white female couplings are seen on the silver screen in films made by young, independent white filmmakers, particularly in comedies, sometimes for shock value. Often no mention is made of the male actor's race, indicating the director is a lot more color blind than his audience. Still, we see almost no affection between these couples as might normally be expected. For about fifteen years, Hollywood has retreated from any depiction of sex in films, worried about an "R" rating or seeming to condone casual sex at a time of the AIDS crises. Young white actresses, with any kind of reputation, are also refusing to do nudity or sex scenes. The movie *Pieces of April* appeared to have reached a compromise when they showed the star, Katie Holmes to engage in sex with her Black boyfriend, Derek Luke, on the bed with her clothes on.

What angers many Black performers is that Hollywood seems afraid of any romance on the big screen. Until recently, Black romance was a huge void in movies starring Black actors. It has lead to a paucity of roles for Black females since they would be the ones playing the girlfriend/wife parts. As male actors have attained some control over their movies, they have insisted on being paired with some female even if they are not allowed to touch. This concern was especially relevant when Hollywood was doing a series of gang banger and drug movies that portrayed only one aspect of Black life. Still, movies that center on Black romance tend to attract mostly Black audiences; sometimes Blacks represent 80 percent of the audience. If the movies are made cheaply enough, it has been demonstrated that they are profitable. The low white patronage of the movies being produced suggests the fear of Black sexuality has not yet disappeared.

The Small Screen

Television is such a conservative medium that sexuality of any kind is rarely seen on it. During the 1950s, the word pregnancy was forbidden and even a married couple had to be shown sleeping in separate beds. When the first Black situation comedy appeared on TV in the 1960s, *Julia*, there was a firestorm of criticism over the star not having a husband, lending fuel to the stereotype of Black families being headed by a single parent. Most Black sitcoms today consist of a married couple. Some of them have featured interracial couples. In a curious move on casting, an NBC television movie was shown about a young woman killed by her lover. It was based on a true story of a Black male who killed his white female lover. Yet, in the television movie, the male's race was changed to white, not an insignificant casting change.

Stories about interracial sex have often had negative perspectives—at least for Blacks. Two episodes of the popular long-running racially integrated drama series *Law and Order*, come to mind. One involved a young White woman whose grandmother died under mysterious circumstances. Only when they discover the young woman has a Black boyfriend do they suspect her of causing the grandmother's death. Apparently, the clue was that if she is twisted enough to be having sex with a Black male, she could also be diabolical enough to kill her grandmother.

The other *Law and Order* episode involved the murder of a young Black male college student in his apartment. Certain clues, like a library book, lead them to an attractive white female on Long Island. This white female is a thinly disguised racial bigot who comments that these "N. . . come out here looking for white girls, wanting to get a piece of this. In their dreams." They find out that she is covering for a friend, another white female college student. This white female has been recently discharged from the hospital where she went for treatment for a broken arm, caused by her father when he found out about her sexual liaison with the Black male college student. The district attorney is able to secure a confession from her that being surrounded by white racists; she defied her family and friends to sleep with him. After making that sacrifice, he intended to break off their relationship. Hence, she killed him in cold blood and later tried to pretend that he had raped her. The D.A. was very sympathetic and agreed to a small amount of jail time for her.

One show on cable television, *Sex and The City*, tells the stories of four attractive young white women who handle sex like a man. They have gone through thousands of men, often discarding them for the most trivial of reasons. One of them, sexy Samantha, has had sex with about three thousand different men in all sorts of physical settings. These women live in New York City surrounded by six million Afro-Americans and Latinos. Until the last year of the show when they did not have to worry about poor ratings canceling them, all these men were white. Finally, the character named Miranda notices there are Black men living in New York City and selects a good-looking Black medical doctor with whom to have an affair. The sex scene would be daring for broadcast television and shows her bare back as she sits atop him.[25]

Sex and the Written Word

While we think of Black culture as largely an oral one, there is a vast body of literature numbering in the thousands of books that fill the shelves of libraries everywhere. In reading that literature, it is obvious that the most life-like, historically accurate, and revealing depictions have come, not from the pens of historians and sociologists but from the works of gifted Black writers and the instruments of Black musicians. In the book *Jubilee*, author Margaret Walker Alexander powerfully captures the essence of what womanhood probably meant to many enslaved Black women. When a ten-year-old girl runs bleeding to Aunt Sally, she gives her some advice about sex and men. "Men ain't nothing but trouble, just breath and britches and trouble. Don't let him feel all over you, now don't let a no-good man touch you, else he'll big you up sho-nuff."[26]

Elsewhere in *Jubilee* are allusions to African-derived beliefs about pregnancy, such as not allowing your feet to touch the ground when your menstrual cycle has begun. Young girls should not straddle the rows in the fields or the crops will shrivel up and die. A pregnant woman should not carry green beans unless she wants them to spoil. Similar taboos had existed among pre-colonial tribes in West Africa. Many Europeans encountered problems in introducing cash crops such as coffee and cocoa because of taboos against women in certain conditions, pregnancy and menstruation, touching certain crops or other living things.[27]

As we have already seen, the blues were often about two-timing women seeking sexual satisfaction from other men. While similar themes run throughout literature written by Euro-Americans, it occupies a dominant role in Afro-American literature. The Literature by Black women that attracted the most attention were the ones describing sexual abuse. It began with the best-selling autobiography, *I Know Why the Caged Bird Sings*, by Maya Angelou which describes her painful rape and its aftermath.[28] Probably the most influential novelist of the 1970s and 1980s was one Alice Walker. Her novel *The Color Purple* was turned into a film that grossed over one hundred million dollars, earned eleven Academy Award nominations and set a record by not earning a single Oscar, a feat many think had to do with the excessively negative portrayal of Black men in the book and film.

The book had already won the Pulitzer Prize for fiction in 1982. Written in the style of Black English, it is a brilliant book in parts. When she described the character Celie's inability to understand her pregnancy and how it came about, it is realistic in light of the nonexistence of sex education or its inaccuracy when conveyed by Black parents. Many Black children were told that babies came from God or were delivered by the doctor in his black bag. One cannot escape the unfairness in the portrayal of Black males. Almost all the Black father figures were portrayed as being amoral and without sexual restraint. Mainly, the book appeared to confirm the worst sexual stereotypes of Afro-Americans. It has led many to wonder why white America has selectively chosen such books to lavish praise upon in the array of books by Black authors.[29]

While Walker's novels were rooted in the South, the books by urban Black males provided no less a negative portrayal of Black men, this time in autobiographies. Even the militant Black nationalist Malcolm X in his 1964 autobiography best seller claimed almost every Black person needed some kind of hustle to survive in Harlem, mostly prostitution, numbers running, or dope peddling.[30] Claude Brown describes the cult of violence among young Black males in his bestseller *Manchild in the Promised Land*.[31] One would think violence was an inherent part of Black culture. The worst was yet to come when Nathan McCall's book came out, entitled *Makes Me Want to Holler*, he discusses participating in gang rapes of young Black women during his youth because he wanted to bond with his peers.[32] Earlier another best seller, *Soul on Ice* by Eldridge Cleaver, had revealed that he practiced raping Black women to prepare for raping Euro-American women.[33]

With these inflammatory books by urban Black males, a wholesale move-ment by Black women into the Feminist camp should have been expected. With the exception of Black female novelists, it did not happen. Probably the best-selling tract on Black feminism was the 1979 book by Michelle Wal-lace, *Black Macho and the Myth of the Superwoman*. Curiously, she does not ad-dress the issue of sexuality except to repeat the often-heard assertion by Black nationalist Stokely Carmichael, "that the only position for the Black women in the civil rights movement is prone." While she accuses Black men of being responsible for the poverty of Black women, her main concern seems to be that too many of them were sleeping with Euro-American women.[34]

Perhaps one of the best-selling Black authors of all time was James Bald-win. Known best as an essayist, this eloquent writer remained on the best-seller list most of his adult life. The nonfiction works did not address sexual-ity but his off-hand comment about the Euro-American male's fear of him marrying his daughter was misplaced. What he worried about was him mar-rying his wife's daughter—he had been marrying his daughter for over a hun-dred years. This was a reminder that the amalgamation of Black women with white men had left many of their daughters in the Black community. Bald-win's novels introduced interracial and gay sexuality in Black literature for the first time in popular books. Eldridge Cleaver tried to make Baldwin's ho-mosexuality an issue but it is Baldwin's memory that is now honored in the Black community.[35]

Notes

1. Roger Abrahams, *Positively Black*. Englewood Cliffs, New Jersey: Prentice-Hall, 1970.

2. Richard Majors and Janet Mancini Billson, *Cool Pose: The Dilemmas of Black Manhood in America*. New York: MacMillan, 1991, pp. 91–102.

3. Bill Wyman, *Bill Wyman's Blues Odyssey: A Journal to Music's Heart and Soul*. London: Dorling Kindersley Ltd., 2001.

4. Ortiz M. Walton, *Music: Black, White, and Blue*. New York: William Morrow, 1972, p. 35.

5. Wyman, *op. cit.* p. 91.

6. Alan Lomax, *The Land Where the Blues Began*. New York: Pantheon Books, 1993, pp. 85–86.

7. Wyman, *op. cit.* p. 90.

8. *Ibid.* p. 131.

9. Bernard Weinraub, "For Disco's First Diva, It's Still Not Last Dance." *New York Times*, November 11, 2003, p. B-1.

10. Cameron Adams, "Slacko Jacko." *Herald Sun*, March 25, 2004, p. 5.

11. Neil Strauss, "Flying above the Shadows." *New York Times*, August 14, 2003, p. B-3.

12. "Black Stars Dominate Billboard's Top 10 Chart for First Time in 50 Years." *Jet Magazine*, October 27, 2003, p. 24.

13. James Haskins, *The Story of Hip-Hop*. London: Penguin Books, 2000, p. 25.

14. Diane Taylor, "Hey Guys, Just Cut the Rap." *The Age*, March 13, 2004, p. A-2.

15. *Ibid.*

16. Hoskins, *op. cit.* pp. 96–97.

17. Jennifer Keeley, *Rap Music*. San Diego: Lucent Books, 2001, pp. 54–65.

18. Nelson George, *Black Face: Reflections on African-Americans and the Movies.* New York: Harper Collins, 1994.

19. Vanessa Williams Snyder, "Is Hollywood Afraid of Black Romance on Screen?" *Marin Independent Journal*, October 30, 1994, p. C-2.

20. George, *op. cit.*

21. Tunku Varadarjan, "Shaft and Foxy Revisited." *Wall Street Journal*, August 9, 2002, p. W-1.

22. Kevin Young, "Blame It on the Boogie: Sweet Sweetback Goes to Crooklyn." *San Francisco Weekly*, May 16, 1994, p. 11.

23. bell hooks, *Black Looks: Race and Representation*. Boston: South End Press, 1992, p. 75.

24. "Denzel Shunned Kissing White Co-star in Virtuosity." *Jet Magazine*, September 18, 1995, p. 35.

25. Caroline Overington, "Carrie Reaches a Climax: Will It Be Big?" *The Age*, January 10, 2004, p. 5.

26. Margaret Walker Alexander, *Jubilee*. New York: Bantam Books, 1967, p. 45.

27. Boris De Rachewiltz, *Black Eros: Sexual Customs of Africa from Prehistory to the Present Day*. New York: Lyle Stuart, 1964.

28. Maya Angelou, *I Know Why the Caged Bird Sings*. New York: Random House, 1970.

29. Alice Walker, *The Color Purple*. New York: Washington Square Press, 1982.

30. Malcom X, *The Autobiography of Malcom X*. New York: Grove Press, 1964.

31. Claude Brown, *Manchild in the Promised Land*. New York: Macmillan, 1965.

32. Nathan McCall, *Makes Me Want to Holler: A Young Black Man in America*. New York: Random House, 1994.

33. Eldridge Cleaver, *Soul on Ice*. New York: McGraw Hill, 1968.

34. Michelle Wallace, *Black Macho and the Myth of the Superwoman*. New York: Dial Press, 1979.

35. K. Ohi, "I'm Not the Boy You Want: Sexuality, Race, and Thwarted Revelation in Baldwin's 'Another Country.'" *African American Review*, Summer 1999.

CHAPTER FOUR

~

Queer and Black in America

While all of human sexuality is a matter of immense complexity, rife with irrational attitudes, contradictions and inequities none is more so than the subject of homosexuality. It diverges from all our other topics as to be incomparable. First, there is nothing more fundamental to a society's organization than the notion of a male and female pairing at some prescribed age to produce offspring that will carry on the society's work in the future. Nothing disrupts this basic function more than same-sex behavior that allegedly threatens the basic fabric of human functions in every society. That is why it has been disapproved and punished more than many other deviations from traditional sexual norms and practices except Black male/white female sexual pairings. Even that most unspeakable act was given societal approval when the United States Supreme Court declared the prohibition of interracial marriages to be unconstitutional in 1969.

Until 1960, every American State had a sodomy law prohibiting oral and anal sexual activities—the only kind gays can practice. It was not until 2003 that the U.S. Supreme Court struck down the nation's remaining sodomy laws, thereby reversing its 1986 decision that ruled that individual states had the right to institute and enforce such statutes. Essentially, it ruled that the state may not legislate its moral code on a minority, that reducing gay relationships to sex acts demeans them, and that they have a right to retain their dignity as free persons.[1] While that decriminalized their conduct it, by no means, gave them legal equality with heterosexuals. A step in that direction was taken when the Massachusetts Supreme Judicial Court ruled in November

2003 that prohibiting gays and lesbians from entering into a civil marriage violated the state's constitution and ordered the ban to cease by May 17, 2004. To counteract the courts decision, the state legislature approved a constitutional amendment to ban same-sex marriage, while permitting civil unions. The amendment requires a second vote in 2005 followed by a vote of the electorate afterwards.[2]

Obviously, it is a dramatic revolution in the legal rights of homosexuals and an issue that will be hotly contested over the next couple of decades. These changes have come about without any great understanding of homosexuality and its impact on society. The gay community has defined itself as a sexual minority with a strong similarity to the Afro-American struggle for civil rights. Certainly, there are parallels. The prohibition on homosexual marriage was comparable to the ban on marriage between Blacks and whites. The courts have used their constitutional power to protect a minority from state laws that they consider discriminatory. Gays have been subject to massive discrimination that may have no bearing on their ability to do a job or on their potential danger to society. In the 1960s, gays adopted many of the protest tactics of the civil rights movement as have every protest movement since 1965. Huey Newton, head of the Black Panthers was one of the first Black leaders to link the Black and gay liberation movements.[3]

Still, there is no shortage of Blacks who dislike the analogy and are quick to point out that gays are a member of the ruling white male class and never suffered the indignities of slavery, separate public facilities, and the like. While that is true in the United States, gays were forced to wear a pink triangle in Nazi Germany and its occupied territories and many were executed along with Jews and Gypsies.[4] There are still Middle-Eastern countries that decapitate known homosexuals. Yet, the differences between the two groups are almost as great as the similarities. While socialist countries supported the liberation struggles of people of color, they have treated gays very harshly in nations like Cuba, the former Soviet Union, and China. Many of the revolutionary leaders such as Frantz Fanon and Eldridge Cleaver were openly homophobic.[5]

Whereas Huey Newton, Martin Luther King, and the NAACP have supported the gay liberation movement, it must be noted that until gays started demanding their rights, they often enjoyed the privileges of Euro-American males. Many have a household income thousands of dollars above heterosexual households and few of the gay males have children to support. This participation in the privileges of Euro-American males was allowed if they were discrete in their sexual conduct. Moreover, if openly gay, they retained the option of going back into the closet and reclaiming white skin privileges. Not every minority has to be poor and gays, in many ways, suffer greater discrimination than Blacks if they openly conduct their sexual lifestyle in many parts of twenty-first-century America.

If it is difficult for Euro-American gays, what about Afro-American homosexuals? It seems that they will suffer the consequences of racism and homophobia—in the white and Black community. Before we address the dual issues around race and sexual orientation, it must be acknowledged that we have no explanation for why homosexuality exists, its prevalence or its dynamics. It is no longer classified as a mental disorder by the psychological associations. Most social scientists have acknowledged that they do not know the genesis of homosexuality. One group of researchers concluded that gays were psychologically as well adjusted as heterosexuals.[6] Given their differential treatment by society, it should not be surprising if some suffered from poor mental health.

In recent years, the conventional wisdom has been that certain generic markers cause homosexuality in men. The research showing this relationship is rather flawed because it is almost impossible to show a connection between genes and behavior.[7] Freud did not see anything particularly wrong with same sex behavior and attributed much of it to arrested development at the adolescent psychosexual stage. Overall, he believed that humans were endowed with the capacity for bisexuality at birth and only the requisites of civilization prevented its expression.[8] Given the current turmoil over gay rights, we should be asking the question of how important homosexuality is to the smooth functioning of human society. The most common reason against it is its capacity to spread and become a majority lifestyle and prevent the species from reproducing. We are told by the religious right that gays cannot reproduce and must recruit and convert others.

The Kinsey studies of the 1940s and 1950s established a benchmark of 10 percent of the male population engaging in some form of homosexual activity. However, that did not mean that 10 percent of American males have a gay identity. The most significant research since Kinsey discovered that only 3 percent of white males identified as gay or bisexual compared to 1.5 percent of Afro-American males. The comparable figures for women were Euro-Americans 1.7 percent and 0.60 percent of Afro-American women.[9] Given their low percentages of the adult male and female population, why would we worry about them swamping the heterosexual population? Everything we know about gays leads to an overwhelming concern for legal equality, not the recruitment and seduction of heterosexuals. Probably all of us have been exposed to them in schools, workplaces, neighborhoods, and recreational areas. Straight women have to worry a lot more about harassment from straight males than from lesbians.

Such rational arguments will not dissuade many of the homophobes out there. The number of severe homophobes is rapidly declining and may even be a minority among Americans under age thirty. The greater tolerance for their lifestyle is largely due to their representation as a largely Euro-American group. Despite the fact that gays come in all colors and classes, they are marketed as a white group. The leadership and highest profile members are almost exclusively white. Given the gains of other "minorities," white America has decided there is no reason that those rights should not be given to the last disenfranchised minority—predominantly Euro-American gays. Moreover, gays have the image as hard working, law abiding citizens who respect the sanctity of marriage as much as other Americans.[10]

Homosexuality and the Black Experience

Male friendships were regarded once by Aristotle as the most perfect of friendships. Indeed, masculine friendships were the only ones that he considered, with the exception of a brief allusion to the possibility of friendship between husband and wife. The average woman, in ancient Greece, was regarded as too ignorant, intellectually, to be capable of deep friendship with anyone.[11] The present state of male friendships is far from what Aristotle celebrated. According to other research, studies and my own, single males have fewer meaningful friendships than most women, with either sex. A couple of reasons for the differences are clear. Women are more likely to be socialized into a nurturing role that complements the friendship role than are men who maintain a certain emotional distance from other men due to the fear of being labeled homosexual or weak.[12]

Homosexuality is the most difficult behavior of Blacks to trace historically. Wherever social contact between persons of the same sex has existed, there has probably been some homosexual behavior. In pre-colonial Africa, there was traditionally a division of labor, separate initiation training for males and females, in addition to economic and sociopolitical associations organized along gender lines. The practice, for instance, of some African tribes of sending young male children off to separate compounds may have produced some homosexual behavior. Such practices are rarely noted in the literature on African society. Instead, a noted Africanist asserts, "Although no proper studies of the problem have been made in traditional African societies, homosexual practices seem to be rare, or only confined to boys and girls before marriage." Part of the reason for this is that the psychological atmosphere from childhood to adolescence prepares one toward the goal of marriage, and a person, therefore directs his sexual development toward a relationship with the opposite sex.[13]

One of the effects of the sexual revolution is the increase in "visible" homosexuality. It is one area in the changing of sexual values that has significant Black participation. However, the increase in people assuming overtly gay lifestyles is largely confined to Black males. It is not known how many people in the United States are exclusively homosexual, but estimates range from 2 through 10 percent of the total population. The nation's prisons are the main places where homosexual preferences are evident. Some Black men who acquired their homosexual behavior as prison inmates because of the unavailability of women continue it after their release. Their reasons for turning to homosexual lifestyles vary, ranging from a desire to escape family responsibilities to acquiring money from prostitution. An interesting side aspect of the sexual revolution is the development in San Francisco of "gay liberation" groups that are so politically powerful that few politicians dare run for office without seeking their support.

Despite a shortage of Black males, relatively few Black women have joined the community as overt lesbians. But since female homosexuals are not as visible as male homosexuals, the number of Black lesbians is difficult to determine. As with the Black male homosexual, many Black lesbians are deeply involved in the white homosexual community. It is not known whether homosexuality is more or less prevalent in the Black population than in the white because there is little data available on the subject for Blacks. Some writers have claimed that Blacks have a greater incidence of male homosexuality than whites. The reason for their belief is that female-headed households in the Black community have resulted in a lack of male models for the male Black children. However, there is no evidence to support this supposition.

After placing obstacles to self-realization in the way of the Black male, America then has its bearers of ideology, the social scientists, falsely indict him for his lack of manhood. There are various sociological and psychological studies which purport to show how Black males are de-masculinized, and suggested in fact, that they may be latent homosexuals. The reason cited is that Black males reared in female-centered households are more likely to acquire feminine characteristics because there is no consistent adult male model or image to shape their personalities.[14] One sociologist stated that since Black males are unable to enact the masculine role, they tend to cultivate their personalities. In this respect, they resemble women who use their personalities to compensate for their inferior status in relation to men.[15]

If the above reasoning seems weak and unsubstantiated, the other studies of Black emasculation are equally feeble. Many of the hypotheses about the effeminate character of Black men are based on their scores on the Minnesota Multiphasic Inventory Test (MMPI), a psychological instrument that asks the subject to determine how over five hundred simple statements apply to him. Black males score higher than white males on the section that measures femininity. As an indicator of their femininity, the researchers cite the fact that Black men more often agreed with such feminine choices as, "I would like to be a singer" and "I think I feel more intensely than most people do."[16]

This is the kind of evidence that the dominant society has marshaled to prove the feminization of the Black male. The only thing this demonstrates is that white standards cannot always be used in evaluating Black behavior. Black people live in another environment, with different ways of thinking, acting and believing from the white, middle-class world. Singers such as James Brown and others represent successful role models in the Black community. Black male youths aspire to be singers because this appears to be an observable means for obtaining success in this country—not because they are more feminine than white males. In addition, music is an integral part of Black culture.

As part of their studies of sexual deviants, the Kinsey group investigated Black homosexuality. They found that Black men were more comfortable around homosexuals and did not perceive them as any kind of threat to their manhood. Consequently, Black homosexuals (male and female) were not as isolated from the Black heterosexual population. They were not relegated to their own bars or social cliques. Also Blacks were more likely to be bisexual than exclusively homosexual.[17]

Homosexuality is difficult to discuss as an option for Black people because it remains a subject fraught with controversy. Even understanding the nature of homosexuality is problematic because the research is permeated by bias. On the one hand, there are those who consider homosexuality to be a genetic disorder and everyone affected by it to be a pervert. More recently, there are those who declare homosexuals to be similar to heterosexuals in order to enhance the civil rights of gays. Some would claim that homosexuality cannot be a viable alternative for Black people because that tendency is formed in early childhood. In interpreting the importance of sexual orientation, we might keep in mind the words of Erich Fromm:

> [T]he very first thing we notice about anybody is whether that person is male or female. And it's the one thing we never forget. Name, telephone number, profession, politics, all of these details may slip from our memory, but never the individual's sex. Therefore our sexual preference linked together, is an important source of a person's identity.[18]

Not only have we failed to understand the causes of homosexuality, but we still know little about its nature. Although no reliable figures are available,

Blacks are assumed to be proportionally representative in that gay population. The majority of gays are assumed to be male, but lesbians maintain a low profile and are less likely to reveal themselves. It appears that the majority of Black homosexuals, both men and women, have less than a college education, although they are well represented, or perhaps more visible, in certain middle-class occupations. Many live in urban locales where the possibility of discovery is less likely, although they can be found in all environments. Certainly, those involved in an openly gay lifestyle live in large cities with sizeable gay populations. Today the most hospitable cities for them in the United States are New York, Los Angeles, San Francisco, and Boston.

A study entitled *Homosexualities* by Bell and Weinberg has attempted to refute some of the stereotypes about gays. Their book provides the source for much of our information about Black homosexuals. In general, they found that Black male homosexuals tend to be younger than their white counterparts, with an average age of 27 in contrast to 37 for white males. They were less educated and employed at a lower occupational level than white gays were. Members of the Black group more often expressed the belief that their homosexuality and homosexual contacts had helped more than hurt their careers. Over two-thirds of Black male gays reported they spent less than half of their leisure time by themselves in comparison to half of their white brethren. Both the Black and white homosexual men claimed to have more good, close friends than the heterosexual men did. A similar difference existed in attitudes about job satisfaction. Black and white homosexuals expressed greater satisfaction with their jobs than did heterosexual men. About half of the Black and white male homosexuals stated they had no regret whatsoever about being homosexual.[19]

It is worth noting that only one fourth of the Black gay males said that all their friends were men. The other gays probably constitute a large proportion of the platonic male friends many single women have. They make very good friends for many of these women because they share some of the same interests and they do not view women as sexual objects. A twenty-six-year-old gay male artist said:

> I enjoy women a lot. I enjoy their companionship without emotional entanglements. I prefer having a platonic relationship with a woman rather than a man. Most of my male friends are gay and our interests overlap too much and we become competitive. I go out to dinners, movies, museums, plays and talk on the telephone with my female friends. They help me keep things in perspective and provide me with a balance to my life. However, they tend to lament the fact that I'm a man lost to them.[20]

Another interesting characteristic of the Black gay lifestyle is the extent of their involvement with whites. Over two-thirds of the Black male homosexuals said that half of their sexual partners had been white.[21] One of our respondents believed race was less important in the gay community. However, he acknowledged that whatever their sexual orientation, whites still have a certain insensitivity to Blacks and cultural differences present problems. Whatever the reason, there is certainly some element of racism among white homosexuals. As a Black male homosexual reported:

> I've learned that in San Francisco's gay bars there's real racism—even overt racism—in terms of just being able to get in gay bars. They ask Black gays for three pieces of I.D. with their pictures on them, but they don't ask whites for that. Or, they have a certain quota and after they've filled it, they won't let any Third World people in. And there are still the sexual myths about Black people. The myth of the Black man as a stud, for example.[22]

Some non-white homosexuals began to confront the racism in gay bars in San Francisco. Since bars are the center of social life for gays, the exclusion of non-whites was of more than passing significance. Non-white gays have demonstrated in front of San Francisco gay bars charging racial discrimination against minority gays. According to a Black gay, "Gay bar owners think it's bad for business to encourage minority gay patrons." In the same city, a rift grew between the straight Black community and white gays over the increasing displacement of Black tenants by gays who are purchasing and renovating homes in the Black ghettos. While the practice, known as "gentrification," is a commonplace practice in other cities, the large number of gays buying up homes in Black neighborhoods has intensified Black hostility to them and created speculation that most low-income Blacks will be moved out of the city in a few years.

There was an interesting racial difference between the psychological adjustment of Black and white male homosexuals, with the Black males more likely to feel less happy at the present time than they did five years ago, to feel more tension, and to feel lonely more frequently.[23] With all these problems, homosexuality seems to be no trouble-free alternative, at least not for Black males. Coupled with the stigma is the fact that many problems heterosexuals face are present in the homosexual world. Among them are the problems of finding a compatible partner. A number of gay males complained they were unable to find a compatible male with whom to establish a meaningful relationship. One male, a thirty-five-year-old social worker told us:

Yes, I've lived with a lover in a homosexual relationship. The first four years were wonderful but the last six months were hell. I'm basically a relationship person. But the society reinforces butterfly relationships, where you light one second for sex. He wanted to continue living together but I wasn't willing. He was conventionally middle-class while I'm more bohemian. He cares what people think and I don't.[24]

While oppressed white groups, such as classes, gender, and sexual orientation can be insensitive to racial issues and people of color, rarely having any more social involvement with them than racial bigots, gays stand out for their involvement with Afro-Americans. Some of the landmark court rulings involving gays were interracial couples. A Florida gay couple denied adoption rights wanted to adopt some Black children with AIDS. It has already been noted that a very high percentage of Black gays had white sexual partners. Whereas sexual relationships can be fleeting, the 2000 United States Census showed an estimated 25 percent of gay and lesbian couples in the San Francisco Bay area were in biracial or interethnic relationships. That figure compares to a much lower number of 7.4 percent on a national basis and 15.6 percent of married couples in California.[25]

Gays may be the only group, regardless of color, to be more stigmatized and face more discrimination in the United States than Afro-Americans face. Racism and homophobia go hand in hand in this country. One study of 369 white middle-class students in grades 3–11 found a statistical link between prejudice against Blacks and bias against gays. Boys, in particular, were likely to have negative perceptions of gays and Afro-Americans. The researcher concluded that it was a matter of power for white boys to look down on all the people they think are at the bottom.[26] It is probable that white gays facing a lifetime of prejudice and homophobia develop empathy for the plight of Afro-Americans and become more compassionate and accepting. One can see this in the city of San Francisco, where gays make up as much as a third or more of the population. It is the only city of its size where 75 percent of the predominantly white electorate voted for affirmative action and against capital punishment.

Of course, not every white gay involved in interracial relationships does so for noble reasons. Some gay white males may be attracted to Afro-American males for the same reasons as Euro-American females, the sexual stereotypes. There were complaints that the controversial photographs by Robert Mapplethorpe of Black males "reduced Black males in their being as sexual, and nothing more or less than sexual, hence super-sexual."[27] It was felt they facilitated the public perception of certain sexual and racial fantasies about the Black male body. These same feelings of being an exotic trophy can exist in the lesbian community and Black lesbians have commented on negative experiences dating white women. Still, even the dating experience is off limits for white heterosexuals who would never consider any social involvement with Afro-Americans. And it would be fair to note that negative dating experiences often occur within the same racial group.

Homophobia in Black America

Given the more liberal racial attitudes and practices of white gays and lesbians, their similar experiences with prejudice and discrimination, we would certainly expect, at the very least, no greater homophobia than found among Euro-Americans. That does not appear to be the case. In most recent surveys, homophobia shows up as occurring with greater frequency among Afro-Americans. We can cite the most extreme cases, both found among Black religious leaders. A Black minister in Florida said he would march with the Ku Klux Klan if the group held a rally against the gays only. He was quoted as saying, "For all the bad the Klan does, they are right about the gays."[28] An Afro-American minister, Eugene Lumpkin, was removed from San Francisco's Human Rights Commission for a series of remarks denigrating homosexuality. Particularly inflammatory was what appeared to be a tacit agreement with the biblical passage that gays should be stoned to death for their "sins."[29]

Although both incidents occurred more than ten years ago, it seems not much has changed among Black religious leaders. Recently, a coalition of Black religious organizations came together to campaign against gay marriages.[30] Much of Black homophobia has been driven by the Black church. Granted, the bible is very explicit in its condemnation of homosexuality and it is regarded as a sin in the religious community. However, the bible was also used as a pretext to defend slavery and the Mormon religion claimed their bible justified Black inferiority until the 1970s. Most Black leaders came out of the Black church and developed their vision of Black freedom on the biblical teachings of their church.

Why would the Black religious community adopt a reactionary position to support the oppression of the most racially liberal white group in the United States? Most of the Black church's members have never been in conformity with mainstream norms on sexuality and the religious institutions that represented them never pursued any vigorous sanctions against them. Perhaps we based our image of the Black church on the movements of leaders like Martin Luther King and Jessie Jackson. Anthony Le Melle reminds us that the Black church has been mostly an accommodating force in American history, that the vast majority of Southern Black ministers urged their flock to completely accept their slave status.[31] We have long known that the white Southern churches did not oppose slavery or the practice of racial subordination. What religious opposition occurred came from outside religious communities. In a historical sense, religious institutions have been conservative in their positions and actions.

Perhaps the most tragic example of the Black minister's default on moral issues was an anti-gay ballot measure in Cincinnati passed with heavy support from Black churches and their members. The religious right spent hundreds of thousands of dollars to elicit the support of Black preachers and their followers. As a result, 51 percent of the Black voters voted to repeal a measure outlawing discrimination against gays. What is so tragic is that the religious right has generally been hostile to all government measures to improve the lives of Afro-Americans, such as the Civil Rights Act of 1960 and Affirmative Action. It is this group of Black enemies that Black ministers find themselves in an unholy alliance. The Cincinnati ballot measure did not ask Blacks to condone homosexuality, only to make discrimination against them illegal. In essence, they voted to repeal a law similar to the one protecting them against racial discrimination practiced by their allies in the religious right. This particular organization, The Traditional Values Coalition (TVE) consists of white, conservative groups who typically support the Republican Party.[32]

As we have been forewarned, the literature on Black homophobia is widely inconsistent. In 1993, an overwhelming 73.3 percent of Blacks refused to support the goals of the Gay Liberation Movement. The figure was only 60 percent among Afro-Americans who had friends or family members who were openly homosexual.[33] In that same year, a columnist claimed that polls on gay civil rights consistently find more support (10–22 percent higher) among Blacks than among whites.[34] Other studies declare there is no difference between the attitudes of Black heterosexuals toward homosexuals than that of their white counterparts.[35] These conflicting results are typical of sex research in general and will not be resolved in this book.

One of the most widely quoted and interesting studies is that of Ernst and his associates. They reported more negative attitudes toward gay men with AIDS but concluded that the difference was entirely attributed to the difference in attitude between Black and white women. Black women were more hostile, they said, because it was believed they were in competition with gay men for Black sexual companions.[36] Lemelle and Battle did not regard the results of their study as valid because the caregiving role of those women should have created more empathy for the social status of gay men. Indeed, the shortage of marriageable Black men would bring about more sympathy for homosexual experiences, especially as many of them would consider same sex experiences later in life due to a shortage of available men. Using a national sample, they found the opposite of Ernst and others. They concluded that feminist and masculinist identity were the most important for distinguishing attitudes of Blacks toward gay males. Essentially, the more important masculinity is to Black males the more homophobic they are, especially if they belong to homophobic religious groups.[37]

In addition to the value of masculine traits, religiosity is a big factor in Black homophobia. Harris, for example, has declared that Black homosexuals, regardless of whether or not they are active participants in faith communities will experience religious—based homophobia.[38] This is important because more than half the population are church members and have a higher frequency of church attendance than do Euro-Americans. The church is the most important institution for Afro-Americans and has a much more important influence on their belief system than it does in white communities,[39] many of these Black churches are religiously fundamental and influenced by the stress on morality of Southern Protestantism in general. The two countervailing forces to Black homophobia are personally knowing gays and high education and income for women. Lemelle and Battle discovered that among Afro-American males, the more frequent the religious attendance, the less favorable their attitudes toward gay men.[40]

If Blacks were indeed more homophobic than Euro-Americans, it would appear to be traceable to Black males, their emphasis on masculinity and participation in the church. We might note that Black male participation in the church is considerably lower than for Afro-American women except for very homophobic religions like the nation of Islam. Its most important leader, Louis Farrakhan, has warned, "We must change homosexual behavior and get rid of the circumstances that bring it about."[41] However, it is not absolutely certain that Blacks are more homophobic than Euro-Americans. In professional circles of highly educated Blacks, the only "negative" comment one might hear about gays is dislike for their analogy to Afro-American discrimination. Otherwise, I have never personally encountered any Afro-American advocating discrimination against any Black gay person. The number of prominent Black gay persons includes Langston Hughes, Lorraine Hansberry, Alice Walker, George Washington Carver, Bayard Rustin, and thousands of other Blacks whose gay identities never impeded them from getting the cooperation of other Blacks. It was more important that they were Black. It is too simplistic to conclude that the moralizing preachers and homophobic lyrics of rap music exemplify deep-seated homophobia in Afro-American communities. Some studies indicate that a higher percentage of Afro-American males engage in same-sex behavior than Euro-American males albeit not self-identified as gay. The point is that these gay/bisexual males largely live in the Black community. Among young Black males, there can be physical consequences. Many years ago, Eldridge Cleaver described Black youths who went "Punk hunting." This involved seeking out gays on the prowl, rolling them, beating them up, seemingly to inflict pain on the specific target selected.[42] According to Howard Pinderhughes, the practice still exists in Oakland and Berkeley, California. We might note that they often target weaker straights and females as well.[43]

We have already noted that sex researchers from the Kinsey Institute reported that Black men were more comfortable around gays and less likely to perceive them as a threat to their masculinity. A prominent professor of Gay and Lesbian history at The University of Chicago claims that when anti-gay attitudes were at their peak in white America—during the 1940s and 1950s—the Black community was considerably more tolerant. Whereas Afro-Americans preferred their gay friends and kin to be discreet, it was much better than in the white community.[44] A Black gay artist of the 1970s says, "[I]t was a limited space but it was there. After all, where else could we go? The white community wasn't that accepting of us. And the Black community had to protect its own."[45]

Could the Black community have become more homophobic since those eras, what happened? Certainly, the Black community is less religious now than it was in the 1940s and 1950s. One possibility is as the discriminatory pressures eased on Afro-Americans, they may have felt more comfortable in discriminating against the one white group where it matters. Perhaps they saw themselves as demonstrating their commitment to "American values" by protesting against a highly stigmatized group or they could be asserting the only privilege they were allowed in twenty-first-century America—the sexual one. After all, we can subscribe to heterosexual values and claim whatever privileges come with heterosexuality. Whatever the reason, Afro-Americans lose their moral high ground by collaborating in the denial of human rights to another group based on the most irrational of reasons—what they do in the privacy of their bedrooms.

Down Low Men and AIDS

The phenomena of Down Low (DL) men is attracting a lot of media hype for what is basically bisexual Black males who deny that they are homosexual.

Indeed, one author of a book on the subject, J. L. King, says DL men actually prefer women but continue to have sex with men.[46] The concept of Down Low was made popular by R. Kelly, he of the child pornography indictment and the singers TLC. It means secret and refers to sexually active men of the hip-hop culture who have sex with both men and women. Their importance in Black life is magnified because they are being blamed for the Black women being infected with the AIDS virus through heterosexual activity. While the sizable number of bisexual men having sex with women has long been known, the media has seized upon the Down Low term to hype it as the equivalent of the Bubonic Plague for Black women.[47]

AIDS has become a crisis in Afro-American communities and is the number one cause of death for Black men between the ages of twenty and thirty-four. This is the only measurement of the disease's impact that is acceptable. Other figures, such as men infected, new infections, are based on estimates. Whereas infections are reported to the Centers for Disease Control, we have no reason to believe all infections are reported and many victims may be infected and do not know.[48] Traditionally, Blacks have used government agencies and are more likely to show up in official data on any number of social and physical pathologies. The disproportionate number of Blacks with HIV infections begs for answers to basic questions.

Why do such a disproportionate number of Black men contact HIV infections from same-sex behavior if they do not represent more than 12 percent of the population in the United States and about the same percentage of the homosexual population? One reason is use of unsterilized needles for illegal drug use. About a third of Black deaths from AIDS result from that cause, a much higher number than among Euro-American men. The reason for the greater drug use is the same as it has been for many decades; poverty, unemployment, hopelessness, and the inability of the government to decrease the magnitude of the drug trade. Instead, they have concentrated on locking up Black consumers of drugs, which has only exacerbated the problem of unemployment, poverty, and AIDS.

Instead of concentrating on the comparatively small number of Down Low men and equally small number of heterosexual Black women infected by them, we need to understand the interplay of race, class, poverty, and homosexuality. It would appear that Black men begin same-sex behavior through two primary institutions. They are over represented in both. About one of every three Black men in their twenties is either in jail, on parole, or on probation. The primary reason they are about 55 percent of the prison population is poverty. There are few, if any, employed or college-educated Afro-American men who are incarcerated for any crime.[49] Even college-educated men who commit crimes are rarely sent to prison. While incarcerated, Black men will be introduced to same-sex behavior; some consent to it, others are forced.[50]

The incidence of same-sex behavior increases in settings that are all-male except for athletic teams. While same sex behavior in the military is consensual, it still occurs with some frequency and Black males compose about 20 percent of those in the largest military branch—the army. Once Black males breach the homosexual barrier they may develop a fondness, or tolerance for it. Hence, they may continue the same-sex behavior once they are in mixed gender life. Some may resort to it for economic reasons, others to obtain money for drugs. Generally, they are responding to economic pressures that do not exert the same influence on Euro-American males who more freely elect to live an exclusively gay lifestyle. So do many Black males but they tend to be middle-class and can afford to be openly gay.

As for the Down Low Black males, they often see being gay in very stereotyped ways; the effeminate, weak, unmasculine model often portrayed in the media. That may be why they deny being gay while engaging in same-sex behavior. That image is not part of their self-definition.[51] To act in such a way is to betray the masculine ideals of Black culture. Be clear that masculinity, as it is defined, is an important part of the collective Black identity. For centuries, Black men were treated as boys, denied even the title of mister. During slavery, all their masculine prerogatives were stripped away by plantation owners. Rations were given to slave women and children were registered in her name. Even in the post-slavery years, they were allegedly under the rule of their Euro-American employers, unable to protect their women from rapacious white men.[52]

Even today, Black males have been denied any real power. Within the family, they were told that women were in control, they were marginal and ineffective figures within their own family. When Black power and its nationalist successors emerged, masculine control became its centerpiece. Yet they never achieved economic or political power. They could win elective office only in cities with Black majorities but never progress to statewide or nationwide elected office. Hence, they had to settle for niche victories—success in the sports and entertainment world. A token number achieved success in the political and economic arena. Otherwise, they adopted the symbols of masculinity, violence, and sexual conquests. Enjoying same sex behavior could not strip them of their masculine identity.

Of course, there are other explanations for Down Low behavior. Gay Advocates have long claimed there is no such thing as a bisexual—only a man who can perform sexually with both men and women. The obvious implication is that such men are true homosexuals and in denial because of the stigma attached to it. Those of us in one camp or the other may not understand how a man can be attracted to both men and women, yet, there is the theory that man is inherently bisexual and is culturally channeled into exclusively heterosexual behavior.[53] Another explanation is that the homophobia among Afro-Americans keeps many true homosexual Black men from coming out as exclusively gay, because Euro-American males are economically secure, they have nothing to lose by coming out of the closet. Conversely, Black males may need their families more because they cannot get support in the larger community. There are no Black gay newspapers, businesses, or political organizations. Few Black gays think they would be welcomed with open arms by the white gay community. One observer has noted that, "that may help explain why many of the Black men who are openly gay tend to be more educated, have more money and generally have a greater sense of security."[54]

The hype over the threat of Down Low men to heterosexual Black women creates a cloud of suspicion over all heterosexual Afro-American men. Since Down Low men are just as masculine as all Afro-American men, there is no way to distinguish them except to catch them "in flagrante delicto." The main alarmist over Down Low men, J. T. King, says women should use their sixth sense, an inner voice that tells them something is "wrong" about a man. If that does not work, he suggests interrogating him or doing some sort of investigation.[55] This advice he is giving goes to a group of women who face any number of hurdles in finding a marriageable male. And, not every male will tolerate interrogations and investigations of his background because 5 percent of the Black male heterosexual population is on the Down Low.

As for the magnitude of the problem, straight Black women infected with HIV comprise about 13 percent of the AIDS victims, while 75 percent of those women allegedly contact the virus through heterosexual activity, their male sexual partners may have contacted HIV from intravenous drug injections.[56] For some reason, the assumption has been made that the male sexual partner had been participating in same sex behavior. The bottom line is that women infected by Down Low men are only 10 percent of the AIDS victims and the other 90 percent of AIDS victims are no less deserving of public attention, support, and treatment. While current medications and treatment have slowed down deaths from AIDS, the real solution lies in the remediation of poverty and racism.

What about the Lesbians?

Lesbians share the social stigma of their gay male counterparts but there are significant differences between the two groups. One of the reasons that lesbians are less visible could be attributed to the possibility that they are less socially acceptable in the Black community. So thinks Audre Lorde, who declares, "If the recent hysterical rejection of lesbians in the Black community is based solely upon an aversion to the idea of sexual contact between members of the same sex—why then is the idea of sexual contact between Black men so much more easily accepted, or unremarked."[57] Another Black lesbian speaks thus about her oppression:

> As a Black lesbian I am in a weird situation. I am oppressed not only by society as a whole, but the Black community too. The Black community looks upon the lesbian as Blacks do upon whites. This is particularly true of Black males who consider lesbians a threat. Black males think that a lesbian is fair game sexually for anybody, because she can't get a man or is turned off by men.[58]

Those Black women who chose lesbianism fared better than their male counterparts. They had fewer transient sexual contacts, for example, most of them had fewer than ten female sexual partners during the course of their homosexual careers, and two-thirds of them reported that the majority of their sexual partners had been persons about whom they cared and for whom they had some affection.[59] In the lesbian culture, youthfulness did not carry the importance it had among male homosexuals or heterosexuals. Because members of the same sex are more sensitive to each other's sexual needs, many lesbians reported satisfactory sexual experiences. This was most evident in the fact that lesbians displayed greater skill in performing oral sex than did men engaged in performing oral sex with woman. Less than two-thirds of the Black lesbians reported that they spent less than half of their leisure time alone. Few of the lesbians encountered sexual problems or contracted a venereal disease. However, Black lesbians were more likely to report poor health and psychosomatic symptoms, to feel lonely more often, and to display more tension and paranoia.[60]

We know no more about the causes of lesbianism than we do about male homosexuality. A theory that covers both groups is that their homosexual orientation emerges in response to past difficulties in heterosexual relationships. It is true that half of the Black lesbians had been married at least once (compared to fewer than 20 percent of Black male homosexuals). And some Black female singles in our study reported that they had considered a lesbian relationship if their relationship with men did not improve.[61]

According to a thirty-seven-year-old teacher, "I'm not ready for homosexuality yet. If men keep playing games with me, I might consider switching in later life. Right now, I still know a few cool dudes." Probably a more typical response to lesbianism is that of a thirty-nine-year-old college administrator:

> Don't worry about me and the Daughters of Bilitis. Somehow I don't think deliberately complicating my life like that would net me anything I'm particularly in need of. For that kind of risk I'd have to be assured of something really great. Knowing what I know about human beings of both sexes and many races I have little hope that anybody can assure me of anything. So, I'll take my chances with my present lifestyle.[62]

Indications are that most Black women live primarily heterosexual lives. Some have recently turned to occasional bisexual experiences. Most of them do this in a clandestine manner—frequently between serious relationships with men. Our interviews confirm a great deal of alternation between men and women.

As previously noted, the most extensive survey of sexual practices since Kinsey found only 0.60 percent of Afro-American women said they were homosexual or bisexual.[63] When Gail Wyatt asked Black women in the 1980s if they had a female sexual partner, about 5 percent of them reported having sex with another woman once. A majority of their sex partners were lovers or friends and the rest were coworkers and strangers. Wyatt claims that the lesbian relationships were self-described as intense, characterized by mutual fondling, manual and oral stimulation that culminated in orgasm for most of the women. As for why these Black women participated in same sex behavior, most often cited was curiosity and the surprise of a seductive attempt by another woman. A third of them reported being in love with or turned on by their female partner. Of the 5 percent who engaged in same-sex behavior, only a third had just one partner and the majority had between two and six partners in adulthood.[64]

When Wyatt conducted her research again in 1994, similar results were found. The lesbian relationship typically began around the age of twenty-two, averaging four sexual partners and generally involved the practice of oral manipulation of the vagina. More than two-thirds of these women engaging in some sex activity were also participating in coitus with a man at the same time. The most important finding of her research was that two of three women denied that the sex alone was their only reason for same-sex behavior. Wyatt suggests that other factors such as the need for love, emotional support, and nurturance may have driven them. A majority of them described feeling guilty about the encounter although that may have been a function of their cheating on male partners. About 10 percent were also cheating on another female partner.[65]

The Wyatt number of homosexual and bisexual Afro-American women is five times higher than in the massive sexual survey. Being based in California, I suspect her research is heavily weighted toward women residing in this state. California is a magnet state for men and women who want to engage in alternative sexual lifestyles. While San Francisco has the reputation as a homosexual Mecca, Los Angeles and even San Diego are equally as tolerant of people who want to "be different"—in a lot of ways. That means straight women might find even a greater shortage of straight men than in other states. Afro-American women may discover that as many as 25 percent of the heterosexual Black men in California are dating and married to women of other races.[66] That creates an even greater shortage than Afro-American women face nationwide. Thus, we may not be able to generalize from Wyatt's sample to the rest of the United States.

However, her research illustrates what we note about Black female sexuality in other chapters. It is very fluid and its purpose is multifunctional. Black women can easily slip in and out of same-sex activity. As I watched a television show, there was a scene with a teenage girl hugging her mother in bed. The culture casually accepts this affectionate behavior between women. How easy is it for two unrelated women to slip into physical sex acts in the context of this bonding between women? Normally, it does not involve penetration. Indeed, it is regarded as "heavy petting" in heterosexual relationships. For Black women, it may involve no shift of female identity or cast any doubt on their femininity. They may not frequent lesbian bars or participate in lesbian political activity. In most cases, they can continue the same-sex intimacy without suspicion, even setting up a household with another woman does not arouse any concerns about homosexuality in the general population unless they are of an advanced age.

Knowing there are such stark differences in how we treat same-sex behavior among women raised the question of the nature of homosexuality. Why doesn't the genetic marker produce homosexuality in as many women as men? Probably, lesbian advocates would explain it as cultural pressures on women to be wives and mothers is much greater. A male finds it much easier—even today—to remain unmarried and childless than adult women. Is it the "maternal instinct" or cultural pressures? In one of the most recent surveys that included homosexual women, The Black Pride Survey 2000, almost a third of Black lesbians reported having given birth to a child. This is considerably higher than the Anglo lesbians (23 percent) who are reported as having produced a child. Some have suggested that parenting among Euro-American lesbians is overstated and understated among Black lesbians. They feel the distinction is important because it refutes the commonly held notion that homosexual and family are two mutually exclusive categories as well as the religious right's attempt to portray gays as intrinsic threats to children. In particular, they feel that restrictive anti-gay adoption policies need to be changed. In some states, the partner of a lesbian mother may be prevented from adopting her child that she has been raising from birth. Given the shortage of adoptive homes for Black children, it may pose a more serious problem for the Black family.[67]

One of the more interesting studies of Black lesbians was conducted by Vicki Mays and Susan D. Cochran. Their sample consisted of 530 self-identified Black lesbians and 66 bisexual women. It was designed to study lesbians only and bisexual women were only a small part of the group under investigation. One caution; the investigators were based in California and the sample is heavily biased in favor of that state. They acknowledge that their sample is not representative. For example, almost half had a college degree and 84 percent were employed at least half-time. The majority self-defined as middle-class, a third had children, a third cohabited with their partner/lover and two-thirds were in a serious/committed relationship. The researchers claimed these were women with a relatively committed lesbian lifestyle.[68]

Women in the majority were in their thirties and said they were first attracted to other women at an average age of sixteen and first engaged in same sex activity around nineteen years of age. Most of them reported sex with a Black woman, two-thirds with a Euro-American woman, and almost 40 percent with other women of color. The median number of sexual partners was nine. What is interesting is that when Black lesbians went outside the race, it was to Anglo women, not other women of color. We must remember that many of these women were in California, where non-Hispanic whites are now a statistical minority.[69] However, it mirrors the interracial pattern we find in the straight Black community. While they did not discover symptoms of depression to be different than for straight Black women, they did show that Black lesbians who are isolated in the Anglo lesbian community more likely to suffer from depression. Those integrated into the Black lesbian community had a greater tendency to experience drug and alcohol problems.[70]

We have no idea how much of Black female bisexuality is a function of the Black male shortage. Another possibility is that some Black women may be engaging in same-sex behavior due to a fear of contracting an HIV infection or some other sexually transmitted disease. The reasons are many and diverse. If they become lesbians because they are disenchanted with men, they may find that it is not a long-lasting solution. Over two decades ago, the best-selling feminist author Michelle Wallace observed, "I don't think that all of these people that are homosexual are born that way. I think that men and women are having problems now with each other and sometimes they think the easiest way to get around that is to go with the same sex; but of course the same problems appear, because they're having problems with themselves and with people in general."[71]

The issue of understanding female homosexuality is made more difficult by the diverse motives of women who become lesbians. It has become fashionable for young white women to have the lesbian experience while an undergraduate in college and later enter into a heterosexual marriage. Some feminists have seen the oppression of lesbians as part of the subordination of women and join them in sympathy. The reality is that lesbians have more in common with gay men and suffer from many of the negative sanctions imposed on same-sex behavior as they do. Lifetime lesbians have pointed out that many of these women are not authentic lesbians and may not be there when crunch time comes. Some years ago Patricia Bell Scott, one of America's foremost Black feminists predicted we would see grey lesbianism among Black women during that time of the life cycle when the shortage of Black men is most acute.[72]

Down Low Black men and bisexual Black women may be part of the social terrain for years to come. Perhaps it is the realization of the notion that we all have the capacity for bisexuality and only the restrictions society imposes prevents us from acting on it. Bisexuality may prove to be the wave of the future and it is interesting to note that Blacks are once again in the vanguard of social change. However, the barriers remain and the rights of gays will not be achieved without a long and protracted struggle. Having gay characters on television programs and finding more positive attitudes toward gays and lesbians in surveys will produce no real change in the rights of homosexual Americans. Afro-Americans have witnessed public opinion equality while continuing to experience the persistence of racial discrimination in the real world. Gays have much to learn from their experience.

Notes

1. Carolyn Lochhead, "High Court Ruling Likely to Usher in New Era for Gays." *San Francisco Chronicle*, June 29, 2003, p. A-4.

2. Harriet Chiang, "After the Wedding Bells, Gays Face Maze of Legal Obstacles." *San Francisco Chronicle*, April 26, 2004, p. A-1.

3. Huey P. Newton, "A Letter from Huey to the Revolutionary Brothers and Sisters about the Women's Liberation and Gay Liberation Movements." *The Black Panther*, August 21, 1970, p. 1.

4. Joane Nagel, *Race, Ethnicity, and Sexuality: Intimate Intersections, Forbidden Frontiers*. New York: Oxford University Press, 2003, p. 142.

5. *Ibid.* pp. 123–125.

6. Martin S. Weinberg and Colin J. Williams, *Male Homosexuals.* New York: Penguin Books, 1975.

7. Ruth Hubbard, "The Search for Sexual Identity: False Genetic Markers." *New York Times,* August 2, 1993, p. A-11.

8. Sigmund Freud, *Three Contributions to the Theory of Sex.* New York: Dutton, 1962 (first published in 1905).

9. E. O. Laumann, et al., *The Social Organization of Sexuality.* Chicago: University of Chicago Press, 1994, pp. 303–345.

10. Elizabeth Mehren, "Homosexuals Finding More Acceptance, Poll Says." *San Francisco Chronicle,* April 11, 2004, p. A-6.

11. "Works of Aristotle, Friendship." *Encyclopedia Britannica* Vol. 2, 1959, p. 459.

12. Robert Staples, *Black Masculinity.* San Francisco: The Black Scholar Press, 1982, pp. 85–101.

13. John Mbiti, *Love and Marriage in Africa.* London: Longman, 1973, p. 35.

14. Thomas Pettigrew, *A Profile of the Negro American.* Princeton: D. Van Nostrand, 1964, pp. 17–22.

15. E. Franklin Frazier, *Black Bourgeoisie.* New York: Crowell-Collier, 1962, p. 182.

16. Pettigrew, *Loc. cit.*

17. Alan Bell and Martin Weinberg, *Homosexualities.* New York: Simon and Schuster, 1978, pp. 34–215.

18. Erich Fromm quoted in the *San Francisco Chronicle,* May 19, 1979, p. 33.

19. Bell and Weinberg, *loc. cit.*

20. Interview document c.f. Robert Staples, *The World of Black Singles.* Westport, Connecticut: Greenwood Press, 1981.

21. Bell and Weinberg, *loc. cit.*

22. "Castro Bars Called Racist." *San Francisco Examiner,* June 15, 2004, p. 7.

23. Bell and Weinberg, *loc. cit.*

24. Interview document.

25. Anastasia Hendrix, "Diversity Flourishes in Gay, Lesbian Couples." *San Francisco Chronicle,* September 15, 2003, p. A-1.

26. "Homophobia, Racism Likely Companions Study Shows." *Jet Magazine,* January 10, 1994, p. 12.

27. Kobena Mercer and Julien Isaac, "True Confessions: A Discourse on Images of Black Male Sexuality." *Ten,* Summer 1986, Vol. 8, pp. 4–9.

28. Evelyn C. White, "Identity Crisis for the Black Church." *San Francisco Chronicle,* January 12, 1994, p. A-1.

29. Clarence Johnson, "Gays, Blacks Try to Cool Tensions." *San Francisco Chronicle,* August 28, 1993, p. A-1.

30. Don Lattin, "Black Clergy Gathering to Fight Gay Matrimony." *San Francisco Chronicle,* May 15, 2004, p. A-7.

31. Anthony J. Lemelle, "African American Attitudes toward Gay Males: Faith Based Initiatives and Implications for HIV/AIDs Services." Unpublished paper, April 2003, p. 4.

32. Donald Suggs and Mandy Carter, "Cincinnati's Odd Couple." *New York Times*, December 13, 1993, p. A-11.

33. "Poll Finds Little Black Support for Gay Movement." *San Francisco Sun Reporter*, October 27, 1993, p. 4.

34. Joan Lester, "The Tension between Blacks and Gays." *San Francisco Examiner*, September 20, 1993, p. A-2.

35. G. Herek and J. Capitanio, "Black Heterosexuals' Attitudes toward Lesbian and Gay Men in the United States," *Journal of Sex Research*, 1995, 32, No. 2, pp. 95–105.

36. Frederick Ernst, et al., "Condemnation of Homosexuality in the Black Community: A Gender Specific Phenomena." *Archives of Sexual Behavior*, December 1999, 20, No. 6, pp. 579–586.

37. Anthony J. Lemelle and Juan Battle, "Black Masculinity Matters in Attitudes toward Gay Males." *Journal of Homosexuality*, 2004, 47(1), pp. 39–51.

38. Whitney G. Harris, "African American Homosexual Males on Predominantly White College and University Campuses." *Journal of African American Studies*, Summer 2003, 7, pp. 47–56.

39. Lemelle, *loc. cit.*

40. Lemelle and Battle, *loc. cit.*

41. David W. Dunlap, "Gay Blacks in Quandary over Farrakhan's March." *San Francisco Chronicle*, October 8, 1995, p. A-24.

42. Eldridge Cleaver, *Soul on Ice*. New York: Dell Publishing, 1968, p. 103.

43. Howard Pinderhughes, personal communication, May 15, 2004.

44. George Chauncey quoted in Benoit Denizet-Lewis, "Double Lives on the Down Low," *New York Times Magazine*, August 3, 2003, p. 32.

45. Glenn Ligon quoted in *ibid.*

46. J. L. King, *On the Down Low: A Journey into the Lives of Straight Black Men Who Sleep with Men*. New York: Broadway Books, 2004.

47. "Men on the Down Low: J. L. King Exposes the Sex Secret that is Devastating Black Women." *Jet Magazine*, May 3, 2004, pp. 32–37.

48. Center for Disease Control cited in Russell L. Stockard Jr. and M. Belinda Tucker, "Young African American Men and Women: Separate Paths" in *The State of Black America 2001*. New York: The National Urban League, 2001: 153–154.

49. *Ibid.* pp. 152–153.

50. Cindy Struckman-Johnson et al., "Sexual Coercion Reported by Men and Women in Prison." *Journal of Sex Research*, 1996, 33(1), pp. 67–76.

51. Denizet-Lewis, *op. cit.* pp. 31–32.

52. Staples, *Black Masculinity. Op.cit.*

53. Freud, *loc. cit.*

54. Denizet-Lewis, *op. cit.* p. 32.

55. J. L. King, *loc. cit.*

56. Stockard and Tucker, p. 154.

57. Audre Lorde, "Scratching the Surface: Some Notes on Barriers to Women and Loving." *The Black Scholar*, April 1978, Vol. 10, p. 34.

58. Ann Allen Schockley and Veronica Tucker, "Black Women Discuss Today's Problems: Men, Family, Society." *Southern Voices*, August-September 1974, 1, p. 18.

59. Bell and Weinberg, *op. cit.* p. 93.

60. *Ibid.* pp. 180–215.

61. *Ibid.*

62. Interview document.

63. Laumann, *loc. cit.*

64. Gail Wyatt, *Stolen Women: Reclaiming Our Sexuality, Taking Back Our Lives.* New York: Wiley, 1997, pp. 163–167.

65. *Ibid.*

66. M. Belinda Tucker and Claudia Mitchell-Kernan, eds. *The Decline in Marriage among African Americans.* New York: Russell Sage, 1995.

67. Juan Battle et al., "We Are Family: Embracing Our Lesbian, Gay, Bisexual and Transgender (LGBT) Family Members" in *The State of Black America 2003.* New York: The National Urban League 2003, pp. 98–102.

68. Vicki Mays and Susan Cochran, "The Black Women's Relationship Project: A National Survey of Black Lesbians" in *The Black Family: Essays and Studies*, 6th Edition, ed. R. Staples. Belmont, California: Wadsworth, 1999, pp. 59–66.

69. Katherine Seligman, "U.S. to Look a Lot like California by 2050." *San Francisco Chronicle*, March 18, 2004, p. A-1.

70. Mays and Cochran, *loc. cit.*

71. Quoted in *Sun Reporter*, August 30, 1979, p. 16.

72. Patricia Bell-Scott, personal communication, August 3, 1984.

CHAPTER FIVE

~

Dating as a Sexual Adventure

Dating as an activity never was deeply rooted in the Black community. It began around the turn of the century among Euro-Americans. Before 1890, it was typical of the man to "call upon" a woman in her parlor, with her parents lurking nearby. Only those men with serious intentions came calling and dating was universally followed by courtship that in turn generally culminated in marriage. Sex would enter the picture for some couples and in the event of a pregnancy, marriage usually took place before the birth of a child. For Afro-Americans, dating was a "catch as catch can" matter. Most of them resided in the South and they had few "all Black" outlets in which to take a date. Since the South had established most entertainment centers as all-white bastions, only the few juke joints and movie houses were available, mostly in the larger cities. In many cities, juke joints were not regarded as appropriate places to take "nice" young ladies on a date.

In the twenty-first century, dating as an activity is more widespread among Blacks but there is talk that it is a dying cultural form. Its relationship to courtship and marriage is very weak. Few Afro-Americans follow lockstep from dating to courtship and marriage any longer. Moreover, sexual relationships may often be an antecedent of dating, if ever it occurs. Both Black males and females reach puberty at a slightly earlier age than Euro-Americans. The average age of puberty is less than twelve these days and sexual activity follows closely afterwards. Some Black children engage in sex play as early as four and five, with neighborhood children, other relatives, even siblings. This sex play begins before they have any understanding of sexuality and its significance in the world. They only know about the plea-sure associated with touching their genitals and the sensation derived from contact with other children.

At an early age, they become aware of sexuality. If they are lower income children, they live under crowded conditions that expose them to the sexual activity of adults. Many in that social class will grow up in single parent households. Typically, the mother, and that parent may still have an active sex life. Older siblings may introduce the child to the mysteries of sex through the example of their own sexual activity, stories about the sexual ex-ploits of others, and their rap music that is played in the room they share. Sexual innocence for the young, lower income child may end before the first grade, certainly long before they can manage to go on that first date. Middle-class parents can protect their children from the intrusion of sexuality into their lives. They may be isolated from older siblings in their own room and their movements and activities closely monitored. Only the "clean" hip-hop music is allowed. Television programs may be controlled and visits by neigh-borhood children closely supervised. Even middle-class parents cannot mon-itor their children 24/7 and they may manage to observe sex-laden scenes in daytime soap operas, see sexuality on cable television, and, when older, fig-ure out ways to watch pornography on the Internet.

Although few parents may allow their children to "date" before age 16, more than half of all Afro-American children will have experienced sex for the first time before that age.[1] Middle schools in America will be filled with a mixture of the sexually naïve with the sexually sophisticated. It does not take long before the naïve are transformed into the sophisticated. Few will be armed with adequate sex education by their parents. Sex education courses tend to be available in predominantly Black inner city schools because few Black parents resist them. In some cases, those sex education classes only re-inforce what they have already learned through experience. Many of the sex education courses include instruction on HIV and AIDS, frightening enough to have a chilling effect on teenage sexual activity where other warnings have been ineffective. Many lower income teenagers will be aware of AIDS victims among their parents' friends, neighbors, and even some of their class-mates. Young girls, if sexually active, learn to demand the use of condoms. Young males, while resisting the use of condoms, find that their use is the only way to gain sexual access to females in their peer group.[2]

What passes for dating among teenagers is going to the shopping malls in mixed gender groups, and going off to someplace private in pairs. Very little in American society tells teenagers that young sexual experimentation is wrong—except in some sex education classes and the church if they belong to one. Their movies, television programs, music, and sports heroes all shape a sexual morality that sexuality in America is okay for everybody. Ergo, very few will graduate from high school as virgins. Peer pressure alone will ensure that fact. Exceptions are men too shy to initiate sexual relationships and those girls convinced that there is a strong relationship between sexual abstinence and upward mobility. At one point, the mothers of middle-class teenagers would have entered college as virgins. But those mothers did not grow up in an environment where the only female virgins were the "uncool" and the "undesirables."

When young Blacks enter the domain of higher education, they also encounter an open door to sexual freedom. Most Americans attend large public universities that have a minimum of rules governing individual student behaviors. Those who live in dormitory residences are free to come and go as they please. Some of the residential halls may be coed dorms where males and females may share rooms or live in the same building. If Afro-Americans elect to attend private Black colleges, there may be some restrictions. Some Black colleges may require freshman to live on campus and they are not allowed to have a car in their first year. Such rules do little to prevent them from engaging in sexual activity. A basic axiom is that sex can take place anywhere there is some privacy and nobody can see you. If both students live in a residential hall, there is generally where they will have their sexual rendezvous. Almost all of them will have roommates who tend to be very cooperative about allowing space for sexual encounters. By their junior and senior year, many students will have pooled their funds and rented an apartment or house together. Each will have a separate bedroom and what goes on in them is not a concern of the other roommates except when boyfriends/ sexual partners become obnoxious.

Despite their advanced ages, very few college students go out on individual dates. It is very common to see college students out in groups or socializing at fraternity and sorority parties. Many college males prefer the group activities because each person pays their own way. College females may like the group date because it is safer. With a group of people, you can let your guard down without feeling vulnerable. Another reason is a fear of intimacy. Many college students will graduate without having entered into a relationship that will culminate in marriage. There is the fear of a divorce that they saw their parents or their friend's parents go through. There is the desire to get established in a career before marriage and children hinder their career prospects. That does not mean four years of sexual abstinence. There is the "hook-up" for casual sex or the sexual encounters that occur without commitment. If a person proposes individual dating, that could presage a step toward the slippery slope of marriage, something they are not ready for—if ever.

Depending on what they do and where they go after college graduation, the college years are the best time to find a mate, particularly for women. Almost everybody in college is close to the same age, should attain the same social class standing, and is unmarried. Once you leave college, a person can be subject to the cruel vagaries of the dating game and its expectations. If a woman goes into occupations like nursing, she will meet a lot of nice women and very old and sick men. The same will be true of schoolteachers in elementary schools where 95 percent of their colleagues are other women and the children cannot date without parental approval. Failing to date and mate in college can leave a thirty-something female sitting in a coffee shop waiting to be approached by Mister Right or hoping to find him in a supermarket, laundromat, or bus stop. In other words, she becomes a participant in the dating game.[3]

The Dating Scene

No matter at what age Black women began one-on-one dating, they will be bedeviled by an inescapable demographic fact: A shortage of eligible men. It begins in high school where the girls are all talking college preparatory or business classes in which to enter the white-collar world. The males are often talking vocational courses or hoping for an athletic scholarship that will allow them entry into a professional sports career. Those not aspiring to be jocks, mechanics, or other blue-collar occupations may be practicing their rhymes to obtain a recording contract as a hip-hop artist. Sadly, some of them will be sidetracked into drugs, petty crime, or simply drop out of school at the legal age of sixteen. The paucity of males joining the females in college is so great that the mothers of college-oriented boys are besieged by Black girls pursuing their sons. In part that is because girls have the freedom to initiate "dates" but it is often a function of the competition for a scarce commodity.

How stiff is the competition? Many parents send their daughters to predominantly Black colleges where they might obtain a degree and a husband. It is one place where the boys will not be distracted by the increasingly available Euro-American female. However, the ratio of Black female to male college students, in the freshman year alone is two to one in twenty-first-century America. At some Black colleges, it is eighteen to one. The ratio will be even lower among those who graduate. Add to her dismal chances the fact that some college males will be involved with a girl "back home" or with one of the wretched townies. The majority of Afro-Americans no longer attend Black colleges. Yet, those who do are overwhelmingly female. Maybe it's because the predominantly white university offers a free ride through college on an athletic scholarship that attracts the Black male. Many are also located nearer their homes in Detroit, New York, Chicago, etc. Almost all Black colleges are private, moderate tuition schools, located in the South, some of them in rural, small towns.

That partly explains why the average Black female graduates from college with just a degree. What about the satisfaction of their sexual needs? The males' tendency toward multiple sexual partners means they may find a sexual partner but there will be a long line of women waiting on the few males available. Among this group of Black women are the most conservative of sexual types in the Afro-American community. They were taught that upward mobility and sexual license do not go together. Instead of nurturing sexual urges, they will spend Saturday nights with a girlfriend or in the library. What they will want is the American dream: a house, nice car, designer clothes, and 2.0 children. They may obtain all of them by themselves but they really prefer a husband to give them those two children. That will require "dating" of some sort and dealing with this tricky issue of sex.

Her chances are not helped by the fact that the prospective pool of husbands does not operate on the same timetable nor have the same ranking of priorities. When the college educated Black male is ready to marry, he has no shortage of available women. Thus, he may bide his time and surely wants the pick of the litter. Meanwhile, there are wild oats to be sown and he is the man to do it. It sets up a system of sexual capitalism with each gender trying to leverage the advantages of their gender. With her, it will be the sexual attractiveness and access. For him, it will be the key to the American dream. He has the college degree, the potential for the middle-class income, and is a commodity in demand.

We must note that the noncollege educated Black woman must address a different set of realities. Many of the men in her class are now in jail, on drugs, or dead. The mortality rate for young Black males is three times greater than that of Black females. About one of three Black males aged eighteen through thirty is in jail, on probation, or parole. We can only guess at the number of young Black men who abuse drugs or alcohol or both.[4] Certainly, some Black males do not go to college and obtain decent paying jobs that do not require a college degree. They do exist, marry early, and have the most stable marriages in the Black community. Because they do have moderate incomes, some are poached by college-educated women.

That leaves comparatively few drug-free, stably employed, Black men for working-class women. If we ask whom they marry—the answer is that they do not. Because most Afro-Americans are working-class, they make up the large majority of the two-thirds of Black women not married and living with their spouse.[5] They do engage in sexual relations, at least long enough to bear children who will be born without a legally wedded husband. It is a pragmatic adaptation to their situation where the real sex ratio of women to men is more than seven to one once you include only the drug free, non-criminal, and stably employed Black males. Their jobs will provide an income of sorts, not a career or much satisfaction. Their only satisfaction will derive from the byproduct of their sexual activity: children. Even that joy may be short-lived as they watch their sons grow into teenagers and are hauled off to jail with their Black peers or die early deaths from AIDS, drug overdoses, and homicides.

Obviously, some women—and men—will fare better. It may help to live in a racially integrated community where there are models of success other than pimps and drug pushers. The women who marry working-class men do live the American dream. Income is pooled. Houses are purchased. There are two-car garages, vacations to exotic places and a college education for their kids. Some of the single women may escape the pink ghetto and obtain jobs in sales that reward hard work. They, too, will have children out of wedlock, often one. The more attractive women in this class may find a husband as the few "decent" men available pick and choose. As for their dating and sex life, there may be little of either. The available men have no money to pay for dates, so it is more a matter of "getting together," generally at her house for meals or drinks. Often, she may have to help him out by buying gas for his car or by paying for gifts. That can be the price of male companionship in poor communities.

Even a decent sex life can be hard to come by. If he has an alcohol or drug abuse problem, he may not be the best sex partner. Not only may he have erectile difficulties but the effects of alcohol and drugs can desensitize him to her sexual needs. Consequently, many of these women rely on their female friends for support and companionship. With no "Mister Right" on the horizon, she resorts to eating fat laden foods as a substitute for love and affection. This, more than everything else, probably accounts for the large rise in obesity among Afro-American women. In part, it is the diet that is rich in calories and fat. It is part of their heritage when they lived in the rural South and got plenty of exercise. Now, they have sedentary jobs and over 60 percent of Black women are classified as obese. It makes them physically unattractive to even the liquored up, drugged, and unemployed Black male. Even the logistics of intercourse can be awkward. One man said that he felt like he was on top of a waterbed.

Within this social class, anxieties and guilt about sex are rare. They are the women who began sexual activity early and continued if they liked a man. For the men, "getting over" with girls was a way of earning respect within the all-male peer group. Very few of these men were monogamous except for a lack of opportunity. Many of the men did have a steady old lady to whom they confined most of their sexual activity. If they had jobs, or when they worked, the expectation might be that they would assist her with the rent or buy some groceries. Sometimes, they developed relationships with her children and took them around the neighborhood. While they may have attempted to cohabit at one time, the problems of alcohol/drugs and other women often make her evict him. During the economic boom years of the 1990s, some of these women married men who had managed to obtain steady work. Welfare reform had forced some of the women to take low-paying jobs and lose some of their benefits. Few of the marriages lasted for long.

Dating Capitalism

After graduation from college, when few of them marry nowadays, these recent graduates returned to their hometowns or settled in new cities. For those who return to their hometowns, many of them move back in with their families. The skyrocketing rents in large cities make establishing an independent residence prohibitive. Females may be more likely to move in with female friends whereas males may prefer the cooking of their single parent mothers. Because the mothers do not have significant others in their lives, they hold on to their adult children as long as possible. However, these living arrangements can pose problems for sexually active young people. Among the older generation of Afro-Americans, the old adage is "if you respect me, there will be no sex under my roof if you are not married." Some females may require the male to find a place for their sexual rendezvous, which could be the nearest motel. That, of course, certainly restricts the number of times they engage in coitus.

When Black college graduates obtain jobs, they find out that the higher paying the job the fewer Blacks work in their office. Most Black women prefer to date Black men due to cultural familiarity and anticipated disapproval of their family if they bring a non-Black person home to meet the family. If she does have a Black coworker, she has to hope he does not work in a supervisory capacity. Many organizations frown on romances between supervisors and subordinates; some define it as possible sexual harassment for the supervisor if there is a complaint. Other organizations forbid romantic liaisons between an employee and clients or customers. That rules out most of the people one might meet in the work world. Despite the rules, many Blacks do enter into relationships with supervisors, clients, and customers. They can only hope that a vindictive former lover does not blow the whistle on them when the affair ends.

Since most of the Black college graduates are female, the chances are that she will not meet many male counterparts. However, if she attended a Black college, she may now meet some of the males who attended predominantly white universities. Where she will meet him is another matter. In many of the large American cities, there is a substantial Black population and they have favorite hangouts. In recent years, Black singles organizations have formed, some of them within churches. Finding Black singles may not be the most difficult part of hooking up. It is matching up people who have reason to be suspicious of each other.

It is the initial encounter that distinguishes the dating styles of Blacks from Euro-Americans. The meeting often begins with the male rap, a conversational style that centers around how good a woman looks, how she turns him on, what he will do for her, what she can do for him, how good in bed he will be to her, and so on. This occurs on the first encounter and is often an explicit invitation to have a sexual rendezvous. It is very different from the style of the white male who may pretend that his dinner invitation is about everything but a sexual opportunity.[6] There is no consensus about how effective the rap is in enticing a Black female into a man's bed. Generally, she is aware of whether she is receptive to a sexual engagement with him and only some poor move will dissuade her or, despite the explicit sexual intention, she may go out with him, refuse to have sex, and wait to see if he returns for a second date.

The rap is obviously nothing more than a male ritual and some Black women protest the insincerity inherent in it. Yet, she is aware of his intentions and does not have to guess about whether he likes her or not. Given that many Black women have few dating opportunities, she may be flattered by the rhetoric and might even believe that he means some of it. No matter how good a rapper he may be, it is unlikely that sex will transpire on the first date—at least not in the twenty-first century. The female notion is that if she sleeps with him on the first date he will think she does it with every male. Since few middle-class Black women are interested in one-night stands, he is politely refused and she waits patiently to see if he requests a second date. Somehow, there is a clear-cut rule that sex on the third date is acceptable to both men and women. Or, she is expected to decline future dates.

After a third date, the question is where they go from there. There is a great gender divide in terms of how men and women interpret dating that culminates in sexual congress. Women see this as the prelude to marriage and he views it as a nice sexual interlude, not a commitment to anything more serious than the next date. There may not even be another date if the sex was unsatisfactory. Maybe he felt that she was too passive during the act, did not talk enough, did not tell him what a great lover he was, or did not have an orgasm. They may not agree on the etiquette of the first sexual encounter. Perhaps she is offended by the lack of foreplay or after play when she wants him to continue fondling and kissing her. Going to sleep immediately after ejaculation is not going to be fondly remembered by her. Some women resent men who do not spend the night, hurriedly puts on his clothes, and rushes off. Any slipup can make your first sexual episode also the last one.

During the 1970s, sexual transactions transpired with no strings attached. Women saw sexual freedom as their right and carnal knowledge did not translate into owning her. In the twenty-first century, a sexual moment can set into motion a complex set of expectations and obligations, often implicit and unspoken. The first and most important obligation is to confine their sexual activity exclusively to each other. Nowadays the pretext is that it is too risky to have multiple sexual partners with all the chances of acquiring AIDS. It is typically AIDS that is the risk, not other sexually transmitted diseases that one is more likely to encounter. Along with that basic obligation is the expectation that weekends will be spent with the sexual partner, that you have first priority on all free time and easy access by phone or e-mail.

All of these assumptions are contingent on both parties being unencumbered by other relationships, and that is more likely to be the case for the female participants. As women soon discover, there are a number of pretenders in their midst. One of them is the married man who is "single for the night." The sophisticated marital cheat is able to mask his marital status by using a post office box disguised as an address, voice mail to collect all his calls and caller ID to screen all his calls. The novice female dater may not notice telltale clues for some dates. Not all the pretenders are married—some have steady girlfriends elsewhere. At least, that relationship can be and often is easily terminated. Men tend to lie about a number of other things, their jobs, ages, and income. If people meet via personal ads or the Internet, a high percentage of people using those devices are deceptive about their personal qualities.

Because the expectation of marriage goes along with regular sexual contact and is as American as mom and cherry pie, few question the appropriateness of women linking the two things. Most men and women enter into sexual relationships without any explicit agreement on what it means. It is understandable that Black women want marriage as the culmination of her sexual relationships over a period of time. After all, marriage represents the fulfillment of her role as a woman. It will provide respectability to their sex life, children within wedlock, a link to their families of origin, and an organized social life. For him, marriage could mean an end to sexual variety, taking on financial obligations of children, a mortgage, and boring social life organized around association with other married couples.

The one reason both men and women might want to marry is to escape the vagaries of the dating game. Although there are more than seventy million singles in America, they are not all going out on dates every weekend. One reason, of course, is that it is very expensive to do so in large cities. A dinner for two can average one hundred dollars by the time the sales tax, tips, parking, or cabs are added up. Going to a Broadway musical concert costs in excess of one hundred dollars for one person in the big cities of New York, Chicago, and Los Angeles. Not only is the expense a problem but not everybody that you date will bring you great joy for the evening. Some will lack a sense of humor, be surly or cynical, bland, supercilious, and any other personality traits possessed by Homo sapiens. If you are a male, be prepared to pay the whole tab unless you make clear that the expenses are to be shared. If you do announce a Dutch treat to her, be prepared to masturbate for your sexual relief that night.

Since women are the decision makers on whether sex will occur, they do not see dating as a sexual opportunity. Very few of them want to continually go out on dates every weekend, have sex on the third date, and repeat the process every six months. We have no reason to believe that women are inherently monogamous. As many as 50 percent of married women have cheated on their husbands, an indication that monogamy may not be their natural state.[7] The conventional wisdom is that it is men who need to date in order to have a sexual opportunity. Women are quite capable of inviting men to their domicile for sexual reasons and dispensing with the preliminaries of a date. Many younger women like the excitement of the new date, getting dressed up and going out after a week dealing with work issues. Many men still pay the full freight for an evening out on the town. Among younger Black college females, that is not justified by income disparities. Those who have graduated within the last ten years have slightly higher incomes than their male counterparts.[8]

Depending on their sexual success, men may enjoy dating more than women. Some may even prefer it as a way of life to the "boredom" of raising a family in the suburbs. Dating, however, contains its frustrations for him; Afro-American women are less likely than are their Euro-American counterparts to believe in sharing the expenses of a date. That means he is hoping for a sexual payoff to justify the expense of dating this woman. After much pleading and begging, she may consent to a sexual moment. He has no way of knowing if she will until her consent at 3 a.m. If she does not consent to a sexual congress, by the third date, he may not know when or if she will consent. Moreover, he may feel he has too much invested to stop dating her. Once sex has transpired, he may have to be concerned about her hearing wedding bells in the near future.

Looking for Mr. and Miss Right

Given that they do not have a lot to choose from, it might be suspected that Black women do not have many standards in their search for a man. What they look for in a sexual partner is typically the same characteristics they seek in a soul mate. As women age, their standards may change for a number of reasons, including dwindling opportunities, to find the right man. Surprisingly, while many of their standards relate to physical traits, a man with a large penis is not one of them. Most Afro-American women claim it is not important to them. Certainly, if she were looking for a soul mate, a man's penis size would not ensure her greater compatibility with him or a long-term relationship. Furthermore, she would not necessarily know which men are well endowed. There are rumors about men with big feet or long fingers having large penises. Those who might know claim that a muscular physique does not guarantee them a large penis. Some women prefer to avoid the large penis brother who, it is claimed, has made sex with them uncomfortable—even painful.

Sex appeal does appear to be more important to Black than white women. In a jet magazine survey of Black women in Chicago, Black women ranked the ten things they notice about men in this order. They were (1) dress/grooming, (2) personality, (3) eyes, (4) mouth/smile, (5) money, (6) physique, (7) thoughtfulness/walk, (8) intelligence/handsomeness, (9) chest, and (10) buttocks.[9] Only four of the desirable attributes are nonphysical ones. I suspect that a handsome man with money might make the other traits irrelevant, while not included in this list. I have found that the ability to dance well and height are traits that Black women value.

Since most Black women actively choose from the men who approach them, their standards reflect what they reject in men. Inarticulate men who lack conversational skills may not get very far. Being bald and very short may find them left off that short list. Anything that might subject a woman to the ridicule of her female peers might cause a male to be rejected. One trait that might cause a male to be rejected by Euro-American women does not seem a big impediment for Black women—obesity. The fat man may be acceptable to many Afro-American women because they, too, are overweight. Or, it could be that a fat mate gives her the ability to eat as much as she likes and not give in to the societal standard of the slim woman. Overall many women have such few choices in mate selection that they are forced to compromise on the standards they have. That is particularly true if her goal is marriage. Even very attractive women acknowledge that marriage proposals are few and far between.

Men, conversely, may have the most exacting standards for a soul mate, even a sexual partner. In the same jet magazine survey, they ranked in this order the things they most notice in women. They are (1) face, (2) legs, (3) breasts, (4) eyes—hair, (5) personality, (6) dress—intelligence, (7) smile, (8) buttocks, (9) walk, and (10) hands—feet—voice—conversation—sincerity.[10] Nobody can accuse them of failing to be superficial. The personality trait would only be noticed if she was particularly dull or "nasty." It is a major reason that physically unattractive women are not among the chosen. It is possible that these are standards for a sexual partner and not a soul mate. However, it is possible that the sexual partner goes on to be a soul mate and that person was selected on the basis of physical qualities.

Among the distinctively Black preferences are legs and buttocks. While some men want women with shapely legs, they also value women with big legs. The model-thin woman is not in great favor, Black women are fond of saying "Black men want a woman with some meat on them." How much meat they want on them is the existential question. They certainly want meat on their legs. In part, that is because legs fulfill part of a sexual fantasy. The area north of the legs is the prize. While large buttocks are currently in favor among Euro-Americans, it has long been a value in the Black community because theirs were bigger than anyone else's was. A Black woman with a "flat ass" may become one of the untouchables, so rare is such woman. Of course, men have managed to sexualize every portion of a woman's body, from her arms, hair, and thighs down to her feet. There are men who do not like women with big feet.

Afro-American men are not big on breasts and a woman small in that area can make it. They seem to be unconcerned about how well a woman dresses, unlike their female counterparts who ranked it the first thing they notice about men. After all, their goal is to get her naked and the clothes she wears into the bedroom will soon come off. When it comes to mate selection time, they will want a woman who is ready for their program—whatever that means. That may be a woman who is trustworthy and will not have sex with other men, a lady that knows how to cook soul food the same way as their mother, or who will work and contribute her income to the household.

One important feature that is notably missing from these lists is skin color. There is lots of evidence that the higher a Black male's educational level and income, the lighter the skin color of his wife. The hi-yellow, mulatto, fair-skinned woman is the most desired by Afro-American males. She combines the physical features of the Euro-American woman with the security and social acceptance of the Black woman. This woman may even fulfill the sexual fantasy of the long taboo Euro-American woman and all the sexual thrills that coitus with her will bring. Among Generation X, the fair-skinned woman may not be as fair. Miscegenation between Black women and white males is much less common and that was the source of the near-white, Black woman. Nowadays the mulatto is more likely the offspring of a Black man-white woman pairing.[11] And that "hi yella" woman is much more inclined to date and marry Euro-American males. Anyway, Miss Ann, the real thing is now available and interracial sexual activity has multiplied a hundred-fold since the 1960s.[12]

As true of Afro-American women, the Black male often selects as a sexual partner the woman who is available. In the Black middle-class, with its sexually conservative cadre of women, one must take sex where one can find it. The danger in that is men are often as overwhelmed by the pleasure of sex that they are convinced they are in love. Assuming the sexual thrill lasts long enough, she will not be content to go from the living room to the bedroom. She will want marriage—he will desire more of that "good sex." The sex will not remain good forever and neither will the marriage. Had he pursued a soul mate instead of a sexual partner the chances of success would have been greater. He had a range of women from which to choose and was guided by his genitals and not his head.

Cues and Seduction

Not all Black males use the "I want to make love to you" approach, particularly with college-educated women. Preferring to use flirting, they rely heavily on cues of romantic interest. By using this strategy, the balance of power shifts subtly to women. Some women view flirting as an end in itself, not a prelude to sexual interaction. Men tend to see the world in sexual terms while women prefer a range of responses to male interest. They may for instance, initially prefer a relationship to develop along the lines of platonic friendship whereas few, other than gay males, of the men they meet are interested in that except under special circumstances. The female perspective may be that you become friends first and that strengthens a relationship that involves sexual congress. Unfortunately, that rarely happens in the real world. A couple may have a harmonious relationship when they are not sexually involved. Once they sexually consummate the relationship, its dynamics can radically change. Friends are limited in the obligations they can impose upon each other while lovers have a complex set of obligations and expectations that did not previously exist. Thus, the platonic friendship only created the false impression they were compatible when it was a function of the absence of sex that allowed for peace and harmony between them.

The most basic cue that women exhibit, that men may interpret as sexual interest, is friendliness. It often depends on who is being friendly. Women in service occupations are friendly as a part of their job. Those same women, if sexually interested are prohibited from dating their business' customers. A few years ago, female employees at Safeway, the grocery chain, complained that the supermarket's policy of having them speak to all the customers in the store had lead to a number of requests for dates from male customers. Women from the southern region of the United States are socialized into a friendly posture and smile a lot.

Men may act on cues only in order to avoid rejection. Yet, some females' cues are so subtle as to be imperceptible. Among Euro-Americans, prolonged eye contact is often a definite cue of sexual interest. Within Black culture, direct eye contact is avoided from childhood on—some trace its origin to Africa. Even lighthearted banter may be seen by women as nothing more than friendly behavior. Many women are socialized, more so than men to smile and be friendly to gain social approval. Being liked is typically more important to women than to men. Of course, many women are using friendliness as a sexual come-on. It lures men into revealing their intentions. Ultimately, he has to act on her cue and it is only at that time that he finds out if he read the cues correctly.

There are also the examples of women who know that a man's primary interest is sexual—and resent it. This woman sends out false signals with coy glances, touching her hair, making physical contact and even using double entendres in conversation. The man can interpret their flirting as a sign to make a move, only to find himself rejected. She, of course, can always claim that she "was only being friendly." Despite the subtlety of their cues, women can also feel rejected if he does not make a move. Once she has experienced the "rejection," he does not get a second chance. The clue could have been as slight as touching her earlobe or crossing her legs. Men are put in the position of being "damned if you do and damned if you don't" when it comes to reading cues of sexual interest in a woman. Individual women can create their sexual cues on the spot and expect a man to know them. The guy with the sexually explicit rap may experience generalized rejection that is less painful than the man who puts his hopes for a sexual interaction in the cues of one woman and is rebuffed.

There are women who feel that their presence in your residence is the only one you need. Otherwise, you receive no other ones. Women's groups deny that a woman in a man's domicile at 3 a.m. is a tacit consent to sexual engagement. This can be the crucial distinction between miscommunication and rape. He had similar experiences where she has entered his domicile, shared alcohol beverages together, and made mild protests when he tried to make physical advances. After a symbolic resistance, she reciprocates his kisses and participates in the sexual act. Conversely, there are lots of women who go inside with a man that have no intention of engaging in sexual congress with him. She may even reciprocate the touching and kissing and expect it to stop there. Unlike some Euro-American women, she will not expect him to accept fellatio or masturbation as a substitute for intercourse. Another reason for relying on cues as a signal of sexual interest and advancing directly to coitus is the conventional wisdom that some women do not wish to verbally consent to a sexual engagement. These women do willingly participate in the sex act after the male acts.

Seduction itself can be a complicated process and here it can be men who make arbitrary rules about when to make the actual physical advances. One man claimed that, if in a woman's residence past midnight he expected a sexual payoff. Another woman reported an episode where a date pulled out his penis and put her hand on it. A very attractive Southern woman went out with an African fellow and returned with him to his one-bedroom apartment. She sat on his sofa while he began piling up chairs against the door to the outside, began taking off his clothes, and when naked put his hand on an erect penis and said, "Here, this is yours." In each of these cases, the woman in question agreed to have sex with the amateur seducer. Generally, a woman sets the stage for sex and usually rehearses the proceeding in her mind. Despite his flawed seduction techniques, she knew that sex would transpire and was agreeable to it.

We rarely think about the fact that there is very little instruction in asking for dates or seduction techniques for men in the United States. Some women report that they have to guide men through the process. Male friends are ready to boast about their sexual conquests to each other but not great on teaching techniques. Men, also, do not want to admit they do not know how to ask a woman out on a date or seduce her after they have gone out. Nowadays, a college-educated male can receive a graduate degree and be in his late twenties and never have gone on a one-on-one date. He had always participated in group dating. If you have a receptive female, there is no real need to sweat the details. The clues of interest will be clear and her availability for sex transparent.

The best of all possible worlds for a man is a sexually aggressive woman. Because of the competition for the scarce available males, she empowers herself to take the initiative to ask for the date and even make the first sexual overture. The Black community has a number of these women whose motto is "Victory goes to the swiftest." Some women may only be aggressive in securing the date, not in pursuing a sexual interaction. By making the first move, she has pretty much agreed to the sexual part—or that is how it will be interpreted by most males. Probably much longer than Euro-American women, the women of the Black community have taken an aggressive stance in pursuing men. Many have not been willing to wait to be selected. They may not know the precise sex ratio but they are aware that "there are a lot more of us than them."

It is these women who are not traumatized by the fact that they engaged in sexual congress with a man they did not love—in some cases did not even like. They are the women some feminists would like to label "quasi-rape victims." Faced with a persistent male insisting on coitus, they proceed to let him have his way to get it over with. Their attitude is "it's only sex." We hear all the time about women who bedded a man because they had orchestra seats at a Broadway musical. It's almost a social contract that if he paid for our dinner, we go to bed. Women often find any number of trivial reasons for engaging in sex with a particular man. In the movie "The Station Agent," Patricia Clarkson's character says, "At age nineteen I once slept with a man because he rolled his own cigarettes." Instead of being victims, these are women who refuse to be defined by their sexuality. They will control it—it will not control them.

The Death of Dating

There are those who regard dating as a cultural anachronism, a relic of an earlier period when a woman had to wait to be called, picked up, and taken out. Some of the members of Generation Y think it is a really weird way of getting to know someone. Yet, group dating contains its own recipe for disaster. How well do you get to know somebody where you are both in a group of ten until you pair off to engage in sexual congress? One of the findings I recall from William Goodes' classic study of divorce, "After Divorce," was that couples were more likely to divorce if they primarily engaged in activities like movies, skating, etc., where they did not have to talk to each other.[13]

Perhaps Generation Y is more comfortable with activities that disguise their shallowness.

Meanwhile, while never that formally structured, dating is on the wane among Afro-Americans. Go to any restaurant with substantial patronage by Afro-Americans and you may see groups of women together and men with their male buddies. Perhaps it means that males cannot shell out the money for two expensive restaurant meals. Maybe the increasing sexual conservatism of Afro-American women means the men are not willing to pay for two meals if the food is all they get. In cities like San Francisco, you may encounter more Black/White couples than all Black pairings. We hear the ritual complaint. She objects to being treated as a sex object to be conquered. Men claim they are being treated as inanimate "success objects" where they are scrutinized for their potential value every time they ask a woman out on a date.[14]

The complaints of women about being sex objects have been around for a long time. In their case, they may not be dating because men are not asking them. We know that college-educated men will eventually marry—most of them to Afro-American women. At any point in time, about 90 percent of college-educated Black males will be married and living with their spouse. Obviously, they are sexually involved with some woman and marrying her. Many of the college-educated women will also marry although a majority will be single or divorced by age forty. Some of those left behind may be physically unattractive, obese, or dark skinned. When I looked at census data for Black women between thirty-five and fifty-five, formerly married, with five or more years of college, there were no Black males available in that category.[15] According to the census Bureau, it meant that the number was lower than five hundred. This was in the 1970s—probably the same today.

Some of this disenchantment with dating reflects the pool of available dating partners. The adult children of baby boomers were raised in very indulgent ways that produced a number of self-centered adults. Unlike the past, where women often kept marriages together, the women are just as selfish as the men. Sometimes, chronological maturity may produce responsible adults. The divorce statistics do not reflect it. Many will avoid divorce because they will never marry, The National Marriage Project, in 2000, found that contemporary twenty-something adults are not looking for marriage partners when they date. Most of them want fun, casual sex, and low commitment relationships.[16]

The date rape hysteria only exacerbated the tension between Afro-American men and women. At the time of the Tyson trial for "date rape," there are no indications of an increase in date rapes around that time. Only a media blitz and women's groups convinced women that all men were potential date rapists. Suddenly women who had been inside your residence dozens of times wanted to meet you outside on the sidewalk—when you were only going to lunch in the middle of the day. The refusal to go inside her residence or yours was the strongest signal yet that no sexual activity would take place on dates. Black men may have responded with the attitude that no play—no pay. Many women do not seem to care. They have an independent income and lots of other single women for companionship. The men will still find girlfriends and wives among the women who will come inside with them. With the world in turmoil, a war in Iraq, terrorist threats looming everywhere, American women think the greatest threat to their security is date rape, AIDS, and teenage pregnancy. Perhaps they will avoid dealing with sexuality only to find it was a false security.

Notes

1. L. S. Jemmott and J. B. Jemmott, "Sexual Knowledge, Attitudes, and Risky Sexual Behavior among Inner City Black Male Adolescents." *Journal of Adolescent Research*, 1990, 5(3), pp. 346–369.

2. Kim Miller, et al., "Adolescent Sexual Behavior in Two Ethnic Minority Samples: The Role of Family Variables." *Journal of Marriage and the Family*, 1999, 61, pp. 85–98.

3. Robert Staples, *The World of Black Singles: Changing Patterns of Male/Female Relationships.* Westport, Connecticut: Greenwood Press, 1981.

4. Ronald D. Taylor, ed., *African American Youth: Their Social & Economic Status in the United States.* Westport, Connecticut: Praeger, 1994.

5. M. Belinda Tucker & Claudia Mitchell-Kernan, *The Decline in Marriage among African-Americans: Causes, Consequences, and Policy Implications.* New York: Russell Sage, 1995.

6. Thomas Kochman, *Black and White Styles in Conflict.* Chicago: University of Chicago Press, 1981, pp. 80–86.

7. Rick Hampson, "The State of Our Unions: Divorce, Cohabitation, and Adultery Have Hurt Institution of Marriage." *USA Today*, March 11, 2004, p. A-1.

8. The National Urban League, *The State of Black America 2003.* New York: The National Urban League, 2003.

9. "Ten Things Women Notice about Men." *Jet Magazine*, May 31, 1982 p. 52.

10. "Ten Things Men Notice about Women." *Jet Magazine*, June 7, 1982, pp. 38–39.

11. Kathy Russell, et al., *The Color Complex: The Politics of Skin Color among African Americans.* New York: Doubleday Anchor, 1992.

12. Kyle D. Crowder, "A New Marriage Squeeze for Black Women: The Role of Racial Intermarriage by Black Men." *Journal of Marriage & the Family*, August 2000, 62, pp. 792–807.

13. William Goode, *After Divorce*. Glencoe, Illinois: The Free Press, 1956.

14. Kevin Chappell, "The Real Object of the Dating Game." *Ebony*, January 2001, p. 16.

15. Staples, *op. cit.*

16. National Marriage Project, *The State of Our Unions, 2000*. New Brunswick, New Jersey: Rutgers University, June 7, 2000.

CHAPTER SIX

~

Sexual Theft and Other Crimes

Probably no aspect of human sexuality is as complex as that of sexual assault or rape. And the Black experience with these phenomena reflects the most inequitable treatment they have received since entering the shores of North America. In no area has American racism manifested itself more than in the lethal penalties meted out to Black males accused of sexually assaulting white women and the lenient treatment of white males that raped Black women. First, we will try to avoid the term rape except in those cases where it is clearly known that the sexual assault involved grievous bodily harm, torture, or murder. Instead, it will be called sexual theft because this crime carries the implicit assumption that women are property—by the perpetrator and the society. As Collins has noted "the very aspect of property is the right of possession, the right to keep someone else from possessing it and the willingness of society to back up those rights."[1]

Women in twenty-first-century America are erotic property just as cattle are agricultural property. We cannot understand sexual theft if we do not know that this is considered the most serious of crimes because the victims are not the woman but her husband/boyfriend or father. The Africans often made the sexual thief pay compensation to the husbands or families of the female sexual victim.[2] This crime also mirrors the double sexual standard that still exists in today's America. Male sexuality is not valued in large part, because men are not owned by women and because underlying male ownership of women is ownership of her reproductive capacity. Thus, our society's property system implies that the property system is much more of males owning women's bodies than the reverse.

While it can be argued that neither husband (if there is one) nor father no longer control a woman's body, the attitudes toward sexual theft are reflective of sentiments forged hundreds, thousands of year ago. It is why sexual theft is the second most heavily punished crime in the United States after murder, despite the fact that the actual damage may be only mental and sometimes only a minor irritation to some theft victims.[3] Moreover, given that female sexuality is often used as a commodity, for leverage with men, she loses market value. Many Americans still think of sexual theft as worse than death. In the film *The Searchers*, John Wayne's character thinks that his niece would now be better off dead since she has been sexually "violated" by an Indian male. How many times do we hear a husband or father on a TV crime show, ask of their murdered wife/daughter: was she sexually molested? Somehow, they can be at peace if she was only murdered.

Again, women's advocacy groups are in an informal alliance with the religious right. By treating the crime of sexual theft as the most serious thing that can happen to a woman, they unwittingly send the message that her only value is her sexuality, that she is defined by it. There are plenty of male rapes every year in North America but it has raised no public outcry.[4] While most of the rapes of men are committed by other male heterosexuals, generally in prison a small number of men are raped by women. The response by other men is "weren't you lucky?" And, women could care less. So, we tell men that their sexuality does not matter and we send the message to women that their sexuality is all that matters. No research I have encountered describes how traumatic sexual theft is for its victims. Given the high percentage of women estimated to be sexual theft victims, it would seem that every woman in therapy is there because of a sexual theft and millions are untreated for the "worst thing that could happen to them."

While sexual theft is harshly punished for the small number of perpetrators arrested and convicted, the punishment was more severe until the mid-seventies. Prior to that time, the punishment was death except that the death sentence was handed out very selectively. In the State of Georgia, until slavery was abolished, the death penalty for sexual theft was reserved exclusively for Afro-American men.[5] Before 1966, Virginia's legal statues reserved the death penalty for the sexual theft of a white woman for Black men while Euro-American men could be imprisoned for no more than twenty years. When fornication was illegal and the law enforced, Alabama's legal codes imposed more serious punishment for people of different races engaged in coitus than for those of the same race. That law held up until 1964 when the United States Supreme Court struck it down.[6]

While the explicit racial discrimination in sexual theft punishment was mostly gone by the 1960s, the discrimination was not. From 1930 to 1964, 89 percent of the men executed for sexual theft in this country were Afro-American men. In one state only, Virginia, every male executed for sexual theft was Black. One analysis of the death penalty for sexual theft revealed the death penalty had been used on Afro-American men by a nine to one ratio.[7] Moreover, 85 percent of all executions for sexual theft have involved Black males and white female victims. Up to the point that sexual theft was abolished as a capital offense, almost all executions in the South were of Afro-American men accused of sexual theft against Euro-American women. No male—Black or white was ever executed for the sexual theft of an Afro-American woman.[8]

Indeed, while sexual theft of Black women by Euro-American men was fairly commonplace in the ante-bellum South, there were few cases of white males tried and convicted of this crime. During slavery, there was no such offense as the sexual theft of a slave woman. During the three hundred years of slavery, Blacks were not allowed to be witnesses against Euro-Americans in a court of law. There were few laws to protect a slave woman against sexual assaults. She was considered the property of her owner and any crime claimed him as the victim. In the nineteenth century, for example, the North Carolina Supreme Court ruled that no white male could be convicted of fornication with a slave woman.[9] Other Southern states required a slave woman have a white witness to the act in order to seek legal relief.

Due to the sexual vulnerability of Black women in the South, the prevalent American stereotype that emerged was that of a sexual seductress. This was in strong contrast to the Southern white woman as sexually pure, a fact that led some behavioral scientists to conclude that Afro-American women tend to draw the unsublimated sexual feelings of Euro-American males. The Black woman was sexually available, unable to make claims for support or concern; by dominating her, men could replace the infant's dream of unlimited access to the mother. White men could always say that a Black woman could not be assaulted, that it was never against her will. Conversely, when a Euro-American woman was found engaged in intercourse with an Afro-American man, it was ipso facto evidence of sexual assault. It was never assumed that she would have voluntarily agreed to such a situation. Any who so admitted were regarded as a fallen woman and declared pariahs in the white community.[10]

Before the political state took over the duty of avenging the Euro-American woman's honor by executing Afro-American men, it was left to vigilante justice. The number of Black men lynched by mobs between 1865–1955 was approximately five thousand, about a quarter of them accused of the "crime" of having touched, approached, or imagined to have looked at a white woman.[11] One of the most famous cases is that of Emmett Till. A fourteen-year-old boy from Chicago went to visit relations in Mississippi during the summer of 1955. He went into a grocery store and made the mistake of whistling at a white female store clerk. Four days later, his body was found in the river. An all-white jury acquitted the two men, who later publicly admitted to the murder, of the crime.[12] Susan Brownmiller, a militant feminist in her book, *Against Our Will*, implies he deserved to be punished.[13]

While Black men could be killed for expressing any sexual interest in Euro-American women, those who were accused of sexually assaulting them were often innocent of the crime. Because Euro-American women discovered engaged in sexual intercourse with a Black male were socially ruined, if they consented to it, they cried rape in order to save themselves. Even those who claimed rape were regarded as "damaged goods" and never received the normal opportunities of marriage offered to "decent white women." One of the most famous cases was that of the nine Scottsboro boys accused by two Euro-American women of raping them. Although the two women were little more than prostitutes the judge ruled that, "in the case of a white woman there is a very strong presumption under the law that she would not and did not yield voluntarily to intercourse with the defendant, a Negro."[14] While a woman's sexual history cannot be used against her now, that was not the case in 1931. All of the nine men were sentenced to death and later had their sentences commuted.

Whereas the harshest sentences were handed out to Black men alleged to have sexually assaulted Euro-American women, the lightest ones were handed out to the few Black men who stole sex from Black women. In one report, it was discovered that only one Black male convicted of sexual offenses against white women had his sentence suspended, almost half the Black men stealing sex from a Black woman were immediately allowed to return to the community. And the estimate is that 90 percent of Afro-American women never report a sexual offense to the police because few think they will be believed.[15]

The Intricacies of Sexual Theft

Probably no act other than forced sexual intercourse exists that produces the irrational response of the citizenry. Other than horse thieves in the old west, vigilante justice was not applied as often to any other crime. It is the only crime in which the victim herself is on trial and suspected of causing the act to happen. It is the only crime that never has a witness other than the assailant and victim. Today the victim's name is not publicly released while the male defendant can be identified and have his name tarnished. Arguably, it is the one crime in which the penalty vastly outweighs the harm done to the victim. There were cases where the male was put to death and the female "victim" was enjoying consensual sex a few days later. It is also estimated to be the most underreported crime in the United States. Obviously, the aforementioned comments indicate that both men and women are disadvantaged by the current status of our rape laws and enforcement.

Unfortunately the public debate on sexual theft has become somewhat one-sided while women continue to experience sexual theft that goes unpunished. Women's advocacy groups continue to insist that sexual theft is the worst act in the United States. Any man can face career extinction if he appears not to take it seriously. One example is that of Gary Barnett, coach of the University of Colorado football team. His former placekicker, a woman, claimed that she had been the victim of sexual theft by a teammate. In the course of discussing her charge with the media, he was asked the question: "what kind of a kicker was Katie"? His response was "Katie was not only a girl, she was terrible. O.K. there's no other way to say it." Somehow, her being a victim of a sexual assault made it too insensitive to say negative things about her ability as a placekicker and he was suspended with pay. It might be noted that he was under scrutiny for a number of irregularities in his football program but the suspension came after that one comment.[16]

On balance, women are by far the most harmed by sexual theft. What I question is whether recent trends do anything to provide a more supportive environment for them. Legally, rape was historically defined as penetration of the vagina or anus with a penis or object without consent. Statutory rape was sex with a minor with his/her consent, by an older person. The minor is typically under age 16 and the older person over age 18 although the ages may vary by individual state. In recent years, the legal definitions of rape have been expanded. A number of states now define nonconsensual sex between spouses as a form of marital rape. Traditionally, a husband had exclusive sexual access to his wife and legal rape was an impossibility. Probably the best reason to charge your husband with marital rape is the punishment will be much greater than the allegation of domestic violence. Very few cases have been brought under this charge and it is questionable that many juries, however constituted, will render a guilty verdict on a woman's husband.

Other changes have to do more with the conditions under which consent is determined or withdrawn. In the year 2003, the Illinois legislature passed a rape law that was the first of its kind in the United States. Under this rape law, a woman can change her mind while having sex. Under this law, if a woman says "no" at any time the man must stop or it becomes rape. In other words, she may consent to sex for ten minutes. If he continues beyond that time, he may be charged with rape.[17] It is not clear why this law was necessary or if a jury will ever find a man guilty for exceeding a woman's time limit. It does demonstrate how the anti-rape lobby can get any law it wants passed. There is no pro-rape lobby. Some women's advocacy groups claim that a woman is the victim of sexual theft if she engages in sex while intoxicated. Being legally drunk means she is incapable of giving her consent. The double standard here is blatant since a greater number of men tend to be legally drunk, particularly Black males, during sexual copulation than women.[18]

The sex police are not finished protecting women yet. Oberlin College passed a regulation obligating its male students to get a female student's permission as he goes to greater levels of intimacy. For instance, if he goes from caressing her thigh to fondling her breast, he must seek her verbal permission. If she does not, I assume she can claim sexual misconduct on his part and the college can expel him. It is unlikely that he will be charged with a sexual offense for fondling a breast without verbal permission by some district attorney. Although I am unsure of the legal standing of this next rape charge, it has been suggested that a prostitute who performs a sexual service and is denied payment has been the victim of sexual theft (literally).[19] Most of these changes in rape laws are unenforceable; few women will press them, even fewer district attorneys will prosecute them, and it is unlikely that many juries will render guilty verdicts if men are indicted.

Furthermore, they trivialize what is a serious invasion of privacy for women. They have the right to control their bodies although one would hope they would not engage in provocative dress or actions to mislead men into thinking they are willing to engage in sexual congress. However, if they do, they have the right to say no. Throughout this discussion, I have confined myself to speaking of one gender as the victim of sexual theft. Many of those laws or conditions do not mention a specific gender. Yet, a male who brings sexual theft charges against a woman is likely to be laughed at. And, France's Supreme Court has denied men the right to even lodge the allegation. In 2000, it ruled that women could not commit the crime of rape because they could not sexually penetrate men. The ruling came about when it overturned a lower court ruling that a woman could be tried for rape for forcing her underage stepson to have sex with her repeatedly between 1986 and 1992. In an earlier ruling, this Supreme Court had issued a ruling that forcing a person to perform oral sex was legally equivalent to rape.[20]

Probably more tragic is the double standard that ignores the fact that an estimated 290,000 men are sexually assaulted behind prison bars each year. That is considerably higher than the Bureau of Justice estimates that there are 135,000 sexual assaults of women nationwide each year.[21] The public view of these male victims is that they are not true "rape" victims, and that they are deserving of their fate because of the crimes they have committed against society. One poll of registered voters found that half agreed that society accepts prison rape as part of the price criminals pay for wrongdoing.[22] Americans that are more compassionate might say that even criminals have the right to control their bodies. Moreover, these are homosexual rapes that could be considered a more serious act. After all, most female assault victims are accustomed to heterosexual intercourse with their consent. Male prisoners are not conditioned to tolerate homosexual intercourse with or without their consent. Some of those in the criminal justice system use the probability of homosexual rape to force suspects to confess and keep those on the outside honest.

Considering all the attention paid to sexual theft by the media, how many women have been the victims of sexual theft. Be warned that the figures are virtually meaningless. In terms of convictions in state courts in 1996, there were 13,559 for forcible rape that year, about 1.7 percent of all felony convictions. Two thirds of those convicted were sent to prison, the rest to jail or put on probation. The maximum sentence length was ten years in prison, more than for any other felony except murder. A startling 1 percent of the felons were female, 70 percent were white, and 27 percent were Afro-American, double their number in the population of men. However, it should be noted that they were a much higher percentage of other felony categories.[23] Another analysis of arrests revealed that they were no more likely to be arrested than white males for the crime of sexual theft. That could be because 95 percent of their victims are Black women and it is suspected they are the least likely of sexual assault victims to report the crime to the authorities.[24]

Chances are that these figures represent only the tip of the iceberg. Depending on the definition of sexual theft, over a lifetime anywhere from 20 to 70 percent of all American women have been coerced into sexual relationships with a man. The highest percentage came from a researcher who claimed that many women had been "bullied" into coitus and felt the effect was the same as "rape."[25] Probably the offender was a boyfriend or husband. What strikes me most about these estimates is that when you combine them with other sexual offenses, i.e., child molestation statutory rape, child pornography, etc., it appears that as many as 70 percent of the American male population could be jailed as sex offenders. If we included various definitions of sexual harassment, it could be 90 percent.

Those figures are the inevitable result of a society that uses female sexuality as a commodity, provides all sorts of sexual stimuli, and criminalizes violations of its moral code. It is the product of a double standard that does not allow women to be overtly sexual, even when they desire to and one that teaches men they are to initiate sexual activity and not take no for an answer. Many women refuse to accept the restrictions on their sexuality even when it is stolen from them. They go on to live their lives and make it an unpleasant part of their past. We can only hope that the thousands of men imprisoned for sexual theft represent the worst of the offenders and not the poorest, least educated men who could not afford competent legal counsel.

Unfortunately, when militant feminists claim that American masculinity models predispose men to rape, sexually harass, and abuse children, they may be partly correct. In the minds of many men lurks the symbolic rapist, who would never assault a strange woman in an alley but gets a certain thrill from the notion of rape. Male movie producers often realize this and include "erotic" rape scenes in their movies. A very good example is this twenty-three-year-old man in San Francisco, who works as a file clerk. He says:

> Where I work it's probably no different from any other major city in the U.S. The women dress up in high heels and they wear a lot of makeup and they just look really hot and really sexy, and how can somebody who has a healthy sex drive not feel lust for them when you see them? I feel lust for them, but I don't think I could find it in me to overpower someone and rape them. But I definitely get the feeling that I'd like to rape a girl. I don't know if the actual act of rape would be satisfying, but the feeling is satisfying.[26]

What he is expressing is the feeling of the powerless male. Women's advocacy groups claim that sexual theft is manifestation of man's power over women. Yet, it is often the most powerless men who steal female sexuality. Black males are the most powerless of all men. When they are exposed to the eroticized Euro-American female, the real hot woman, they know she is not available to a man of his color and class. Thus, he displaces his lust to women of his own race, who are more vulnerable and available. Intuitively, he knows that stealing the sexuality of a woman of the master race will bring the greatest punishment. He can kill a Black man or woman and receive less punishment than stealing the sexuality of a white woman.

Definitions and Denials

Most surveys of sexual assault encounter problems of subject recall, definition, and measurement. One very famous study was *Ms.* magazine's "Campus

Project on Sexual Assault" directed by Mary Koss. According to this study, 28 percent of the female college students had been victims of "rape" (15 percent) or attempted rape (12 percent) an average of two times between the ages of fourteen and twenty-one. These were Koss's definitions; two subsequent articles claimed that only 27 percent of the students Koss defined as "rape" victims believed they had been raped.[27] Adding to the confusion, 42 percent of the alleged victims reported they had sex again with the purported offender on a later occasion. Almost half the students classified as "rape" victims labeled their experience as "miscommunication." One critic of these studies claiming huge numbers of women have their sexuality stolen says, "By exaggerating the statistics on rape, advocacy research conveys an interpretation of the problem that advances neither mutual respect between the sexes or reasonable dialogue about assaultive behavior."[28]

Even when some women claim sexual theft, there are a couple of reasons to question their veracity. Nancy Friday found a number of white women had fantasies of having their sexuality forcibly taken. Friday's explanation was that such fantasies remove responsibility from the woman dreaming of a sexual assault. By imagining herself in the hands of a fantasy rapist, she enables him to do her bidding while appearing to be forced to do what he wants. Ultimately, she cannot be blamed since she is overwhelmed by a force stronger than she is.[29] It was the early 1970s and a number of these Euro-American women had dreams of being sexually attacked by a Black man. According to Friday, "the first thing a (white) woman does in the Black man fantasy is to remove the guilt by making it a 'rape.' Being raped allows her (helpless) self more wholeheartedly into the act, so that every determined thrust can be read as one of struggling protest. After that the black man's rumored size and skill can go to work on her."[30]

Of course, a rape fantasy does not mean a woman wants her sexuality stolen and Friday now claims that women no longer need these fantasies because the guilt does not exist or is not as strong. While women advocates want us to believe every woman who cries rape, saying no woman would fabricate a lie about sexual assault. The reality, unfortunately, is that false allegations are much more likely in sexual theft cases than other felonies. One of the most exhaustive studies of sexual assault reports to the police was conducted by Kanin. With the cooperation of the police department in a small metropolitan community, he looked at rape charges over a nine-year period. This police agency vigorously pursued all rape claims and the woman had to admit no such rape had occurred for it to be classified as a false allegation. An astounding 41 percent of the total disposed rape cases were officially declared false during the nine-year period (N = 45). The reason for these false allegations fell into three categories: (1) The need to provide a plausible explanation for the consequence of a consensual sexual interaction, (2) revenge against a rejecting male, and (3) an attention/sympathy getting device.[31]

The comedian Richard Pryor used to joke about white cops in his hometown of Peoria, Illinois rounding up black men for a lineup because ugly white women had accused some Black male of sexual theft. This material may have come from some real-life experiences. In two of the false allegations in Kanin's study, one involved a white married woman, with a Black lover whose condom broke and her husband had gotten a vasectomy. Another case involved a thirty-seven-year-old white woman who reported she had been raped "by some nigger." The truth was that she feared her boyfriend (white) had given her "some sexual disease" and wanted to be sent to a hospital to "get checked on."[32] This, of course is a continuation of the trend toward Euro-American's falsely accusing Afro-Americans of crimes such as murder and rape because they know that such fabrications are easily accepted.

Probably the most famous case in recent times of a false rape allegation was that of Tawana Brawley, a fifteen-year-old Black female from Poughkeepsie, New York in 1987. She claimed that she was abducted, raped, and left covered with racist graffiti by a group of Euro-American males who included police officers and the assistant district attorney handling the case. Al Sharpton, now a nationally known civil rights leader defended Brawley and branded as racist anyone who suggested she might not be telling the truth. The speculation is that she had spent the night with her boyfriend and was afraid of her parent's reaction. After a long investigation, a grand jury found no evidence indicating Brawley had been attacked. This assistant district attorney later won a sixty-five-thousand-dollar defamation judgment against Sharpton, who never apologized for defending Brawley.[33] In 2004 a thirty-eight-year-old woman reported she had been gang raped by St. John's University basketball players, most of them Black. Later, she admitted she made up the story after the players refused to pay her one thousand dollars for sex. She was charged with prostitution, attempted extortion, and filing a false report. Typically, nothing is done to the women who filed false rape reports.[34]

What we have here is a huge percentage of alleged "rape" victims filing false allegations and an even higher number, it is assumed, of legitimate sexual theft victims never reporting the crime. When the victim is Euro-American and the assailant (alleged) is Afro-American, few in the white community will question her claim. Yet, a number of Afro-American males have recently been exonerated by DNA tests and they had white victims. Most Euro-American women have their sexuality stolen by white males and most sadistic rapists and lust murderers are Euro-American males. In terms of numbers, the vast majority of sexual thieves are Euro-American males. Not only are women unsure if a sexual theft has occurred, men are in absolute denial about having stolen a woman's sexuality. In the massive sexual survey, only 2.8 percent of the men report forcing a woman sexually and 1.5 percent of the women surveyed admitted to forcibly stealing a man's sexuality.[35]

There were a few surprises in that last survey. One of them was the low rate of forced sex by women living in central cities and a comparatively high rate for those living in noncity urban areas (suburbs). Among the women reporting forced sex, a majority of them said the person forcing them was a lover or spouse. Others were men the women knew well and only 4 percent of the men forcing them were strangers. It must be noted that the researchers used the term "forced sex" instead of rape and still found 22 percent of the women being forced by a man. Surprisingly, the percentage of Afro-American women being sexually forced (19 percent) was lower than that of Euro-American[36] women (23 percent). One possible explanation is that Afro-American husbands (not lovers) may be less inclined to sexually force their wives. After all, she contributes a higher share of their household income than do white wives. The researchers also note that a number of the women who report being forced were more likely to be unhappy and to find sex less enjoyable. It suggests they were more likely to reject a spouse's sexual overtures and were subsequently forced.[37]

Sexual theft in the Black community is a complex matter. Afro-American women were historically allowed to express sexual interest. However, their desire to engage in sex has never rivaled that of Afro-American males. In lower income communities, men are known for taking what they can get. His masculinity is often defined by the number and quality of sexual conquests. There is little protection for young females in their environment. The police are more concerned about drug busts and gang wars. A female may willingly engage in intercourse with dozens of males but finds herself forced by one particular male. When she reports it, her former lovers will blow the whistle on her and the police may do a ritualistic search for the man.[38]

Previous ethnographic research revealed that a young Black female has little chance of escaping forced sex at a young age. She is surrounded by young men who have nothing to lose. They are the ones who will die at an early age, be imprisoned at a young age and drop out of school, and be an absentee from the labor force most of their adult life. Stealing a girl's sexuality is the least of their worries. Chances are that she will not report it, if she does, won't be believed and if convicted will receive very little jail time. Additionally, she runs the risk of retaliation by their male friends if she continues to live in that same community. Nowadays, they are heavily armed and dangerous. In San Francisco, witnesses to crimes have to be relocated if they agree to testify against crime suspects. The penalties for forced sex can be greater than the penalties for some of the drug charges. In California, where a third felony conviction sends you to prison for life, a sexual assault victim faces the wrath of a man with nothing to lose.

Why do Afro-American women run the risk of filing forced sex reports? Nothing I have read indicates they are inclined to make false allegations except for Tawana Brawley and those against celebrity males. One reason is to protect their reputation. A male who stole her sexuality may boast about it to his male friends as a voluntary sexual conquest. To defend herself, she makes an official report to the police. Even if he is not arrested or convicted, it indicates that he lied and it inconveniences him. Another factor is mere outrage at the sexual exploitation involved in him "taking it" without her consent. It makes it more difficult to attract a boyfriend or husband if it becomes known that she is "damaged goods." While Black males are known to refer to females as bitches and ho's, in reality they divide women into categories of "not nice" and "nice." The "not so nice" females are the ones they exploit and the "nice" girls become their lady, the one they like or love. A woman whose sexuality has been stolen—and it is known—becomes known as a "not so nice" woman. One other factor that provokes an assault claim is the male's contempt for her sexual code. He may have stolen the sex on the first date when she expected him to wait until a later time.[39]

Besides the fear of violent retaliation, Afro-American women have other reasons for not filing forced sex charges. One is the obvious factor that they will not be believed or the criminal justice system is indifferent to the sexual theft of Black women. In many cases, the offender is a boyfriend or acquaintance that she does not want to get into trouble. Occasionally, the community may pressure her not to file charges in order to avoid sending another young Black male to prison, particularly if he is known as a "good boy" who is kind to his mother. A big reason for lower-class Afro-American women is, although undesirable, sexual theft is not the end of the world and they want to go forward with the rest of their life. One interesting aspect of sexual theft among this group is that the male offender often requests to see her again.

Celebrity Theft

Perhaps the most famous rapist in the United States was a man named Willie Horton. He and white racism gave the presidential election of 1986 to George Bush. The elder Bush campaign ran pictures of Horton, a Black man and his white housewife victim over and over on television. It seems that Horton had been paroled by Bush's presidential opponent, and had raped a white woman while on parole. The not so subtle message was that, if elected president, Dukakis could not be trusted to keep white women safe from Black male rapists. Many consider it the key to Bush's presidential victory. Before he died, Bush's campaign manager apologized for running the ad and pandering to the racist sentiments of Euro-Americans.

Black male celebrities are treated differently than their more pedestrian brothers, who are subject to discriminatory treatment in the criminal justice system. When the formerly famous basketball star, Jayson Williams, was acquitted of killing a limousine driver, despite eyewitness testimony, it showed that American jurors are loathe to convict their sports and entertainment heroes of the worst crimes possible. Although even celebrities are presumed to be innocent at the outset, Williams "accidentally" killed the chauffer in front of witnesses and was not convicted of aggravated or reckless manslaughter.[40] The explanation is that he had a nice persona and the jury felt that he did not mean to harm him. In the year 2003, the star of violent movies, Arnold Schwarzenegger, ran for governor and more than sixteen women claimed he groped or sexually harassed them over the last three decades. He admitted to the behavior and said he was sorry if the women were offended. Not only did he win the governor's race by a large margin, 43 percent of women voted for him. Men were largely unmoved by the allegations and heavily voted for him.[41]

Of course, the election was held in California where film stars are treated like royalty. Still, we must raise the question: why have Black celebrities been so involved in alleged felonies, many of them of a sexual nature? Almost all of them are men and most come from the field of music and sports, areas that are dominated by Black males. At least two white celebrities, Robert Blake and Phil Specter, are currently under indictment for the murder of intimates. They are stars of the past and the media has not shown that much interest in them. The public is much more interested in the trials of Michael Jackson (child molestation) and Kobe Bryant (forcible rape).

Mike Tyson is the one exception to male celebrities being acquitted of a felony. In 1991, he was convicted of sexual theft of an eighteen-year-old Black beauty contestant and served three years of a six-year sentence before being released on parole. What made his case different? Unlike the other defendants, Tyson had a long record of crimes and abuse of women. Some said he fit perfectly the stereotype of the savage brute who failed to adhere to the norms of civilization. Had he been Muhammad Ali or George Foreman, it is unlikely he would have been convicted. Still, he seems to sincerely believe he was innocent of the assault allegation, even blaming her charges on the fact that he did not walk her back to the limousine after the intercourse. When asked about his victim recently, he said, "I just hate her guts, I really wish I did now. But now I really do want to rape her."[42]

Kobe Bryant, one of the nation's most prominent basketball stars, did not have Tyson's problem. Accused of the sexual theft of a nineteen-year-old hotel concierge in Colorado, he has a wife and child and had a clean-cut image with no record of any kind of scandal in his past. He had an aggressive, white female attorney determined to earn the big bucks he is paying her. His accuser found out the downside of allegations against a sports hero. Although she is Euro-American and he is Afro-American, millions of whites rooted for him. One of them might have been on his jury. One example of what she faced is a man from Switzerland who had offered to kill her if paid three million dollars. He was arrested.[43]

The racial angle came out in the preliminary phases. A white supremacist group distributed fliers headlined, "Don't have sex with Blacks." Where the alleged sexual theft occurred, Bryant did run the risk of being tried by an all-white jury.[44] But Colorado is not the state of Mississippi. Bryant's white female attorney raised the race issue. According to her, "my client stands accused of a very serious crime. There is lots of history about Black men being falsely accused of this crime by white women."[45] That part is true but didn't mean some nineteen-year-old white woman in Colorado is one of them. However, her history and behavior did not make her the best theft victim. She flirted with Bryant when he checked into the hotel, went to his room late at night without a job-related reason, and consented to kissing and minor petting. She had attempted suicide earlier and Bryant's attorney declared she had sex with two other men around the same time.

Meanwhile, legal experts said it was predicted that race would be introduced in such a high profile case. Jurors were given a hook to hang their reasonable doubt on. One law professor claimed it is the start of a very blatant race-card strategy.[46] Many white journalists questioned the procedure of hiding the victim's identity while everyone was aware that Kobe Bryant was the alleged assailant. Depending on the progress America has made in race relations, the race issue might have freed Bryant in a way unexpected. How many Euro-Americans, particularly men, were bothered by the fact that the alleged victim flirted with Bryant, even consented to kissing him? Did they think no "decent white woman would do that and she got what she deserved"?

As true of most sexual assault cases, it was her word against his denial that she was forced. Nobody knows but Bryant and his accuser what happened in that hotel room. The public knew and liked him and she was an obscure, anonymous woman in a small town in Colorado. As for the consequences of accusing a popular sports hero of a crime that many Americans were divided on, it was reported that she was forced to quit school, could not live at home or talk to her friends, and received hundreds of e-mails or phone calls threatening either death or mutilation. According to her mother, the alleged victim lived in four states in six months.[47] Finally, the charges were dropped when the alleged victim refused to testify in the case. She reached an out-of-court settlement with Bryant, leaving many to believe her real goal was money; others feel that he bought his way out of a jail term. If the case had gone to trial, few felt she would have been vindicated.

Group Sex

A group of men sexually assaulting a lone woman is truly deserving of the term rape. There are few circumstances where there was miscommunication or consent on the woman's part. It is an inherently traumatic act for the female victim and almost no cases of false allegations. The incidence of group rapes is not unknown to Afro-American males. Curtis reports that 25 percent of all Black rapes involve two or more offenders. He explains they are likely to occur during or after Black social gatherings. These group rapes are most likely to result in injury to the female victim. He surmises that the most dangerous rapists are also the least afraid to go it alone.[48]

Group rape is not a race-specific phenomenon. Currently, public notice is viewing gang rapes by members of athletic teams in Australia and Britain. Wherever men are isolated in a particularly macho culture, group assaults against women are fairly typical. The most common are group rapes committed by military soldiers, particularly against foreign women. Almost every war fought by every nation has involved gang rapes of the foreign women. Often, women of their own troops will be assaulted. We know that men in groups will often commit acts that they would not do alone. Group sexual assaults are fostered by male bonding among closely knit male fraternities such as sports teams and street gangs. Because Afro-Americans are more likely to belong to those groups, gang rapes can happen with great frequency.

Of course, there are cases where group sex is consensual. Women's advocacy groups claim that even consensual group sex is nothing more than rape. As for why women would consent to participating in group sex, some claim that it is the message of feminism telling women they have the right to be as lusty as men. In the case of athletes, there are a lot of women who are sports groupies. By allowing members of the team to bond by "using" her body, she could feel that she is part of the team. Some women actually use group sex as a way of being "loved." We must never forget that a woman's sexuality can be used in so many different ways.[49]

Even the current governor of California, Arnold Schwarzenegger, has claimed to have participated in a "gang bang" involving some male friends and an Afro-American woman. By his account, the woman emerged into the Venice Beach Gold's Gym naked and consented to group sex.[50] It was in the 1970s and the sexual revolution brought about a number of daring acts by women, and group sex was just one of them. Whereas women's advocacy groups want to declare group sex as akin to rape, they cannot criminalize sexual activity that women voluntarily participate in because they dislike it. However, Nathan McCall, a best-selling author acknowledges that he participated in "Trains" (gang rapes of Black women). His explanation is that "even though it involved sex, it didn't seem to be about sex at all. Like almost everything else we did, it was a macho thing."[51]

Other Sexual Crimes

For years, the conventional wisdom has been that, apart from rape, there was less sexual deviation among Afro-Americans than among their Euro-American counterparts. Probably the statistical data confirms that and is more consistent than in other aspects of Black sexuality. In terms of official statistics, white youth were more likely than Black youth to be victims of sexual abuse (13 percent vs. 7 percent).[52] Yet, we know that these sexual crimes are vastly underreported. Wyatt's research found that 20 percent of Afro-American women had childhood sexual experiences that involved an older adult fondling their bodies in an attempt to engage in coitus with them. In earlier research, she had discovered that 57 percent of Afro-American women had experienced childhood sexual abuse compared to 67 percent of Euro-American women.[53]

Childhood sexual abuse is often widespread among males too. We have all read of the massive sexual abuse occurring in the Catholic Church and other organized religions. One expert has declared that one in six Afro-American men has reported being sexually abused.[54] In an analysis of Black and white sex offenders committed to a hospital for mentally disordered sex offenders, one researcher discovered that white sex offenders were more likely to have a male victim (27 percent) than Black sex offenders (8.5 percent). Black offenders were inclined to engage in vaginal intercourse with their female victims, to use force more often, and to have somewhat older female victims than the white offenders. When they controlled for the offender's occupation, most of the social differences disappeared.[55]

Given the prevalence of these sexual abuses, we need to consider a few facts. Many of these childhood sexual abuses are fairly minor in nature. They include exposure of the penis, masturbation in front of the child, rubbing genitals against the victim's body to attempted or completed intercourse, and oral and anal sex. Almost all the research is dependent upon subject recall. What a woman recalls at age thirty-five and her feelings at age twelve may be very different. Comedian and actor Billy Connolly told his biographer that his father sexually molested him between the ages of ten to fifteen. He comments that "the most awful thing was that it was kind of pleasant, physically you know, that's why nobody tells."[56]

We have no idea what the consequences of child sexual abuse are, particularly for males. Wyatt speculates that they are at high risk for school health and other psychological problems as a result of childhood sexual abuse. She suggests that female abuse victims develop distrustful feelings toward men. What her research uncovered was that females experiencing body contact in childhood had voluntary coitus 15.4 months earlier than did women with no contact or sexual abuse. They were also more inclined to participate in necking and petting behavior at earlier ages, to have a larger number of sexual partners during the teenage years, and to have briefer sexual relationships.[57]

What about male childhood abuse victims? Strangely, Latino and Asian teenage males claim to have been more physically and sexually abused. About 1 in 8 report they were abused by a family member in their own home and the sexual abuse they experienced was recurring. In comparison to their female counterparts, most of the teenage boys had not talked with anyone about it. About 15 percent of the abused boys said they had thought of suicide. Forty percent of them experienced symptoms of severe depression. What is so strange is that Asian and Latino boys generally fell below Euro-Americans and Blacks on most sexual variables except this one. The sexual abuse rate was 9 percent for Asian teenage males and 7 percent for Latino boys compared to 3 percent for white and Black males.[58]

Whereas it appears that the pathology of child sexual abuse is weaker among Afro-Americans than other racial groups, it is still too prevalent for the Black community. Children are the most available and vulnerable of all demographic categories. The people (typically men) who molest them are in a position of trust. Once an impressionable child has been sexually molested, it leaves an indelible imprint. Here are one woman's memories of a childhood about fifty years ago. She recalls:

A child's memories should be happy ones; some of mine are not. Uncle Richard, Aunt Lillian's husband, used to take me for rides in the country with mama's permission to his mama's house out in ballyhack. He put his huge penis on my bald headed vagina, rubbed and rubbed it until wet sticky stuff came from nowhere. While I looked up at the stars and ate my candy bar.

On another occasion I can see me licking the chocolate ice cream cone he bought me while he is on his knees licking between my legs. Can you image that, a grown man wanting to f . . . a little girl. He made me feel that I was not that good person Grams always made me promise I would be, and I never felt the same again. I became somebody else and a very unpleasant sort.[59]

This society has very little tolerance for child molesters. Even other criminals behind prison walls dislike them and prison authorities are often forced to isolate them from other prisoners. This did not look good for Michael Jackson, who was accused of multiple counts of lewd or lascivious acts with a child under age fourteen. While it was another case made murky by weak evidence, Jackson's history of paying a child's family fifteen million dollars to drop another child sexual abuse allegation worked against him. Furthermore, he was known as one of the most eccentric entertainers in show business. Even with his vast wealth, he could not have claimed that it was socially acceptable to sleep with young boys in his bed, particularly if some of those children claimed he sexually molested them. At the same time, we might have been more comfortable with some of these allegations if we did not know that fifteen million dollars is a strong incentive for a child and his family to fabricate these child sexual abuse allegations.[60] Ultimately, he was acquitted of all charges by a jury with no Blacks on it. His alleged victim and the victim's mother simply lacked enough credibility for the jury to convict Jackson. There is speculation that his career is ruined and he has temporarily moved to a Middle Eastern country.

With regard to other sexual offenses, little is known about incest in Black families. Obviously, those family members molesting close relatives are committing incest. Still, our own definition of incest includes the definition found in most developed nations, sexual relationships between siblings, parents, and children. Although a number of American states define incest as intercourse between first cousins, many African and Middle Eastern countries prefer those close kin to marry each other. Very few of the other cases have come to our attention. One recent case did involve a Black man who fathered two children by his own daughters. This same man murdered nine members of his own family, an act that must be regarded as contrary to all the norms in the Afro-American community and an unusually rare act.[61]

While not a crime, sexual harassment has claimed a number of Blacks as its poster child. First, it is a workplace regulation that forbids the sexual harassment of mostly female workers. The landmark case of sexual harassment involved a Black female bank employee whose supervisor fondled her in front of other employees and even raped her on other occasions. The most famous case of alleged sexual harassment involved a Black male candidate for the U.S. Supreme Court, Clarence Thomas, and his former subordinate, Anita Hill. He was appointed by the United States Senate and went on to render a number of adverse decisions against the Afro-American community.[62]

Unfortunately, sexual harassment policies are deeply entrenched reflections of the double sexual standard in the United States. Almost anything of a sexual nature, (e.g., jokes, photos) can be interpreted to be sexual harassment. That is why as many as 90 percent of women say they have been sexually harassed in some surveys. On some college campuses, some women advocacy groups tried to classify all professor/student romances as sexual harassment, even if it was consensual. Their reasoning was that any unequal power relationship meant the female student could not freely consent to a romantic relationship because she was overwhelmed by his power as a professor. At one point, San Francisco City College tried to prohibit any social interaction between students and faculty outside the classroom.[63] The power differential exists in other workplace settings where an executive can be found guilty of sexual harassment if he asks a female subordinate to have dinner with him. Lunch would be acceptable. By virtue of these rules, almost all American men are guilty of sexual harassment even if they later married the woman.

Notes

1. Randall Collins and Scott Coltrane, *Sociology of Marriage and the Family: Gender, Love, and Property*. Chicago: Nelson-Hall, 1995, pp. 34–35.

2. Boris De Rachewiltz, *Black Eros: Sexual Customs of Africa from Prehistory to the Present Day*. New York: Lyle Stuart, 1964.

3. Bureau of Justice Statistics Bulletin, *Felony Sentences in State Courts, 1996*. Washington, D.C.: U.S. Department of Justice, 1996, p. 3.

4. Cindy Struckman-Johnson, et al., "Sexual Coercion Reported by Men and Women in Prison," *Journal of Sex Research*, 1996, 33, pp. 67–77.

5. Coramae Richey Mann, *Unequal Justice: A Question of Color*. Bloomington, Indiana: Indiana University, 1993 p. 122.

6. *Ibid*. p. 122.

7. *Ibid*.

8. William Bowers, *Executions in America*, Lexington, Massachusetts: D. C. Heath, 1974.

9. Coramae Richey Mann and Lance H. Selva, "The Sexualization of Racism: The Black Rapist and White Justice." *Western Journal of Black Studies*, 1979, 3, pp. 168–177.

10. Jacquelyn Dowd Hall, "The Mind that Burns in Each Body: Women, Rape, and Racial Violence" in *Powers of Desire: The Politics of Sexuality*, ed. Ann Snitow, et al. New York: Monthly Review Press, 1983, pp. 328–349.

11. O. Demaris, *America the Violent*. New York: Cowles, 1970.

12. Laura Parker, "Justice Pursued for Emmitt Till." *USA Today*. March 12, 2004, p. 4A.

13. Susan Brown Miller, *Against our Will: Men, Women, and Rape*. New York: Bantam, 1975.

14. Hall, *op. cit.* p. 336.

15. Mann and Selva, *op. cit.* pp. 168–177.

16. Bob Frantz, "Buffaloed," *San Francisco Examiner*, February 23, 2004.

17. "Change of Mind Law passed." *San Francisco Chronicle*, July 30, 2003, p. A-3.

18. Neil Gilbert, *"Realities and Mythologies of Rape."* Society, May-June 1992, 4, pp. 4–10.

19. Terri-Lee D'Aaron, "I'm a Hooker: Every Woman's Profession" in *Gender Basics*, ed. Anne Minas. Belmont, California: Wadsworth, 1993, pp. 381–382.

20. "Court Rules Women Incapable of Rape." *San Francisco Examiner*, June 27, 2000, p. 10.

21. Stephen Donaldson, "The Rape Crisis behind Bars." *New York Times*, December 29, 1993, p. A-13.

22. Struckman-Johnson, *op. cit.*

23. Bureau of Justice Statistics Bulletin, Felony Sentences in State Courts, 1996. *Op. cit.*

24. Stewart J. D'Alessio and Lisa Stolzenberg, "Race & the Probability of Arrest." *Social Forces*, June 2003, 81, No. 4, pp. 1381–1397.

25. Gilbert, *loc. cit.*

26. Tim Beneke, "Men on Rape" in *Gender Basics: Feminist Perspectives on Women and Men*, ed. Anne Minas. Belmont, California: Wadsworth, 1993, p. 356.

27. Robin Warshaw, "I Never Called It Rape" in *Gender Basics, op. cit.*, pp. 358–364.

28. Gilbert, *op. cit.*

29. Nancy Friday, *My Secret Garden: Women's Sexual Fantasies*. New York: Pocket Books, 1973, p. 121.

30. Friday, *op. cit.* pp. 186–191.

31. Eugene J. Kanin, "False Rape Allegations." *Archives of Sexual Behavior*, February, 23, 1994, pp. 81–93.

32. *Ibid.* p. 86.

33. John Wildermuth, "Sharpton Says He Wants Party to Stop Acting like GOP." *San Francisco Chronicle*, January 17, 2004, p. A-2.

34. "St. Johns President Says Players to Blame in Scandal." *USA Today*. February 9, 2004, p. 4-B.

35. Edward O. Laumann, et al., *The Social Organization of Sexuality*. Chicago: University of Chicago, 1994, pp. 336–346.

36. *Ibid.*

37. *Ibid.*

38. Lynn A. Curtis, *Violence, Race, and Culture*. Lexington, Massachusetts: D. C. Heath, 1975, pp. 69–83.

39. *Ibid.*

40. David Steele, "Williams: Too Cool to Convict." *San Francisco Chronicle*, May 3, 2004, p. C-1.

41. Vicki Haddock, "Surviving Scandal." *San Francisco Chronicle*, October 12, 2003.

42. "Tyson Talks about Rape Accuser in Recent TV Interview." *Jet Magazine*, June 16, 2003, p. 46.

43. Alexandria Sage, "Murder for Hire Arrest in Kobe Bryant Case." *San Francisco Chronicle*, September 19, 2003, p. A-4.

44. "Racist Fliers Circulated throughout Town of Kobe Bryant Case." *Jet Magazine*, September 1, 2003, p. 48.

45. "Kobe Bryant's Attorney Plays Race Card in Court." *San Francisco Chronicle*, January 24, 2004, p. A-6.

46. *Ibid.*

47. Tom Kenworthy, "Trial Urged in Bryant Case: Accuser Says She Faces Continuous Death Threats." *USA Today*, March 26, 2004, p. A-1.

48. Curtis, *loc.cit.*

49. Debra Jopson, "Sex and the Team Player." *The Age*, March 6, 2004, p. 4.

50. Lance Williams and Carla Marinucci, "A Raunchy Interview Bedevils Schwarzenegger." *San Francisco Chronicle*, August 29, 2003, p. A-1.

51. Nathan McCall, *Makes Me Wanna Holler: A Young Black Man in America*. New York: Random House, 1994.

52. United States Department of Justice, *Children as Victims*. Washington, D.C.: Office of Justice, May 2000.

53. Gail Wyatt, *Stolen Women*. New York: Wiley, 1997.

54. "Sexual Abuse: Speaking out on the Silent Shame." *Jet Magazine*, April 5, 2004, p. 19.

55. S. A. Kirk, "The Sex Offenses of Blacks and Whites." *Archives of Sexual Behavior*, 1975, 4, pp. 295–302.

56. John Lahr, "Scot of the Antarctic." *Good Weekend*, March 20, 2004, p. 19.

57. Gail Wyatt, "The Aftermath of Child Sexual Abuse of African American and White American Women: The Victim's Experience." *Journal of Family Violence*, 1990, 5, No. 1, pp. 61–81.

58. Tamar Lewin, "Study Finds 1 in 8 Teen Boys Abused: Highest Rates Reported by Latinos, Asian Americans." *San Francisco Chronicle*, June 26, 1998, p. A-6.

59. Phyllis Meadows Jones, "His Plan." A Masters of Arts thesis presented to Hollins College, Salem, Virginia, May 2000, pp. 9–10.

60. "Michael Jackson Calls Child Molestation Charges Lies." *Jet Magazine*, December 8, 2003, p. 16.

61. "Incest and Polygamy in House of Horror." *The Australian*, March 15, 2004, p. 15.

62. Lynn Norment, "Black Men, Black Women, and Sexual Harassment." *Ebony*, January, 1992, pp. 120–124.

63. Pamela Burdman, "S. F. City College Wants to Institute a 'Dating Ban.'" *San Francisco Chronicle*, February 27, 1998, p. A-23.

CHAPTER SEVEN

~

When Races Copulate

The most interesting thing about interracial sexuality is the fear white America had of it. In the beginning of British colonization, the Africans freely mated with English indentured servants and some even married them. Before the alarm at the rate of Black/white marriages, male slaves were encouraged to marry white women since the children from such unions were also slaves. These children became part of the organic property of the slave-master. After the abolition of slavery, all the Southern states passed laws prohibiting "race mixing." Southern politicians found it easy to gain elective office by running on a platform to prevent the "mongrelization of the white race." Thousands of Black males suspected of sexually consorting with white women were lynched and castrated by white mobs and their genitals mutilated. The taboo on miscegenation was so strong that some Southern states had laws enslaving white women who had children by a slave.

Euro-Americans justified these Nazi-like practices as necessary to protect the purity of the white race. This ideology was facilitated by white stereotypes of Black males lusting after white women and Black women were regarded as sexually promiscuous and ardent for sexual mating with Euro-American men. However, the fear of Black sexuality was not restricted to the South. More than half the American states passed laws against miscegenation, whose violation could be punished by imprisonment up to ten years. In New York City, white mobs protesting the draft into the Union Army to fight the civil war hanged Afro-Americans, denuded them, and mutilated their genitals. There are also examples of white women being killed if they consented to sexual congress with a man of African origin.[1]

When we speak of interracial sexuality, it pertains to Black men and Euro-American women. The taboo on race mixing was applied to white men and Black women only if they attempted to marry. Otherwise, Black women and Euro-American men freely engaged in coitus since the first female slaves disembarked on the shores of the United States. Many slave women were coerced into sexual relations with their masters; others did so out of desire. Hence, interracial sex became a prerogative of the white male, a symbol of his authority and power. Relations between a white woman and a Black man were an affront to the white male's power. Sex, in other words, was a weapon used to keep Blacks in submission. Ostensibly, the movement to keep the white race pure lacked any scientific basis since many authorities consider race a social construct. The whole population of the world is hybrid and becoming increasingly so. At any rate, the pace of miscegenation in the past almost certainly casts doubt on any pure race theory for the United States.[2]

Obviously, the Black population cannot lay claim to any purity of its population. Estimates range up to 90 percent of Afro-Americans having some strain of Caucasoid and Mongoloid blood. The most recent and highly publicized episodes of Thomas Jefferson and Strom Thurmond siring children by Black women are but two examples of miscegenation by the elite, particularly in the Southern states. Moreover, many of these children produced by Southern white males were fair in skin pigmentation and decided to move quietly into the white population and become part of them. Several celebrities have recently admitted Black ancestry: Carol Channing, Lauren Hutton, and Peter Ustinov. There may be millions of other whites who are unaware of their Afro-American heritage.

The stereotype of Black males as sexually superior has been exploited by both Black and white males. One of this nation's classic essays was written by the esteemed writer, Normal Mailer, in the late 1950s. Entitled "The White Negro," it promoted the idea of the hip Black male and his lack of sexual inhibition as exhibited in his music that symbolized sexual orgasm. While Mailer seems to be advocating that other whites imitate this style, giving up the pleasures of the mind and giving into the pleasures of the body, it was only another way of saying Black men were not very intelligent.[3] The other writer, himself Afro-American, was Eldridge Cleaver, who proposed Black sexuality as a "revolutionary force." Using himself as an example, he became a rapist once he left prison. He began the rapist career by practicing sexual assaults against Black women and graduating to Euro-American women. To him, rape was an insurrectionary act, a way of defying and trampling upon the white man's law, upon his system of values. He raped white women, he says, to get revenge for the Euro-American male's sexual abuse of Black women.[4] Before he died, he developed a prototype of male pants, called Kleavers, which would accentuate the Black male's penis.

His sexual philosophy was no less inflammatory than other ideologies of the Black Panther Party, of which he was a leader. It was earlier than his entrance on the world stage, in 1968 when Euro-American women had any significant association with Black males as a group. During the 1960s, a large group of educated, single white females came from "up North," to work in civil rights campaigns alongside Black civil rights workers. When young people of opposite sexes are thrown together, sexual relations are an inevitable result. It was the carnal knowledge of the Northern white women that fueled the ire of Michelle Wallace in her feminist tract, *Black Macho and the Myth of the Superwoman*.[5] Many of the Euro-American women went on to join the women's movement. A few wrote of their experiences in the civil rights movement, that they encountered numerous sexual proposals from Black male civil rights workers. If they rejected the proposals, charges of racism were leveled at them. Sleeping with them elicited accusations of sluts and whores while incurring the anger of Afro-American women in the movement. Moreover, Southern whites, already resistant to pleas for racial democracy claimed the interracial relations only proved their contention that black males crave white flesh.[6]

Taboos and Conflicts

Those were not the only authors to comment on the Black man/white women pairing. The noted writer, Frantz Fanon, penned that the Black male living under racial oppression wants to be white. He wants to take the place of his oppressor. While he can never change his skin color, the desire to engage in sex with a white woman reflects his desire to be white. When this man of color embraces a white woman, he is embracing freedom and is empowered by it. This Black male, so constituted wants to be validated as white and who but the white female can do that for him?[7] Another Black leader, Malcolm X regarded white culture as decadent and insisted that the Euro-American female's sexual practices were part of that decadence. That vein is reflected in his comment that "Black women have to be drunk to do what white women do sober."[8] Presumably, he was thinking about oral sex, a rare practice among Black women in the 1960s when he said it.

Since the interracial taboo focused on Black men and white women, it is not strange that these two groups have a certain curiosity about each other. Inflaming this curiosity are the sexual stereotypes mutually held by Blacks and whites about each other as sexual partners. Nancy Friday, the writer, spoke for many Euro-American women when she wrote, "The Black man is cut out for sexual fantasy. Everything about him, real and imagined, throws fuel on the fire. He's forbidden because of his color. His penis has been endowed with mythic proportions and the story's been around for years that his expertise at screwing comes close to Black magic." Certainly, none of these stories came from Black women. She goes on to say that "all Black people are promiscuous . . . white people think. They're always screwing or they're about to. They reek of sexuality."[9] This was written in 1973 when lots of sex was a good thing and Blacks allegedly did more sex than anybody else did—or so whites thought.

While Euro-American women may have been attracted by the sexual stereotypes of Black men, the Afro-American male was equally attracted by the concept of sacred white womanhood applied to all white women as far as Blacks are concerned. Especially in the South, the penalties for having sex with a white female were extremely severe. Her forbidden fruit status could only add to the natural attraction that most men have for the opposite sex. What is taken for granted by most white men became a rare pleasure for Black males. What is rather bizarre is this magnetic attraction to the Euro-American female has nothing to do with anything she does sexually. Her whiteness is her value and it is only skin color and hair texture that sets her apart from Black women. Otherwise they have the same equipment and nobody would know a woman's race if they are in a totally dark room.

For men, however, women do not have to demonstrate any special skills for men to enjoy the pleasures of sexual engagement. Obviously, a physically attractive face and moderate body size in a woman under age forty may be an expectation. While Euro-American women may no longer be the rarity to a man who has been around the block a few times, her comparative inaccessibility is still working in her favor in attracting Afro-American men. They are simply not as available to Black males as women of their race are. Although some studies have shown as many as 45 percent of Euro-American women have dated men outside their race, that would include the legally white Latino males and Asian men. It may have been only one date for her to have the experience and otherwise she is available only to Euro-American men. The massive sexual survey revealed that 6 percent of Euro-American women had engaged in sexual activity with Afro-American men and 19 percent of Black males had experienced coitus with white women.[10]

Given the ratio of white women to Black men, that is a substantial pool of white women who have participated in sexual relations with Black males. The percentage may be higher since many Euro-American women may not want to reveal their interracial sexual liaisons to a research interviewer. At the same time, it indicates that 94 percent of Euro-American women have never engaged in sex with a Black male. The absence of interracial sexual activity does not mean an antipathy toward it. If a white female does not live in a large industrialized state, inside a large city, it is unlikely she will ever encounter a Black male that she can meet and date. Still, given the anecdotal reports by Black males to this author, the overwhelming majority of Euro-American women are off limits to them. That renders the white females who will date them more attractive because so many women of their race are unavailable.

Our focus is on sexuality while almost all the research on interracial unions involves marriage. Is there a significant difference between interracial couples who marry and those who only date for a limited time? We think so! Many of those who married start off in a sexual relationship, find they have much in common, and decide to marry. If you ask the members of interracial marriages, they will claim marriage happened because they fell in love. Certainly, they did not do a cost-benefit analysis, especially about the risks of divorce. Interracial couples have a much higher divorce rate, especially Black women/white men, than couples of the same race.[11] It is not just a clash of different cultures but societal barriers that make them risky. For example, one spouse's family of origin may help to keep a marriage intact when it is a same-race couple; when it is an interracial couple, they may have a hands-off attitude.

The person, often the white partner, who confines the interracial relationship to sexual activity only may not want to experience the difficulties of an interracial marriage. In particular, she may not want to bear children by her Black partner. When compared to same race couples, interracial couples are less likely to have a child in common.[12] There may be any number of reasons for this fear of the white partner about bearing a biracial child. Despite the trend toward a biracial identity for the child of an interracial marriage, the child will be regarded as Black by most people, especially if the child has Black features. That means an uncertain future for her child. Furthermore, in the event of a divorce, it brands her forever as a partner in a Black-white relationship. It will be a problem finding a white male to marry if she has a Black child.

There can be other problems with interracial unions. Whites are privy to backstage behavior of other whites while Blacks are protected from racial jokes, slurs, and pejorative comments due to white fear of racial harassment lawsuits. The white partner's interracial marriage may not be known and she will bear all the negative comments about the man she goes home to. Even she may be subjected to innuendo about her marriage to him based on the sexual ability his race is reputed to have. Given her anticipation of the magnitude of problems a marriage will bring, she stays in a time-contained relationship and then moves on to dating white men. A few women of European descent confine their dating exclusively to Black males for different reasons. Many claim it is purely an accident that the only men they have dated for ten years were all Black. Some say they find Black men less sexist. Often these women only date, not marry Black males.

Of course, the Black male partner may not want the complications of an interracial marriage either. Many Black families disapprove of their family members marrying outside the race. Black females, in particular, tend to be very antagonistic toward Black men married to Euro-American women.[13] Again, we turn to the late basketball star, Wilt Chamberlain:

> It used to be that any Black man who dated a white girl was looked up to by other Blacks, the white girl was a tangible symbol that he'd made it and that he could thumb his nose at whitey, and all Blacks shared, vicariously, in his triumph. Now, it's just the opposite. Many Blacks say you should date Black girls exclusively, to prove that you're proud of being Black. So, where I used to get a lot of phone calls from strange white girls who would go out of their way to let me know they were white, I now get a lot of calls from strange Black girls who go out of their way to let me know they're "soul sisters."[14]

We have no idea how many white sexual partners that Black males have accumulated. Many of them were very casual. White women have complained they would go to bed with them and they would not be heard from in another two through four weeks. That is not a race-specific pattern. These are free-floating unmarried Black males who do not want long-term commitments. The advantage of their interracial dating is that many of their Euro-American sexual partners do not either. America has not made enough progress in race relations to make marriage a comfortable situation for Euro-American women or Afro-American men. About 80 percent of Afro-Americans live in neighborhoods where their neighbors look like themselves. Blacks and whites often inhabit different social worlds where never the twain does meet. There are liberal environments with cosmopolitan racial relationships. They include cities like Berkeley, San Francisco, Los Angeles, New York, and Boston. If they go outside those cities, what they will encounter are strongly entrenched patterns of spatial and social segregation by race.[15]

Making Contact

Before Blacks and whites can form a sexual liaison, they must first make connections with each other. Here, the normal pattern of initiating the relationship is reversed. Because most Euro-American women are inaccessible, he will not typically make the first move because the risks of rejection are fairly high. That means the roles are reversed—she must make clear that she is available to him. Her normal cues of body language and direct eye contact may not work because those are unfamiliar signals to him. Hence, she will have to use excessive friendliness, touching, flirting, and flattery. In the 1970s, the Euro-American female might be fairly aggressive. One man told of a woman who came over to his apartment on some pretext and asked if she could see how he could kiss. Another man told us of a woman who came over to his desk with a copy of Playboy magazine and turned to the centerfold. Rarely did they play the coquettish role so often enacted by Afro-American women.

Some Black males take the initiative with Euro-American females and live to regret it. It is his approach more than his race that she objects to. Kochman cites the case of a Black male student, in a newly desegregated high school, who approached a white female student and began to tell her how "fine" she looked, what a great "lover" he was, and how much he could do for her. She walked away from him and later filed a sexual assault charge. His approach and her response had little to do with race. In Black culture, it is typical of men to express an open sexual interest in a woman while the white female's values lead her to be offended by a direct interest in sex. While the charge of sexual assault was an extreme reaction, it could certainly lead to a sexual harassment charge if he attempted it with a white female colleague in an office.[16]

White women are accustomed to sexual intent being inferred circumstantially. Offering to come to a woman's apartment to fix an appliance is one example. Her acceptance of such an offer indicates some availability since it is presumed any male's objective is to have sex with her. Black males will allow a woman to express sexual interest in him while Euro-American women are not expected to directly convey a sexual interest because the white male is likely to regard her as sexually promiscuous. A Euro-American male would likely never consider marriage with a woman so sexually aggressive, although he will use her directness as a tool to have sex with her. Black women will have a similar problem with a white male who uses a pretext to seduce women. The Black woman is not accustomed to sexual availability being determined by subtle cues and may not be sure if he's sexually interested in her. White women will let him lead the way and allow the circumstances to dictate the presence of a sexual intent.[17]

Not only do Black males believe that women, too, are generally interested in sex but his culture allows them to express that interest in a direct way and to be sexually assertive. She is not less respected for expressing that interest. More importantly, she retains the right to discriminate among men and to reject a male's proposition of sexual engagement. Black men will assume that all women have an interest in sex but an individual Black woman may not be interested in sex with him. Rapping is a ritual for Afro-American males and may be practiced indiscriminantly on any number of Black women he encounters. Thus, they will be subject to many more refusals of their sexual propositions than women who accept them. What is important is that she makes some response to his rap and doesn't ignore him. The Euro-American female does not know how to respond to a Black male's rap and normally would not entertain such a direct sexual proposal from a white male lest she be thought of as a whore or slut. The Black woman suffers no such allegations because her culture permits her to have an interest in sex, express it, and still retain the right to deny sexual access to a specific Black male's sexual propositions.[18]

In white culture it is still the case, for most women, that women are socialized to be passive and sexually receptive in relation to men and rely on men to lead the way. In response to a Black male's rap, she does not possess the verbal skills to respond in a way he is accustomed to hearing. Women may be disadvantaged in a situation where they are expected to be polite and spare a man's feelings. Whereas a white male will employ an indirect approach by inviting her to dinner, she can freely refuse by saying she is busy and, in future requests never manage to have free time to accept his invitation. If she accepts his invitation, it is implied that he has been given the opportunity to make sexual advances and that she is sexually available. With the Black male's more direct approach, she is only allowed a plea not to be bothered or ignore his proposition. Some Black men are successful with Euro-American women because they do not have the skill or tactics to deny his very explicit invitation to sexual congress.

We may note here that not many Euro-American women had to be pressured into interracial sexual activity during the years when white women were sowing their own oats. During the high-flying 1970s, white women came into their own sexually and permissive norms of sexuality became the norm during that era. They were able to have sex with whomever and whenever they wanted. Black men became the flavor of the decade. In certain contexts where the Blacks were low in number, Euro-American women had to form a line to taste their sexual favors. Hans Sebald's study of interracial sexual activity on the campus of Arizona State University, located in Phoenix, Arizona, presents one of the extreme examples during that decade. Arizona had a very small Black population and many of the Black male students at that university were on athletic scholarships. Athletes were normally a sexual magnet for Euro-American women and Black athletes, in particular, were in heavy demand. His Black male sample often reported hundreds of one-night stands with Euro-American women during four years or less as students on that campus. One student cited an example of going to the library, encountering a Euro-American woman and engaging in sex there in the stacks.[19]

That was in the permissive 1970s. Now the Euro-American woman does not respond to the Black stranger. Indeed, that stranger is perceived by almost all white women as the potential rapist and criminal. The media has launched a culture of fear among American women about the risks to their safety. The majority of American women live in fear of being robbed or raped. They rarely go out at night alone and some do not go out at all. Most have become the human equivalent of pack animals. Not only do the media depict a country where all women are at risk but the scores of books designed for women urge them to take all kinds of precautions, get instruction in the martial arts, and arm themselves with mace, knives, and guns. American women are frightened and Euro-American women are the most frightened of all. In very subtle ways, the media tells them the person to be most frightened of is the Black male. Although most media no longer mention the race of criminals, they do not have to. His picture is there on the TV screen and in the newspaper. Consequently, whenever a Black male is near a Euro-American woman on the street, she clutches her purse and gives him a wide berth on the street. It does not matter if the male is 16 or 90 years of age, she is afraid of him. Black males report that they hate walking anywhere because they encounter this constant fear among Euro-American women wherever they go.

Whereas Euro-American women over the age of twenty five meet potential white male lovers at bus stops, supermarkets, laundromats, and other public places, they do not respond to sexual proposals from Afro-American males in casual settings. They may date Black males that they meet on the job, through friends, or in their apartment building. Otherwise, there is the chronic fear of the Black stranger. Even the most liberal of white women share this fear. It is, in most cases, a race-specific phenomenon. Although Black women live in high-risk neighborhoods, most do not experience this generalized fear of the Black male stranger. They know what white women do not: most Black males are not rapists and criminals. They realize that a fifty-year-old male carrying a bag of groceries does not intend to rob or rape them when they ride up in the elevator together.

Push and Pull Forces

Sociologists often use the concept of push and pull factors in studying domestic immigration. The push factors will be those forces such as a draught, mechanization of agriculture, loss of manufacturing jobs, etc., that push folks to migrate against their wishes to another environment. The pull forces will be those attractive elements in the environment to which they are migrating, such as racial diversity, high paying jobs, cultural amenities, etc. If we apply these concepts to interracial sexual activity, we will note the promotion of the white female as a sexual icon is a big pull or attraction for the Afro-American male. In the last twenty years, America has promoted the eroticization of the white female. She is the one we see in skimpy clothing in billboards, television, magazines, and the movies. Hollywood films can be singled out for making her almost the exclusive sex symbol because Blacks rarely make love on the big screen, even in the movies that feature them as leading men. There has been some effort at racial diversity but almost all the sexually tinged advertising involves a non-Hispanic white woman, who only makes up about 60 percent of the female population. This increasing eroticization of the white female is worldwide.

We have already mentioned the Euro-American woman's inaccessibility as part of her attraction. She is aware of being the desired sexual object of men of every race. That can make her arrogant and self-centered. Yet, her passion is reserved for the Euro-American male because that is where the money and power are. In almost every ad placed by white women in personals ads, looking for sexual partners and males, it mentions her race and her desire to find a man of the same race. Despite their greater similarity to her, Latino and Asian men are further down the sexual food chain. When she strays across the color line, her choice is inevitably an Afro-American male. The percentage that beds other men of color is much lower. At one time, she was not the desired sexual object because Euro-American women were not regarded as "sexual." She was perceived as the dutiful wife and mother of his children. Only when she declared herself sexually liberated did the Euro-American masters of the media decide she would be marketed as a sexual commodity.[20]

Adding to the allure of the Euro-American women is the fact that the standards of beauty in America are all about those traits white women have in abundance. Asian women cannot match her in height, blondness, bust size, and white skin. Latino women often cannot match her in blondness and skin pigmentation. The Black woman, with rare exceptions, cannot compete on the basis of skin color, long, straight hair, blondness, and big legs. Among dark-haired people the world over, the blond has become a global symbol. In the Black female community, there is the prevalent belief that all she brings to the marriage table with Black men is white skin. In her book on how to find and keep an employed Black man, Julia Hare says, "these brothers can find a white woman in the dark. Some of these floosies they come up with—obviously just because they're white—can look like they just came out of a cave, because the brother was 'shonuf,' dealing in the dark. Heard one fellow say 'it's okay if she's obese, it just gives him more white to love.'"[21]

This notion that only physically unattractive Euro-American women are attracted to Black males, because they cannot find a comparable white male may have some validity. Even within the white race, women may compromise their standards if they cannot find what they want. Thus, white women may marry older white males; middle-class white women may marry working-class white men. Some of the interracial marriages may be mismatches on the surface. He may be a Nobel-winning physicist and she works as a waitress at a restaurant, yet men marry down all the time since a woman's occupation and income are not as important to him as they would be to a woman. Black women may think every elite Black male should be married—if they must—to somebody who looks like Britney Spears and has lots of money. When it comes to finding a Britney Spears type the Afro-American millionaire is competing for her hand with white male billionaires.

When it comes to finding a sexual partner, the Euro-American woman may have different standards. It is possible that she has accepted the myth of Black male virility and wants to give it a try. If she is looking for that, his income and educational level should not matter. Whom she winds up with may be a function of the environment she finds herself in. If she is a college student, chances are that he will also be a college student or perhaps a Black professor on the campus. Women do not often screw down even if it is only a sexual dalliance she wants. If she wishes to have coitus with an Afro-American male, chances are that it will be an executive, not the office janitor. Given that Black males have less education in general than white women, it is telling that the Euro-American woman winds up with a Black male that has the highest level of education and income within his racial group.[22]

Speculation has long been rampant that the Euro-American woman is exchanging her whiteness for his education and income. It is difficult to accept the notion that she brings nothing to the table except white skin. Her manner of dealing with men may be pleasing to them. If a student, she may offer to type his term paper—maybe even write it. We know that she is more likely to perform fellatio on him than a comparable Black woman is. Many white females are heavily socialized into ways of pleasing a man. The writer, Naomi Wolf, wrote about practicing oral sex on a coke bottle in order to be good at it.[23] Black women swear that the Euro-American woman allows him to be irresponsible and get away with bad behavior, whereas they would call him on it. Whatever the speculation, only the two individuals can know their motivation for entering an interracial relationship. Furthermore, the intermarriage rate of Asians and Latinos is far higher than that of Afro-Americans.[24]

Then, there are the push forces that can be pretty much reduced to disenchantment with Black women. Julia Hare recounts her conversations with Black men about why they were dating Euro-American women. Some insisted that Black women are too uptight and don't want to engage in kinky sex, preferring to stick to the missionary position. Others claimed that the Black woman demands too many things whereas a white woman will let him alone, give him money on the side, and allow him to drive her car.[25] By "kinky sex," Hare presumably means oral sex, the one sexual technique that white women are known for and Black women are reluctant to do. While more than 90 percent of Euro-American women engage in oral sex, it is not because they have much gusto for the practice.[26] Many do not like it and do it because they know men desire it. Nancy Friday once said the best way to please a man is through oral sex on a national television program.

On occasion, Afro-American males can cite other reasons for dating/marrying the Euro-American female. On a subliminal level, it may be due to their resentment of white women who rejected his overtures in the past. Because he may see sexual intercourse as a way of defiling a woman, this is his retribution. Others have actually claimed that they married white women to extract revenge against the Euro-American male. He relishes the look on his face when he sees his precious white female, who could be his mother or daughter, on his arm. Perhaps the racial bigot will be incensed by the sight but it is doubtful that any white male of sound mind loses sleep over the sight of one white woman on the arm of a Black man. Moreover, more rational people have theorized that the white elite are happy to see an interracial couple because it suggests the Black partner has embraced Euro-American values and will not go off on a separatist tangent. Both Black males appointed to the United States Supreme Court were married to nonwhite women.

Black women largely escape criticism for their liaisons with Euro-American males because they would be susceptible to the push factor of a shortage of Black males. Julia Hare says that a Black woman on the verge of an interracial marriage may wonder, if Black men are thought of as sexually superior to the men of other races, why does she have to be consigned to crossing the color line to something inferior.[27] We know that Afro-American women are reluctant to date and marry white men because of the historical abuse meted out to her people by the ancestors of these men. Or, at least, that is what they claim. When doing my research on college-educated Black singles, I was surprised at how many of the women had dated and had sex with Euro-

American men. Many of the Black women dating and marrying Euro-American men today say they hear the tick of their biological clock and, if they want children, have to marry what is available. We might raise the question of why they do not try men from the Caribbean or even Asian and Latino males. Also of interest may be why so many Black female celebrities had white husbands such as Lena Horne, Pearl Bailey, Diana Ross, and others. After all, these very attractive and wealthy Black women did not face a shortage of Black males willing to share their millions.

The male shortage notwithstanding, many Black women are sexually attracted to Euro-American males by the same pull forces that pull Black men in that direction. White men are not as sexually marketed as white females; they are certainly the sex symbols that men are allowed to be. The Tom Cruises, Brad Pitts, and John Travoltas are the sex symbols of the twenty-first century. However, those are not the white males Black women will have access to although Brad Pitt once dated another Black female film star. At one time, Afro-American women wanted to marry white men in order to have light-skinned children. Unlike white women in interracial marriages who refuse to have children by their Black spouse, those women wanted to and had children. If their children were light-skinned enough, they would also go into interracial marriages. Very few of the lighter-skinned children of interracial marriages went on to marry men and women of African descent.

Is There a Sexual Difference?

After all the furor over keeping Black men and white women apart, what happens when they meet in the bedroom? In a physical sense—not much. Sex is sex and the men and women of their race had the exact same body parts. A Black comedian jokes that the Black male will try harder with the Euro-American woman because he has a reputation to live up to. In most interracial situations, she will discover that his penis is no bigger than those of her white lovers except that there are more Black men in the super large category. It's doubtful that many white women are seeking out well-endowed Black males because she chooses them on the basis of their social status more than any other criteria. Even if she gets a man with a big one, it will not particularly lead to increased sexual satisfaction. And, some women find that sex with a well-endowed man can be uncomfortable.

Still much of sexuality is mental. She finally is in bed with a man that white dominated society would not allow her to have. Not only might they kill him if caught, they would severely punish her if she agreed to the sexual relationship. This is her ultimate rebellion against her parents, her friends, and her country. If he is trying hard to live up to his image as a super stud, so much the better. They are living in the moment and a large penis is the last thing she cares about. One respondent from Nancy Friday's sample provides a description of the feelings of many Euro-American women:

> I have always found sleeping with Negro men very satisfactory (even when it isn't satisfactory) because they are so sexy by virtue of their forbiddances. I mean . . . wow, if your mother found out . . . I was talking about Negroes. There's a whole number one can do on one's self about them (they are never really good at it in person as they are in my head), which is part of our gross national guilt about Black/white relations. I kind of like it when I imagine some heavenly looking Black guy telling me I'm nothing but a white bitch. . . . The Black-white love affair thing is always more exciting because of the taboos connected with it. Dialogue is important anyway in lovemaking and Black guys can usually come up with some very exciting talk.[28]

Her Black male partner may be equally as excited about breaching the long held taboo on sex with a woman of the master race. As he looks at her creamy white flesh, her long hair cascading over her head, he is aware of the harsh penalty meted out to his ancestors for even touching white flesh. Now, the same woman who is loved by the white man is loving him, and touching him in previously forbidden areas. Given how difficult it can be to elicit fellatio from a Black woman, he marvels at the touch of her lips on his sexual organ and thinks that he has gone to a heaven designed especially for Afro-American men. This exhilaration pertains to his first time with a Euro-American woman. If he has sex with her over a hundred times, he starts to hear the B. B. King song, "The Thrill is Gone."

As Euro-American women soon find out, he will tire of her quickly and move on to other women. Some of those other women may also be white or he could return exclusively to Black women after satisfying his curiosity. Some Black males confine all their sexual relations to Euro-American women. Some of America's sports icons were among them: O. J. Simpson, Tiger Woods, and Reggie Jackson. Perhaps it takes some Black males longer to get over the mystique of the white woman. A number of Black men complain that Black women are too conservative in the bedroom. One of these men was Wilt Chamberlain, who said, "Black women also tend to have more sexual hang-ups than white women do—and I don't like any sexual hang-ups." Explaining why he dates more white women than Black women, he goes on to explain that "many Black girls grow up thinking of sex as furtive and dirty, and they can't respond as fully as they should to a man. Many of them even insist on making love quickly and in the dark."[29]

Any Black women reading his book must wonder where he found the Black women he dated. There are nuanced differences between the races. White women do seem to be more comfortable with all their clothes off. Black men may find that they have to take off all a Black woman's clothes. White women have complained that Black men do not want to spend a lot of time on foreplay and can be too rough in their lovemaking. And, many of them comment on the fact that they do not like to give head (i.e., cunnilingus). Black women have complained about white men being the silent type, saying very little during the sex act. When they do talk, it is never as colorful as the Black male. While not a complaint of many, there were Black men who felt that Euro-American women were too reserved and silent during their lovemaking.

What about the Others?

There are other racial groups in the United States besides Blacks and whites. Latinos actually outnumber Afro-Americans as of the 2000 census. Most Latinos live in the same states and cities in America and, unlike Euro-Americans, typically attend the same public schools as Blacks. Yet, there is very little sexual interaction between these racial minorities. Black women were more likely to engage in sex with Latinos than Anglo males. One does find in California significant socializing among these different racial groups in the most racially diverse state in America. Black men in California also have the highest percentage of intermarriage on the American mainland (Hawaii excluded).

One reason for the low level of sexual interaction is that Blacks and Euro-Americans are by far the most sexually liberal groups in the United States. Until recently, many Latino women had chaperones and being a virgin was very important within their culture. Very little is known about Asian sexuality except that they are, on the average, more conservative than Black and Anglo women are. White males, unlike their female counterparts do engage in sexual activity with Asians, enough so that a huge number of Asian females have out-married to them. In premarital interaction with Anglo males, most Asian females have to adapt to their more liberal sexual values. That typically means sex after a few dates and employing a variety of sexual techniques.

While there is not a perfect correlation between racial groups engaged in sexual activity and those who marry, they are often the same. If we look at the substantial intermarriage rates for the state of Hawaii, we find that the most numerous Black male outmarriages are to Euro-American women. What is so strange is that most of the women in Hawaii are of Asian descent.

That is partly explained by the fact that the majority of Blacks living in Hawaii are members of the United States military. Chances are that most of the women they work with are Euro-American and that is whom they marry. Furthermore, Asian women are not taboo to Black men and Asian women are inclined to have sex with men that they hope to marry. Their families will accept outmarriage with a white male but severely disapprove of out-marriage to Black and Latino males.

Latinos are themselves racially mixed although a large majority is listed by the U.S. Census Bureau as Hispanic whites. Many of them come from countries where the mixture is white and Negroid. That would make them Black by the racial definitions of American society. Yet, the census classifies them as white. Due to their racial mixture and willingness to have sex outside their racial group, many are probably available to Afro-American males. It seems Afro-American males do not have much of an interest in them and prefer to deal with the forbidden white woman. Of course, it is also possible that Euro-American females are more aggressive in pursuing Afro-American males and Latinos wait to be asked. Black women are more likely to have engaged in sex with Latino men and my guess is that most are Puerto Rican.

In the future, I expect unions between Black males, Asian, and Latino females to increase. They have minority status in common although the issues are very different for each group. Presently Blacks resent the encroachment of Asians and Latinos on low-wage, unskilled jobs. In particular, they see themselves in competition with Latinos for housing, jobs, health care, and affirmative action slots. It does not help that Latinos are often white in appearance and have the option of operating as white in the Anglo community. Still, Latin America is a model of racial amalgamation and has easily integrated with people of color for centuries. As a racially mixed and low socioeconomic group, they have the most in common with Afro-Americans. While Asian Americans, through hard work and education, have attained middle-class status, Asians often find themselves opposing affirmative action because they think they benefit little from it and often are disadvantaged by it.

Still, Afro-American men can rest assured that Asian and Latino females are not attracted to them by myths of their sexual virility and gigantic sexual organ. They will, consequently, have to be taken seriously since they will not want a time-contained relationship. These women of color do not have a social world that Black men cannot enter. There is no historical record of Asian and Latino men lynching and castrating Afro-American males over alleged sexual involvement with their women. These women will be in the struggle for racial parity over the course of a relationship, not advocating civil rights for Blacks one year and in the women's movement the next year.

Already, people of color in the state of California have joined together to vote for Black political candidates and fight against referendums to roll back the gains of the civil rights movement. White women, on the hand have often joined with Euro-American men to support reactionary measures on the ballot.

I have restricted this discussion because it is not clear what Black women will and can do in terms of a future alignment with other racial groups. We know that they resist going outside the Black community for sexual partners or mates. At times, we hear that they have no real options, that men of other races are not interested in them. Maybe that is partly true. While Euro-American women can select men on the basis of their socioeconomic status, white males are selecting women by physical standards and femininity fit. Asian women are acceptable to them because they are considered ultra-feminine and willing to please a man. Black women, as often portrayed in the media, are depicted as being the opposite. Asian and Latino men are also looking for the feminine, subservient female when considering wife candidates. At the same time, Black women have almost a monopoly on the available Black males. Nationally, of those Black men who marry, 95 percent choose Afro-American women.

As for Afro-American men and white women, I expect an incremental increase in the rate of intermarriage. Despite the availability of Black men on their socioeconomic level, the stakes are still too high for her to forsake the benefits of white skin privilege for an iffy marriage with an Afro-American male. White America will still punish her for crossing outside racial lines whereas Euro-American males can do it with impunity. That is why we can list any number of white male celebrities who have married Black women and no white woman of American birth has ever done so. All the A-list female celebrities who have tasted Black flesh publicly are European or Australian.

For many Euro-American women, interracial sexuality was just a fad. We now see many of them coming out as lesbians. The hard-core interracial loyalists are mostly in the gay and Jewish community. Gays identify with the underdog status of Blacks, as they encounter discrimination on every level in American life. A number of them have dated Black gays and lesbians. Partly, it is easier for them because they have nothing to lose. They are already so stigmatized for being gay that heterosexuals will hardly notice or care about them having a Black partner. Jews empathize strongly with Blacks after being subjected to discrimination everywhere they have gone. Having six million of your faith killed only because they were Jewish has really sensitized them to the folly of race hatred. Even now, racial bigots often target them for homicide in the case of serial killings based on race. Although they represent only 2 percent of the American population, Jewish women have always rep-resented a large percentage of the intermarried.

Interracial sexual activity will continue as Generation Y comes of age. They are the white youth buying the rap records, wearing Black designed clothing and admiring Black sports heroes. It is said that they are the least racist of white Americans. Perhaps they will allow women of their race the latitude, the right to pursue a relationship with a man of their choosing. Maybe the men of Generation Y will find the positive personal qualities of Afro-American women sufficient to overlook the fact that they do not meet the physical standards of European beauty. Perhaps the best thing they can do is work toward a true multiracial society, where people are judged on the content of their character and not the color of their skin.

Notes

1. Martha Hodes, ed., *Sex, Love, Race: Crossing Boundaries in North American History*. New York: New York University, 1999.

2. Naomi Zack, *Race and Mixed Race*. Philadelphia: Temple University, 1993.

3. Norman Mailer, *The White Negro: Reflections on Hipsterism in Advertisements for Myself*, ed. N. Mailer. New York: Putnam, 1959, pp. 374–375.

4. Eldridge Cleaver, *Soul on Ice*. New York: Dell, 1968, pp. 25–29.

5. Michelle Wallace, *Black Macho and the Myth of the Superwoman*. New York: Dial Press, 1979.

6. David Allyn, *Make Love, Not War: The Sexual Revolution: An Unfettered History*. Boston: Little, Brown, and Company, 2000, pp. 89–90.

7. Frantz Fanon, *Black Skin, White Masks*. New York: Grove Press, 1967.

8. Quoted in Robert Staples, "Has the Sexual Revolution Bypassed Blacks." *Ebony*, April 1974, 29, pp. 111–114.

9. Nancy Friday, *My Secret Garden: Women's Sexual Fantasies*. New York: Pocket Books, 1973, p. 186.

10. Edward O. Laumann, et al. *The Social Organization of Sexuality: Sexual Practices in the United States*. Chicago: University of Chicago, 1994.

11. United States Bureau of the Census, *Interracial Couples: 1960 to the Present*. Washington, D.C.: U.S. Government Printing Office, 1999.

12. *Ibid.*

13. Y. St. Jean and R. E. Parker, "Disapproval of Interracial Unions: The Case of Black Females" in *American Families: Issues in Race and Ethnicity*, ed. Cardell K. Jacobson. New York: Garland, 1995, pp. 341–352.

14. Wilt Chamberlain and David Shaw, *Wilt: An Autobiography*. New York: MacMillan, 1973, p. 260

15. M. Belinda Tucker and Claudia Mitchell-Kernan, "New Trends in Black American Intermarriage: The Social Context." *Journal of Marriage and the Family*, 1990, 59, pp. 209–218.

16. Thomas Kochman, *Black and White Styles in Conflict*. Chicago: University of Chicago, 1981, pp. 74–87.

17. *Ibid*.

18. *Ibid*.

19. Hans Sebald, "Patterns of Interracial Dating and Sexual Liaison of White and Black College Men." *International Journal of Sociology of the Family*, 1974, pp. 23–36.

20. P. Dixon, "In Search of the Black Man's Blond: Physical Beauty and the Caucasian Standard in African-American Heterosexual Relationships." *Griot*, 1996, 15, pp. 33–40.

21. Julia Hare, "How to Find and Keep a Black Man Working" (BMW). San Francisco: The Black Think Tank, 1995, p. 33.

22. United States Bureau of the Census, *loc. cit*.

23. Naomi Wolf, *The Beauty Myth*. New York: Simon and Shuster, 1996.

24. Grace Yoo and Robert Staples, "Intermarriage" in *Encyclopedia of Sociology*, 2nd Edition, ed. Edward F. Borgatta and R. Montgomery. New York: MacMillan Reference, 2000, pp. 1407–1415.

25. Hare, *op. cit.* p. 37.

26. Laumann, et al., *op. cit.* pp. 264–265.

27. Hare, *op. cit.* p. 30.

28. Friday, *op. cit.* pp. 190–191.

29. Chamberlain and Shaw, *op. cit.* p. 262.

~

CHAPTER EIGHT

Sexuality of the Rich and Famous

Being a celebrity in America is akin to being a member of the royal family in Great Britain. The cult of celebrity is stronger here than anywhere in the world. The doings of celebrities, their deaths, births of their children, and dating relationships may occupy the front page of newspapers, lead the local TV news, and pervade the Internet. Entire magazines are devoted to them and more than a million dollars has been paid for the exclusive photos of their weddings or newborn children. Photographers make a handsome sum taking pictures of their comings and goings. If they live in the two media capitals of the world, Los Angeles and New York, very little of their lives remains private. Unlike ordinary citizens, we know about their presumed sex life because of the inordinate attention paid to it in gossip columns, kiss and tell books, and magazine articles. When their careers have wound down, celebrities will reveal sexual secrets in a lucrative autobiography.

Prior to 1960, only a handful of Blacks would have qualified as rich and famous. Most behaved with great rectitude and scandalous behavior was rarely reported in the media. Today, there are hundreds in that category, perhaps thousands depending on the standards used. Fame in the twenty-first century is very different from notoriety in the 1950s. With the fragmentation of the entertainment industry into niche markets, there are very few superstars, who are Black, that are known to 75 percent of Americans or 100 percent of Black Americans. Michael Jackson and Bill Cosby would register instant recognition. Knowledge of other celebrities is contingent on your age group, your music, TV, and movie tastes. Unfortunately, scandal can confer high visibility on some Blacks. Thus, O. J. Simpson is widely known as is Janet Jackson, Kobe Bryant, and Mike Tyson. On a worldwide basis, Muhammad Ali is regarded as the most famous man in the world, in a category of his own.

In terms of sexuality, you do not need to have instant recognition by a hundred million Americans. Being revered by five million Blacks who buy your records and watch your films and television shows is sufficient to endow you with a different sexual lifestyle. Moreover, being rich without fame will not bring the same advantages to a man. There is not the same glamour attached to wealth as to fame. A rich person may be seated ahead of others at a restaurant, especially if a large tip is given to the maitre d'. Celebrities are not only seated ahead of others but may not have to pay for their meals and will be fawned over by the staff and owner. Some celebrities have fame—not wealth—as we find out when they declare for bankruptcy, listing three hundred thousand dollars in assets and ten million dollars in debts.

While there are millions of Euro-Americans who are wealthy through business dealings and inheritances, a majority of wealthy Black Americans are entertainers and athletes. Even the one Black billionaire made his fortune through a Black cable TV network and now owns a professional basketball team. When you read interviews with Euro-American celebrities, the men admit that a primary motivation for attaining fame was to increase the number and variety of women they had sexual access to. Most Black males were driven by a desire to escape poverty and believed entertainment and sports were the only avenues open to them. Black women want the money that comes from show business success and the adulation that fame brings. While women are not driven by sexual reasons to attain fame, it does provide them with a better class of sexual partner and allows them to call the tune in a relationship. It also means they will not face the typical problem of ordinary Black women—finding a husband with a job.

What distinguishes the Black male celebrity from ordinary Black men is the supply of sexual partners exceeds the demand. There are thousands of women very anxious to have sex with a famous Black man. They are motivated by a number of reasons. Some actually fantasize that the star will even marry them and they will forever enjoy a life of luxury and respect from others. If she works as a customer service representative for some company, her chances of actualizing her dream are slim and none—unless she meets him before he becomes a star. More-practical women will settle for the one-night stand and something to brag about to their friends. Most of the "older" male film stars are married to women they knew before becoming stars or are dating women of other races. Some of the younger male music stars will marry women in the entertainment world and almost none of them remain married forever.

The easiest celebrities to meet are the athletes. Many of them earn a higher income than show business types although their careers will be shorter. Anybody can buy a ticket to a sports event and wait around after the game is over. About half their games will be played in their home city and they can be easily located. Depending on the sport, many of the athletes are young and single. Baseball players tend to marry early and stay married. Of course, many are willing to engage in extramarital affairs and those affairs often take place on the road. Superstars may be surrounded by a large entourage, often comprised of young men who were friends during their poverty years. If a woman wants to join the inner circle of the superstar, she will sleep with a member of the entourage. Very little security exists among the sports groupies as there are always new and younger women waiting for sex with the superstar. Because athletes spend so much time on the road, they often settle on one woman to come home to. Most of them do not live in the city they play in during the off-season and the ones who do are likely married or cohabitating with children.

Meeting the lone celebrity is not an easy task for the woman who wants to have sex with one. In the 1950s and 1960s, celebrities were subject to the same laws of racial segregation as ordinary Black folks. Thus, they lived in the same neighborhoods, their children went to public schools, and they had to stay in Black hotels when on the road. Nowadays, they live behind gated walls, their children attend expensive private schools, and they can only be seen at special events. We are discussing the celebrities who live in Los Angeles, New York, and Miami. A number of them live in other cities and might be more easily encountered. Even when they go to clubs or other special functions, VIP rooms are set aside for them. The folks in the VIP rooms will be those with connections, power brokers and other celebrities from different venues.

The sexual agenda of male and female stars can be very different. Both will be surrounded by an entourage. These entourages will consist of relatives and hometown friends who may perform specialized tasks for the celebrity. This seems especially true of Black celebrities. It is a way of providing a payday to needy kin and friends who "knew them when." In the case of female stars, their role is to erect a barrier between her and interlopers. Sometimes they do this without their knowledge because they fear any romantic/sexual involvement could mean the loss of their positions. Whereas the male celebrity wants his posse to select choice females for him to bed, he may select the women himself and use his aide to invite her to a private meeting.

Monogamy is not a strong suit of the male celebrity. Marriage is no obstacle to taking advantage of the abundant sexual opportunities available to a star. Two of the superstars, Bill Cosby and Michael Jordan, had their infidelity revealed by the women they had as paramours. One was a basketball star, the other a comedian/TV star. Jordan's affair was facilitated by the fact he played many of his games on the road. He also was known to travel to different cities for gambling and golf games. Cosby went on movie locations and gave comedy performances in various locations. Probably most celebrities own more than one residence, which also enables them to carry on affairs with ease. A common reason cited for the celebrity divorce is how much time they spent apart. What is left unspoken is he spent the time apart with other women.

Celebrity Status and the Dating Game

Comparatively few celebrities have lifelong marriages. Some have been married to the same person for a lengthy period and have conducted a number of affairs during the marriage. The advantage of the male celebrity is that women are attracted to his fame, wealth, or power. Almost all the American presidents since the 1930s have been proven or rumored to have engaged in extramarital affairs. This includes the president who was impeached for lying about his sexual indiscretions in the oval office. There is no reason to believe they were any different from other married men. They simply had more, perhaps explicit, sexual opportunities. The male celebrity views these sexual opportunities as a perk that comes along with fame. What is the sense of having fame and not being able to indulge your sexual fantasies? Their wives are often codependents in their adulterous affairs. Very few of them terminated the marriage after the affairs were revealed. These were women who luxuriated in reflected glory, who liked the idea of being married to a powerful, famous man. A divorce would secure for her some of his wealth but the doors his fame can open would now be closed. If she divorced him, she is now just a former wife while the interloper might sit in her place.

For those celebrities that are single, sex and the dating game are fraught with risks.[1] The newly arrived celebrity is inherently suspicious of new people he/she meets after becoming a celebrity. The late Wilt Chamberlain, in his autobiography *Wilt*, explains, "I've had more than my share of 'friends' who only wanted to exploit my name and leech off me. That's why I'm so suspicious now, and take so long to make new friends. I've just been burned too many times to be open and trusting with everyone I meet." That suspicion may be doubled for the female star, which worries that a potential lover is really after her money. At least the male celebrity is comfortable with a woman being after his money and is willing to shower her with money and gifts. Some women celebrities, with money, may still feel that the man in pursuit of her should pay for everything. She may be willing to have sex with him but does not want his intrusion into her financial affairs.

That attitude can create quite a conundrum for the female star. When they do marry, it is often to men in show business or those men described as "wealthy businessmen." Unlike the male stars, many of the female celebrities allow their lovers/husbands to manage their career and finances. The other option they have is to date and have sex with another celebrity. This supposedly prevents the problem of fortune hunters in her midst. If they marry, such marriages inevitably fail—for obvious reasons. He is accustomed to having his ego stroked and so is she. There generally are not enough positives in a relationship for it to last long. The men seem to have greater success at marriage—on the surface—while it is difficult to think of many famous Black women in long-term marriages, especially in recent years.

Comparatively few Black women have been involved in the sexual scandals surrounding male celebrities. Lena Horne did have to endure the allegation by the boxer, Joe Louis, that they had an affair while she was married. Diana Ross, the singer, finally acknowledged that the child thought to be sired by her Euro-American husband had actually been fathered by Berry Gordy, the boss of Motown Records. The blues singer Bessie Smith had lesbian affairs when Euro-Americans did not care about the sex lives of Black Americans. The singer Roberta Flack has often been rumored to have had an affair with the reverend Jesse Jackson while he was married. Nonsexual scandals have taken their toll on female stars, such as Whitney Houston's and Dionne Warwick's substance abuses, Halle Berry's hit and run accident, and Dorothy Dandridge's suicide. Of course, it must be noted that the overwhelming majority of Black celebrities are men.

Celebrities dating other celebrities are not always what they appear. Sometimes these matchings are arranged by publicists in order to get publicity. Gays may go out on dates with straights to ward off any suspicion about their sexual orientation. Usually, stars who go to a popular hangout are there to see and be seen. Hordes of photographers surround these places and take pictures that crop up in the tabloids and entertainment magazines. These same magazines pay well to employees of restaurants, nightclubs, and hotels to supply information on celebrities in their establishment. While we cannot know which celebrity dates are real dates, we are even less certain about whether they involve sex. Many celebrities, when asked, will say they are just friends and questioning is rarely intrusive enough to ask specifically about a sexual relationship. A refreshing response by actress Sandra Bullock, when asked about a serious relationship with actor Hugh Grant, was "nothing has been penetrated anywhere."

The Setting

Whether you can maximize your celebrity status is often contingent on the venue in which you work. Film and television stars are theoretically most disadvantaged because they are employed in venues not accessible to the public. Movie stars in particular shoot their films in remote locations, sometimes in Canada and Australia, for up to a year. The only time the public can locate them is at movie premieres, award shows, and occasional charity functions. Of course, they may not be interested in ordinary members of the public anyway. A movie set, generally closed to the public, can contain more than a hundred people working on the picture. Big-budget films may employ hundreds of people as extras. Married stars may be away for months while their wives remain at home. There is lots of downtime on movie sets while stars sit in a private trailer waiting to be called. Anyone reading the gossip columns knows the stories of stars having a romance (i.e., sex) on the set of every film they make. One explanation for the actresses constantly exchanging sexual partners on each movie set is it lends a greater "authenticity" to their love scenes.

Another reason is that actresses may lead the occupational groups in nonconformity. They are more likely than other Americans to smoke cigarettes, engage in substance abuse, get divorced, and hold politically liberal views. The same is true of actors. Another factor is they tend to be physically attractive people and that adds to the sexual allure. Nowadays, being successful and making money for the studio conglomerates is all that matters. Any number of female stars have bore children out of wedlock. Their public is rather tolerant of most behavior although arrogance is frowned upon. Because they are financially independent, women in Hollywood have long violated the norms that average women live by. That is part of their appeal to their fans: they do not have to live by the same rules as everyone else.

Television stars live in a slightly different world. The broadcast networks, where the money and fame is the greatest, are a much more conservative medium. Since their shows are sponsored by large corporations that can be easily pressured by large interest groups, the image of their television stars can be a factor in their success. Movie stars can be involved in all kinds of scandals and continue to command top dollar. Just an intemperate remark about people of color, women, gays can lead to a celebrity's suspension—even

termination from a TV show. However, television stars are not as closely followed and the public may not care about moral indiscretions—just members
of the religious right and moral crusaders. TV stars may also earn a sizeable
portion of their income from doing commercials and a clean image does not
hurt.

The stars of television shows tend to shoot their shows in the same location for about eight to nine months. If they work on a scripted show, they
may work as many as twelve hours a day, six days a week. It is not an ideal
environment to find an abundant supply of sexual partners. On situation
comedies, you are often working with the same people each week and an office romance can be risky. You do not have the same large number of people
that are employed in theatrical films. The people in television, particularly
the women, are generally more conservative. One reason they work in television is because of the steady income despite being less challenging than
theatrical films and live plays. While having no empirical data, we suspect
that the television people are more likely to be married and hold politically
conservative views. Other than being on a wildly successful TV show, the
lead actors are typically not as known to the public as are movie stars, nor as
revered. That may lead the stars of television to seek out sexual partners in
more conventional outlets such as private parties, bars, and clubs.

Stars in the musical field represent the prototype of the sex-seeking person of fame. First, more than the other entertainers they are perceived as sexual symbols. They are mouthing lyrics about love, sex, passion accompanied
by sounds that stir the savage beast. One of the biggest obstacles to Black
male crossover success in music is the record company needed to market a
sexual symbol, not just the music alone. Since a large number of record buyers were Euro-American females, that was not socially acceptable. It may be
only a coincidence that, until recently, some of the biggest Black male
singing stars were rumored to be gay or were blind. Based on attendance at
their live shows, the majority of their fans appeared to be Black for Black
male singers. Euro-Americans often purchased the records but did not go to
the live concerts.

Anyway, it is for the male singers that the term "groupie" was invented.
Women would linger backstage after performances, and wait to get autographs or to take photos with their favorite singers. The groupies hoped to be
invited to the parties in hotel rooms and aspired to have sex with the man of
their dreams. It is no accident that the most sexually active entertainers were
the male singers such as Elvis Presley, Mick Jagger, and Jimi Hendrix. They
could be more easily found than the other types. When not performing on
the road, they were at leisure and could be found in various venues. With the

exception of Elvis, they seem to mingle more with the public. Also, women would follow them from city to city, after engaging in sexual relations with different members of the tour. It is their sexual shenanigans that are responsible for the term, "sex, drugs, and rock and roll."

Black male singers were just as sexually active—only not as much written about as their Euro-American counterpart. B. B. King, the King of the Blues, admits to eight children born to different women. Little Richard wrote about his wild bisexual affairs on the road. Chuck Berry was jailed for transporting an underage woman across state lines. Sam Cook was killed by a motel owner during a night of cavorting with a prostitute at her hotel. We have already mentioned the sexual adventures of Black female singers. While there have been no recent sex scandals concerning them, it is worth noting that they and their Euro-American counterparts are using their sexuality more than ever, from the scanty clothing to the lyrics in their songs. One singer, Toni Braxton, was proclaiming her total abstinence from sex while wearing barely enough clothes to prevent her arrest for indecent exposure.

Most of the bigger names among Black female singers have reputations for being sexually active—although nowhere near the extent of their male counterparts. There does not seem to be the female equivalent of a groupie, mostly because men can rarely penetrate a female singer's phalanx of protectors. Female singers do have the advantage of being totally surrounded by men, including members of their orchestra, roadies, agents, and managers. Very few women serve in those roles although a few singers have female relatives handling them. As true of the men, female singers can be more easily located than other entertainers can. A number of them have married men outside the music business. We cannot forget the most sexual of them all—Tina Turner. It has been noted that her autobiographical film *What's Love Got to Do with It* portrayed her as an innocent young girl when she met a Svengali like Ike Turner. In reality, she had a young child born out of wedlock when she met him. Ike has also alleged some wild sexual episodes with other men after they met.

After the singers, athletes are best known for their sexual exploits. As true of the entertainers, a whole section of the daily newspaper is devoted to their activities. Those activities increasingly cover off-the-field acts. In many cities, the most famous local resident is a good performing athlete. Many cities have four major sports, baseball, football, basketball, and hockey. When those teams participate in their championship playoffs, they are often covered on the front page. There are cities where young college athletes are the focus of much attention. All local television stations have sports coverage and there are numerous sports cable networks and weekly magazines. Sports stars can transfer their fame to other areas, such as movies, when they become very admired for their sports feats. There are distinctions between athletes and those in the entertainment field. Almost all of the stars are men, most are young, and the careers are much shorter. Moreover, their fame, while real, can be regional rather than national. And, their sexual exploits are not routinely a part of sports coverage. Only when their sexual activities become part of some court action or criminal prosecution do we learn of it.

As already explained, athletes are the most accessible of our rich and famous. Although far from rich, the college athlete can be nationally famous and the most accessible of them all. They have to live on campus and attend classes with other students. None of the barriers erected by other celebrities are available to them, if for no other reason than they have very low incomes. On a certain level, athletes can be a greater part of American lives than other celebrities, who are seen as larger than life. We can see them often, up close, and regard them as the most talented in the world of the famous. Certainly, they are richer than the average American. The average professional athlete earns more than two million dollars a year in baseball and three million in basketball. The top stars, most of them Black, will earn as much as twenty million a year in salary. Athletes in individual sports, such as Mike Tyson and Tiger Woods, may earn as much as eighty million a year. In some cases, they earn more from product endorsements than their on-field efforts. We might also mention that there are considerable more Blacks earning high incomes from sports than the three branches of entertainment combined. And their salaries are highly publicized.

Starting with the very young college athlete, the sportsman has easier access to women than other men do. Some regions of the country are sports crazy and athletes are treated like gods. In some areas, it begins in high school and continues through college. The most attractive girls on campus seek them out, flirt with them, and have sex with them. In the case of the star athlete on campus, her motivation might be to snare him early and cash in on the big bucks he will earn later. It also elevates her status on campus to be the college quarterback's girlfriend. This is one reason that professional athletes have attractive wives although they married at early ages. In baseball, men become stars at a late age and are typically married by that time. Of course, marriage does not need to prevent a man from taking advantage of a sexual opportunity. Again, Wilt Chamberlain reveals in his autobiography, "of all those players (in his fourteen years in the NBA) there was only one—Paul Arizin—who really seemed content with his marriage and didn't use our road trips to find new ways of cheating on his wife all the time."[2]

In the same book, Chamberlain claims that sports jocks, like rock singers, have their groupies, girls who hang around all the time, hoping the star will speak to them, sign autographs, and have sex with them. Chamberlain claims that he never liked the sports groupie types and, immediately upon noticing one heads in the opposite direction. One reason he avoids them, he writes, is that he would not take some other athlete's sexual hand-me-down.[3] This man created quite a stir in the sports world when he claimed to have engaged in sex with twenty thousand different women. Considering his age at the time, those who calculated that number figured he could only devote about four hours a day to activities other than sexual relations. While his number was obviously a huge exaggeration, it did illustrate the easy access athletes have to sexual partners.

Unfortunately, that easy access may have led to a sense of entitlement among some athletes. College athletes have been accused of a disproportionate number of rapes on university campuses and other highly publicized crimes have involved professional athletes such as Mike Tyson, Kobe Bryant, and O. J. Simpson. There are almost no female athletes to consider in terms of sexual scandals. Women's basketball does not have a large following in the United States and only professional tennis has any Black female stars. Not only have the Williams sisters not been involved in any sex scandals, there is no indication that either has ever been on a date or had any sexual contact. Both sisters are members of the Jehovah's Witness faith. Despite the appearance of being asexual, Serena Williams has been accused of flaunting her sexuality on the tennis court. Some onlookers commented that she was dressed like a whore.

The Perils of Being a Celebrity

Along with the advantages of celebrity status in securing numerous sexual partners, are the risks attached to the abundance of sexual access. While some of these risks are not unique to celebrities, they are played out on a much larger stage and can do emotional and financial damage to those involved. While these risks are generally attached to male celebrities, there is one risk both men and women share: the kiss and tell syndrome. In the normal course of events, a woman can be trusted to be very discrete about her sexual partners and only confide the news to her chosen friends. With the celebrity partner, she may broadcast the news from the highest hill. Not only will she tell everyone whom she encounters, her report may be paid for by magazines like *The National Enquirer* and *The Star*. It is lucrative, of course, depending on just how famous the star is. Despite the fact that Elvis Presley had bedded over a thousand women before reaching the age of twenty five, a couple of his sexual partners were able to get books published on their relationship with him. Many men, if not married or otherwise attached, do not care unless the woman claims he was sexually inadequate. Female celebrities, however, are bothered by men who kiss and tell. The tabloids may be more interested in a lesser female star because there will typically be fewer salacious stories about her. Even dating another celebrity may not deter the kiss and teller, as Britney Spears found out when Justin Timberlake revealed he had broken her hymen.

While lots of men impregnate women who later sue them for child support, celebrities are particularly vulnerable to the paternity suit. Whereas the celebrity may be looking at a one-night stand with the woman in question, she may be thinking of a unique economic opportunity. DNA tests are pretty conclusive in proving paternity nowadays and the celebrity may be obligated to pay hundreds of thousands of dollars for a night of pleasure. The amount he pays these days will not necessarily be based on the actual cost of supporting that child. Instead, judges are deciding the amount of child support based on the lifestyle of the celebrity. If his child would go to an exclusive private school, take dancing lessons, etc., the out-of-wedlock child may be entitled to the same.

Obviously, some women become accidentally impregnated with a celebrity's child and needs financial help in raising that child. One can still raise the question of why she engaged in sexual relations without adequate contraception—or did not require him to use a condom. If she is a woman of average means, becoming pregnant with a celebrity's child means the child has a better pedigree and she may not have to work another day in her life. Despite the foolproof tests, some women file false paternity claims against celebrities. She may have engaged in sex with the celebrity and another man during the same menstrual cycle. Not knowing which one is the father, she uses the same formula as others when selecting which person or institution to sue—choose the one with the deepest pockets. However, there are also cases of women who lodge paternity suits that never had sex with the celebrity. Such women are numerous enough that the National Basketball Association maintains a list of such women in every NBA city. In a few cases, the celebrities have filed counter suits against women who file false paternity suits.

In cases of an accidental pregnancy with a woman that a celebrity had a substantial relationship with, he often agrees to provide financial support for the child and proudly recognize it as his own. Indeed, it appears as if every NBA player has children by a woman to whom he is not married, enough that is has become a standing joke among sports announcers. We have no idea of how many women impregnated by celebrities have an abortion. Given the financial costs, it illustrates how much men dislike using condoms when they would rather pay the thousands of dollars to support a child than experience reduced sexual pleasure. Of course, it is possible that some women tell them that they are using some form of contraception. The late Elvis Presley had such a fear of paternity suits, having settled a few, that he practiced coitus interruptus (no ejaculation) with a regular girlfriend.

One risk that is pretty unique to the rich and famous is extortion. Generally, this happens to men in stable marriages. Two of our most famous celebrities, Bill Cosby and Michael Jordan, were the victims of extortion attempts. In the case of Cosby, it was a woman who claimed to be his daughter deriving from an adulterous relationship more than twenty years earlier. Rather than pay, he reported her extortion attempt to the police. By doing so, his sexual relationship with the mother was exposed. Still, by not giving into her extortion methods, he spared himself future extortion requests from the same woman. Despite Cosby's plea for leniency, the extortionist and an accomplice were sentenced to several years in jail. Cosby expressed regret about the adultery, his wife forgave him, and his career does not appear to have noticeably suffered.

The stakes were higher in Michael Jordan's case when a paramour claimed that he promised to pay her five million dollars. When he refused, she sued him and exposed their adulterous affair. Since she had nothing in writing showing a promise of five million dollars, she won nothing. The exposure did damage his marriage and there was a brief separation.[4] He continues to endorse products and any decline in endorsement income may be attributed to the fact that he has now retired as an active player. Another famous basketball player, Dr. J. (Julius Erving) had a long ago extramarital affair revealed when the daughter born of the affair gained attention as a professional tennis player. He also was considered a class act in professional basketball and his marital infidelity came as a shock to many.

Finally, allegations of rape, sexual molestation, and child pornography may not be a risk for a celebrity as much as it is for the alleged victims. We do not know if they were accused of these crimes because they were celebrities or that they engaged in these sexual aggressions because they felt, as celebrities, they were above the law. We do know that all of the accused have denied any guilt and the one convicted continues to claim his innocence. It is also true that the alleged victims have received substantial financial remuneration for their alleged sexual exploitation. The only celebrity, of national stature, actually convicted of a sexual crime was Mike Tyson, former heavyweight champion, who was found guilty of raping a nineteen-year-old beauty contestant in Indianapolis, Indiana. Despite his high paid legal team, he had a questionable defense strategy, claiming that he had such a bad reputation for roughing up women that her willingness to go to his hotel room was a tacit consent to have sex. A racially mixed jury found him guilty and he served several years in a state prison. The alleged victim sued him in civil court and got an out-of-court settlement in excess of one million dollars.

There have been numerous high profile Black celebrities who have been given jail sentences. They include Richard Pryor, Chuck Berry, Vida Blue, Congressman Mel Reynolds, Hurricane Carter, Malcolm X, James Brown, and others. Most did not involve sex crimes and their offenses occurred before massive media coverage and televised trials. Wealthy and famous people have gone to jail in the past. Still, a lot more poor people who are innocent are sentenced to prison because they lack competent legal counsel. The few wealthy and famous Blacks who escape punishment for crimes they commit pale before the millions of Blacks who are victims of an unfair and racist justice system.

Other Considerations

We have already mentioned that the Black celebrity has access to a "better" class of sexual partner than the average American. Among those different from the garden variety of sex partners will be Euro-Americans. With their wealth and fame, they will be more attractive to average Euro-Americans than ordinary Black Americans. Thus, we can speculate that any Black celebrity who so desired has engaged in sexual relations with a person of European descent. In the cases of a few Black celebrity males, it appears that is the majority of their sexual partners. That would include men like O. J. Simpson, Tiger Woods, and Jimi Hendrix. We, of course, have no idea of the identity of their European descent sexual partners unless they too are celebrities and it appears in print.

The obvious place to start is with the Euro-Americans married to Black Americans. They include some of the biggest names in the entertainment world although some are no longer married to them. Among them are Clint Eastwood, Robert De Niro, Billy Bob Thornton (divorced), Roger Ebert, David Bowie, Vic Damone, Tom Clancy, and Boris Becker. Those who have dated Black women are Mick Jagger, Robert Loggia, Ted Danson, and Carl Bernstein. Those are fairly prominent European-descent men who have married or dated Black women. Apparently, Euro-American women face career death if they marry Black men. The list starts and ends with Tyne Daly, once the star of her own TV show and now in a supporting role on another TV series. Now divorced from George Sanford Brown, she continues to "date" Black men based on the companions we see at award shows. Whereas an A-list actor like Robert De Niro has had two Black wives, no American-born woman of such stature has ever dared to marry a Black male. Two very marginal white actresses married Black superstars, Sammy Davis Junior and Sidney Poitier, and lost their movie careers immediately afterwards.

Two Black males stand out in terms of their interracial dating. Because of the time in which he crossed racial lines, Sammy Davis Junior took the greatest risks. We only know the names of his two most famous sex partners because he married one and the other liaison is well known in many circles. Mai Britt, the Swedish actress, had starring roles in a couple of movies before meeting and marrying Sammy. Being Swedish, she didn't share the racial consciousness and prejudice of most Euro-Americans. She faced career death due to her marriage and never starred in another movie. Kim Novak, a major star in the 1950s had the sense to carry on a clandestine affair with Sammy. The story is that her studio, Columbia Pictures, threatened to shoot him for good if he ever saw her again. That ended their sexual dalliance and he kept quiet about it until he wrote his second autobiography in the 1980s. Sammy was able to bed such prominent white actresses because he was the only Black allowed in an exclusive group called The Rat Pack, headed by Frank Sinatra and Dean Martin. That gave him a social connection to leading white actresses, a few who fell for his charms.[5]

Another Black male who dates the rich and famous is Lenny Kravitz. He is a biracial singer whose music has great appeal to Euro-Americans. In his dating style, he has demonstrated a tendency to cavort with high profile women, many of them foreigners. He had a "serious" relationship with Nicole Kidman until she discovered him cheating on her. Some of his other celebrity conquests include Gina Gershon, Natalie Imbruglia, and Kylie Minogue. While Nicole Kidman is a major star, many of the other women are better known in Europe and Australia except for Gina Gershon, a B-list actress. Nicole Kidman's publicist spent a lot of effort denying they had a relationship, although she at one time lived in his New York apartment, until her ex-husband Tom Cruise exposed her.

Euro-American celebrities probably learned from the case of Joyce De-Witt, a white female star of the TV series *Three's Company*. When word came out of her romantic involvement with a Black actor, she lost her product endorsements. When the TV show ended, her two co-stars went on to future fame and she fell off everyone's radar. Still, a few high profile Euro-American celebrities have been known to date Black men. Madonna has pushed the envelope more than any of them have, dating a number of Black males, including Dennis Rodman and even having a child out of wedlock by a rather olive-skinned Latino. Kim Basinger is rumored to have had an affair with Prince, the singer. Joan Collins, in one of her autobiographies, writes of an affair with the singer Harry Belafonte. The European actress, Nastassja Kinski, had a child by the composer Quincy Jones. After her career was pretty much over, Doris Day had an affair with Maury Wills, the baseball player, as he claims in his autobiography. Other Euro-American celebrities have been seen with Black dates, such as Anna Kournikova, but that does not necessarily translate into a sexual involvement.

While we have focused on sports and entertainment stars, political and civil rights leaders have had great fame and visibility in the public eye. One of the most famous men in American history is Martin Luther King. After his death, FBI tapes revealed a series of liaisons with women other than his wife. When the idea of a national holiday, named after him was being debated, political conservatives opposed the idea because he was not "morally fit" for a holiday due to his marital infidelities. In the more current scene, the Reverend Jessie Jackson was found to not only have impregnated a woman associate but to have placed her on the payroll of a civil rights organization without being seen to have done any work for them.

The litany of sexual misconduct by America's rich and famous could continue ad infinitum. What it illustrates, particularly for men, is what the ordinary person would do if presented with the same opportunities and prospects. There is no reason to think celebrities are different from ordinary Americans except in the ability to actualize their sexual desires. Even women might be more sexually liberal if they had the financial independence and sexual choices of female celebrities. Perhaps one exception to this assessment is the tendency of celebrities to experiment with unusual sexual acts because the abundance of sexual opportunities has deprived them of any sexual challenges. We need not envy their inability to sustain long-term relationships because they do not sexually need them. They may never rest easy because of the lingering fear that they are not loved for who they are as much as what they are—rich and famous.

Notes

1. Wilt Chamberlain and David Shaw, *Wilt: An Autobiography*. New York: MacMillan, 1973, p. 256.

2. *Ibid.* p. 264.

3. Luaine Lee, "Celebrities Are a Bit Wary of the Dating Game." *Dallas Morning News*, October 14, 1997, p. 8-C.

4. "Jordan Scores Victory in Court: Lawsuit against Star Thrown out." *Jet Magazine*, June 30, 2003, pp. 48–49.

5. Wil Haygood, *In Black and White: The Life of Sammy Davis Jr.* New York: Alfred A. Knopf, 2003.

CHAPTER NINE

∼

Prostitutes, Pimps, and Pornography

Prostitution arose in Western society because of our hypocritical attitude toward sexual behavior. Theoretically, we had a single code of sexual conduct that sexual relations were to take place only between a man and a woman married to each other. In reality, men were permitted sexual activity with women other than their wives. Since the male's violation of the sex code could not take place without a female partner, prostitutes traditionally provided them with their illicit sexual pleasures. For performing this service, women usually receive money or its equivalent. In turn, they were denied community respect and made themselves ineligible for a "respectful" marriage.

Because these disadvantages attend the role of prostitute, most women reject the job. Women who become prostitutes have usually done so because of their impoverished circumstances or because they were forced to do so. Black women who became prostitutes originally did so for the latter reason. As slaves, they had to submit to their masters and received no compensation. However, some white slave masters saw the opportunity for commercial profit in peddling the bodies of their female slaves. As a result, there was in the South a considerable traffic in Black women for prostitution. Particularly desirable was the mulatto woman, herself a result of earlier miscegenation between a white man and a Black woman.[1]

After emancipation, the flagrant sexual abuse of Black women by white men decreased. However, the amount of organized prostitution among Black women increased because it was the only means that some Black women had

157

of supporting their families. And, these Black women met a need of white men. As one writer asserted:

> For the young white man, Negro or mulatto girls existed to initiate him into sexual experience. Later he might set up one such girl as a concubine and produce a family. Or he might continue to indulge himself throughout life whenever opportunity presented itself. The point to bear in mind is that despite legislation, official sexual propriety, and Christianity itself, the Southern white had embarked upon the systematic prostitution of Negro women.[2]

Although many factors compelled Black women to become prostitutes, the most important one was the need for money. As an economically deprived group, they were subject to enticement into sexual relations with white men of considerable means. While they may have disliked the idea of intercourse with them, their family could not be supported with high moral values. Some domestic servants, for instance, supplemented their low incomes by having intercourse with the man of the house.

But other variables enter into the Black woman's decision to become a prostitute, assuming that she does decide and is not forced into the role. Included in her reasons may be a desire to get back at white women. A woman with this motive revealed, "Well, these white women may high hat us, but we sleep with their men just the same. We may have to cook for them, but we get back at them in this way." If their vengeance is not directed toward white women, it may be aimed at what they consider pulling the white man down. Sex relations it is said, strips the male of any claim to immortality.[3]

It is also quite possible, that some Black women enjoyed their sexual liaisons with white men. With the cultural restrictions on their sexual behavior very weak, Black women may have received transitory gratification from their sexual relations with white men. Unlike white women in the South, for whom chastity was a cultural imperative, Black females could yield to their sexual impulses more freely. Prostitution, although socially degrading, may have given some Black women sexual pleasure as well as money.

Whatever advantage the Black prostitute may have gained is cancelled out by the loss of social esteem. Women who play-for-pay are looked down on everywhere. Although she often performed a service for chaste white women by allowing white men to release their prenuptial sexual urges upon her, opprobrium she receives. Universally despised, she makes herself ineligible for marriage by her sale of passion. A tragic example of her plight is recorded thus:

A Black told me of a childhood sweetheart whom he had once wanted to marry. He left town for a time and when he returned met this girl again. She had become a prostitute. He asked her if she had known what was in his mind when they were boy and girl together, and told her he thought then that she would make a good wife for some man someday. The girl regretted that she had gone too far now ever to be able to marry, and said it was the fault of her God-mother who turned her over to men before she was grown up.[4]

But, as Frazier noted, the human relations between the Black and the white race tended to dissolve the formal and legal principles upon which segregation was based. Sexual relations broke down caste barriers and paved the way for a relationship based on individual merit and not racial membership. Sexual attraction produced at times genuine affection and the protracted relationship created between the white male and Black mistress an enduring sentiment. The intimacies of sexual relations and the birth of children symbolized the ultimate triumph of the deepest feeling of human solidarity.[5]

In most cases, the women had no real choice in the formation of these unions. Thus, the real losers in this situation were the women of the South—Black and white alike—who were the unwilling victims of a Southern value system that demeaned their humanity and subjected them to exploitation by white men.

The Prostitute Moves North

Most authorities agreed that around the turn of the twentieth century most prostitutes in the South were Black, while the prostitutes of the North were white. As one writer states, "In the North, prostitutes were a social and professional group, while in the South they were a racial group." In other words, even lower-class white women of the South were allowed to retain their virginity until marriage whereas even some middle-class Black women were sacrificed to the white man's lust.

Along with the general immigration of Blacks from the South to the urban areas of the North went large numbers of Black prostitutes. This is reflected in the statistics of arrests for prostitution by racial ancestry. In 1914, Black women constituted 16 percent of the total number appearing in the morals court in Chicago. In 1929, Black women totaled 70 percent of the women arraigned before the moral court. Viewing these figures, one writer concluded that "if the percentage of colored women in the total load of the morals court continues to increase, the court will in a few years become practically an agency dealing with Negro female sex delinquents."[6] Although we do not know the exact figures, one could speculate that some years later this is precisely what has happened.

The increased number of Black women involved in prostitution is reflected in a number of studies. One survey found that 54 percent of the arrests of all women for prostitution in New York City were of Black women, and that the rate for Black women was ten times that for white women.[7] When the Kinsey group interviewed 390 Black female prisoners, they discovered that 56 percent of these women admitted to or had been convicted for prostitution prior to their confinement.[8]

Racial discrimination and problems of poverty have made prostitution more common among Black women than among white women. But differences in the degree of prostitution among Black and white women tend to be hidden by their different sphere of activity. With sufficient accuracy, we can designate the typical Black prostitute as a streetwalker and the white prostitute as a call girl.

Call girls are regarded as the "aristocrats of prostitution." They live in the most expensive residential section of our large cities; they dress in rich, good taste and charge a minimum of five hundred dollars per sexual contact. Unlike the streetwalkers, they are selective about customers, entertain clients in their homes or apartments, and assiduously avoid bars and restaurants patronized by other prostitutes.

Black prostitutes are much more subject to arrest than the white call girls are. As one-observer comments:

> Since it is easier to observe immoral conditions among poor and unprotected people, Black prostitutes are much more liable for arrest than white prostitutes. White women may use the big hotels or private apartments for their illicit trade, but the Black women are more commonly forced to walk the streets.[9]

The low status of Black women generally prevents them from becoming call girls. The clients of call girls are usually white men who want the call girl to be a part of their social life. Often these clients require an entire night of a girl's time, maybe taking her out to a nightclub as part of the arrangement. Most call girls are found in the better cocktail lounges and restaurants where the presence of a Black woman would be suspect. Police officers have been known to arrest Black females solely because they find them in the company of white men. Ordinarily a white woman can approach white men without having her motives questioned.

Sometimes, there is a thin line between a prostitute and a good-time girl. The Black community does make distinctions between a hard-core professional prostitute and casual pickups available for a good time. Often the dividing line is based on the customer. One who caters to white men and middle-class Blacks would be considered a professional. Those who deal only with lower-class Blacks are held to be nonprofessional. The exchange of money for sexual services is seen not so much as a commercial transaction but as a token of appreciation for a good time.

In Soulside, for example, there are bars where more than drinking takes place. One important reason for frequenting these bars is to meet members of the opposite sex. In essence, these bars are pickup places where any woman may be approached for sexual relations. Most of the women in these places are prostitutes or semi-prostitutes. But they are not strictly out for money. One of them, named Ruby, occasionally lives with one man or another for a time. Men also use her apartment as a lounge, particularly during the winter when it is too cold to be outside much.[10]

Men with perverted sexual tastes often seek out prostitutes to satisfy their tastes. Sadists and masochists form a part of the prostitute's clientele and their peculiar needs must be catered to. Beatings administered by the sadist are common for the prostitute, though sometimes the beating is purely symbolic and not carried to the extent of causing pain. A Black prostitute remarked that men only tried to hurt her once in a while and usually it was the white men who did it.[11]

Beatings bring a higher price, and some impoverished Black women are forced to undergo such treatment for their bread and butter. One Black hustler explained that white tricks pay a hundred dollars to beat a prostitute. Sometimes, she says, they hit you so hard you land in the hospital. Other men who attain sexual gratification in bizarre ways that defy description usually have a need to degrade the woman before they can enjoy her. And it is probably easier for them to vent their pernicious sexual urges upon Black women because they consider these women to be less than human. As one white man told a Black prostitute, "Gal, there's two places where niggers is as good as white folks—the bedroom and the graveyard."[12] One sociologist has even declared that prostitutes receive money not only for their sexual services but also for their loss of status in the community.[13] They fail to consider that prostitution is a crime punishable by imprisonment in this country and that in most cases only the woman is arrested.

The only open prostitution left in the United States is frequently found in the Black ghetto. Many hotels and brothels exist there and it is a usual sight to see a dozen streetwalkers on every corner. One reason for this situation is the dual standard of law enforcement in this country. The police maintain a much less rigorous standard of law enforcement in the Black community, tolerating their illegal activities such as drug sales, prostitution, and street violence that they would not tolerate elsewhere. Moreover, investigations of the police force in certain large cities have revealed a close collaboration between the men in blue and the peddlers of vice in ghetto communities.[14]

The recent increase in crime in the streets has made prostitution an unsafe trade. One woman who dropped out of the profession said that it had become a holy hell. Many women have been mugged or killed by criminals who roam the streets at night. With the recent reluctance of ordinary citizens to venture into the inner cities at night, prostitutes have become the victims of muggings and killings. Sometimes the trick takes her money after the act of coitus, adding insult to injury.

Women who become prostitutes face a multitude of problems. Men have been known to say that females never face starvation because they can always sell sex if they cannot do anything else. Such statements ignore the realities of the prostitute's life. Not infrequently, it is the male pimp who gets the greatest monetary gain from the sale of the prostitute's body. And even though prostitution may be lucrative for a while, the passage of time takes its toll on the pulchritude of most prostitutes, as it does on that of all women. When she reaches a certain age, the prostitute becomes less desirable as a sex object to most men. If she stays in the hustler's underworld, she then resorts to performing degrading services for emotionally disturbed men that all other women refuse to perform.

What happens to the prostitute in her declining years? According to Iceberg Slim, many of them become lesbians, and some become the pimps of lesbians. In some cases, they become the operators of bordellos. But in too many cases, prostitutes have become hooked on narcotics. Many of them wind up in mental institutions. Prostitutes have a very high suicide rate, and, in general, do not earn very much.[15]

A woman who shares her body with all types of men inevitably encounters the occupational hazards of promiscuity, venereal disease, and AIDS. Some 30 percent of the Black prison women in the Atlanta sample, most of whom were former prostitutes, had sexually transmitted infections.[16] The more recent increase in venereal disease can hardly be attributed to prostitution. Indeed, most public health authorities agree that prostitutes are usually conscientious about avoiding venereal disease and seeking treatment if they do contract it. Prostitutes, also, are rarely the transmitter of AIDS to their male clients.

Changes in the World's Oldest Profession

The turn of the twenty-first century had witnessed thirty years of significant change in the sex for pay trade. After 1970, a liberalization of sexual values and practices meant that many American males—Black and white—did not have their first sexual experience with a lady of the night. Suddenly the prostitute was in competition with the girl next door, who was providing the same service for free. Even some Black males, especially in the middle class, no longer had to pay to play. The civil rights movement created new and better job opportunities for younger Black women, removing millions of them as the source of sexual providers for Southern white males. With younger women free to sexually experiment before marriage, it appeared that prostitution as a trade would die out for a lack of customers. Yet, it survived and may have even flourished in one of the most permissive eras of the European occupation of North America.

For a number of reasons, too complex to explain here, men still had need of the services of sex industry workers. These men were sometimes testosterone ridden young males, who now had access to their female counterparts. Not every young female was eager to have sex and not every male knew how to negotiate for it. Prostitution had the advantage of easy visibility and availability. It was a simple transaction of paying money of a requested amount and engaging in sexual intercourse until you received physical relief. That made it appealing to married men, who lacked access to a paramour or did not want the possible complications of an extramarital affair. Some married males wanted sexual practices their wives refused to do— or who even refuse all sexual activity. Along with the socially inept, elderly, physically unattractive males were members of the military who did not have a girl in every port. Moreover, the fact that many of the men not in that category seemed to be enjoying an abundance of sexual opportunities stimulated the desire of onlookers to pay for what other men were receiving "for free."

While Black prostitutes had a number of white males from the suburbs as customers, they faced an array of competitors other than the predominantly white call girls. Prostitution could be found in a number of different forms that provided a security not found among the dusky streetwalkers. Massage parlors and escort services became very popular. Not all of them contained prostitutes; enough did to satisfy a growing male clientele. Bordellos or houses with sex providers also existed, with very upscale madams such as Heidi Fleiss, the Hollywood madam, and the Mayflower madam and her Park Avenue stable of very cultured girls. Many of the women working in these placcs were very mainstream, college students trying to pay tuition and suburban housewives looking to pay for a family vacation. In recent years, women from Asia, Latin America, and Eastern Europe have joined their ranks, some of them forced to do so.

Some of the new migrants satisfy the desire of Anglo males for an exotic sexual partner. Black prostitutes continue to walk the streets hoping to attract men willing to venture into the most dangerous sections of America's largest cities. Occasionally they may even have the opportunity to service a celebrity. Such was the fate of Divine Brown, who was approached by one of the movie industry's most handsome stars, Hugh Grant, on the streets of Hollywood. Being British, he was very polite and complimentary, saying he had heard a lot of "nice" things about Black women. Unfortunately, his jovial manners did nothing to persuade Divine to lower her price to sixty-five dollars for full intercourse, which is all the money poor Hugh had in his possession. She did agree to perform oral sex on him, which, unfortunately, was witnessed by a member of the Los Angeles Police Department. After being arrested, paying a fine, he profusely apologized on the Jay Leno Show, and resumed his fine acting career with no known repercussions other than the end of his eight-year relationship with Elizabeth Hurley, one of the world's most beautiful women. Divine Brown became a minor celebrity in her own right, gave interviews to the media, and posed nude for a national magazine.

We should not look for a film based on Divine Brown's life anytime soon. Although the majority of women arrested for prostitution in the United States, for the last twenty-five years, have been Black and Hollywood loves hookers on the screen, having awarded ten Oscars to women playing them— all were Euro-American. The public adores women playing prostitutes on the big screen and actresses compete to play those roles. None of them played a common streetwalker and, with few exceptions, had some sort of relationship with their clients. In films, these women are portrayed as exciting and dangerous, their male clients as handsome and wealthy. Although Black women are not given awards, they certainly are seen as prostitutes on TV and in films quite often. Many Black and Latino actresses complain that the only roles offered to them are drug addicts and prostitutes.

The AIDS hysteria has been a mixed blessing for many Black prostitutes. They have lost customers due to their fear of contracting HIV from prostitutes. However, most sex-industry workers are very diligent in requiring male customers to use barrier methods during sexual activity. The same fear of AIDS has had a chilling effect on the willingness of mainstream women to engage in sexual activity, thus reducing the sexual opportunity for many men, forcing them to pay for a woman's sexual services. Women who are in the hooker role may be disproportionately infected with HIV because they are overrepresented among the nation's drug users. It is the drug consumption that has radically altered the rules of the prostitute's trade.

The use of illegal drugs has long existed in urban Black communities, a situation that was largely ignored by law enforcement since the users were largely members of the unemployed underclass. Only when the turf wars over the drug trade brought about an epidemic of gang wars and homicides have they taken serious action. The introduction of cheaper and more dangerous drugs increased the users and the risks. In the past, drug consumption was largely confined to males in the Black community. Circa 1980, women became drug users big time. The effect was seen in the number of Black mothers having their children removed from them by the courts and often placed with grandmothers and in foster homes due to the mother's neglect. This was unprecedented since Black mothers had given their lives to protect their children in the past. Their addiction to crack cocaine and heroin made them concerned only with their next fix. When they had no money to pay for the drugs, they offered their bodies in lieu of cash. In effect, they became prostitutes to support their drug habit. Because of their desperation to obtain drugs, they might agree to sex with high-risk men without protective measures.[17]

There is very little glamor in the Black prostitute's life. Prostitution is a miserable occupation that exposes the Black woman to every sordid side of the human personality and to all the social ills that exist in human society. Prostitutes are usually prey to the problems of drug addiction, alcoholism, mental illness, venereal disease, and AIDS. They are exploited sexually and economically, by the pimp, the customer, and the police. Their entire lives are not the carefree and happy ones depicted in the motion pictures and books. Instead, they live in a constant state of insecurity and most of them wind up penniless. They represent the epitome of womanhood abused to the level of a thing.

The Pimp as a Cultural Icon

The concept of a pimp has such currency nowadays, with constant references to "pimps and ho's," that many young people may think it refers to a woman's sexual partner. Certainly, it is a concept attached uniquely to a man of great sexual abilities in the Black community. The rapper, Snoop Doggy Dog, often has his pimp accompany him on stage to accept awards for his music. The pimp has been immortalized in songs like "Stagger Lee," the man who shot Billy over a game of dice. Rumor has it that the posse or entourage of celebrities contains a man who plays the role of a pimp, in this case one who procures women for the star and other members of the posse. These various meanings divert from the most literal definition of the term, which is a paid companion to whom the prostitute gives her earnings in return for certain services. Since this role exists in relation to an illegal activity, its performance depends on an oral agreement between the prostitute and her pimp.

Because the rappers popularizing the concept of a pimp grew up in lower-class sections of the inner city, he played a larger than life role in their lives. As the Black middle class abandoned poor ghettos for the fringes of cities and suburbs, the models of success left in those communities were often the drug dealer and pimp. They were the men with the flash cars, fine jewelry, and designer clothing. The pimp, however, did the drug dealer one better! He had a stable of women trailing alongside him. He combined the most desired values among young Black males: sex and money. No matter the reality, among a group of males with the public image of sexual masters, the pimp was king. Since he had control of women who engaged in sexual acts with dozens of men each week, it was assumed the pimp had the sexual techniques that pleased a lady of the night and kept her under his spell.[18]

Based on folklore and popular media, being a pimp is a Black man's job. Certainly, the white public believes the vaunted sexuality of Black males would translate into a job convincing women to sell sex for money. Considering that prostitution is defined as providing sexual services in exchange for money and takes a variety of forms, from a woman who "borrows" money from a lover she just met to the exotic dancer who may bed a customer who left a big tip, it is not clear that the majority of prostitutes in the United States are Black, only that most women arrested and jailed for that crime are. If a pimp is interpreted as the manager of the sexual services for sale, many whites are involved in the same process. Many prostitutes are independent entrepreneurs who manage their own affairs. Some of them are Euro-American women such as the Hollywood and Mayflower madams. For large scale enterprises connected to gambling, gentleman's clubs, escort services, massage parlors, Euro-American men are very much in control. One of the few legal places of prostitution allowed, two counties in Nevada, the famous Mustang Ranch, was owned by a Euro-American male.

What distinguishes the Black pimp is his visibility, nature of his role, and style. Black women are still seen as the nation's prostitutes because they are the streetwalkers visible to many who see them soliciting customers—or who are themselves solicited. The media, news, film, and television portray most prostitutes and their pimps as Black. Occasionally, there is the big arrest of a white female ring of hookers whose existence is so rare that the madams get their own TV movie and book deal. Mostly the authorities ignore large-scale white and Asian prostitution because it is not very public and can involve pillars of the community. Police offers may be bribed and often receive free sexual services.

The Black hooker is very public and so is her pimp, who may perform recruitment of customers and protection from them. His style is one of flamboyance and showmanship. Their clothing style was very much on display in the Blaxploitation movies of the 1970s, with the big hats, long coats, and pump shoes. Nowadays, their favorite arenas are the marquee boxing matches where they show up with flashy clothes, cars, and a stable of their women. Then there is the nature of the pimp's role, which can be ambiguous at best. Unlike the Euro-American managers and owners of sexual services, the pimp has some kind of emotional relationship with the prostitute. Sometimes he provides the only human relationship with continuity and meaning for her. Hookers, like all women, have their affectional needs and the pimp provides them with all that they get. In addition, her status within the in-group of prostitutes may depend on the way she keeps her pimp; whether he drives a Jaguar or a Ford is important to how he is perceived in the community.

However, it is the emotional content of their relationship that is important to her, not his vaunted sexual ability. Engaging in sexual activity with as many as twenty men a day leaves her with little desire for "free sexual activity."

It is the affectional attention provided by the pimp that is important. He may not have any different sexual techniques than her customers. What he does have is the time to be ardent and diligent in their sexual activity. Moreover, he can kiss her, something a paying customer is prohibited from doing. What the pimp does not do is remain monogamous. In most cases, she knows that she is part of a stable although made to feel the most important when they are alone together. This is a practical matter, for him to keep his lavish lifestyle he must maintain the role of pimp to more than one woman. Call girls may earn as much as five thousand dollars a night. Streetwalkers may earn less than two hundred and fifty dollars a night and less in the Northern cities during the winter season.

What services does the pimp provide for the money he receives? A major function is protection from rogue customers, who refuse to pay, rough her up, or threaten to call the police. The United States has experienced more than one case of serial murders of prostitutes in its large cities. When arrested, which can be often, the pimp has to provide bail money to get her out of jail. When the police become vigilant, the pimp may try to recruit customers in a more subtle manner. Sometimes the pimp will be her drug dealer, if for no reason than to prevent clients from enticing her to engage in unprotected sex in exchange for drugs. The pimp himself may have a philosophy of being drug free in order to maintain control over his stable, many of whom have drug addictions. In past years, the pimp found abortions for a pregnant member of his stable when abortions were illegal.[19]

There is a downside to the pimping profession. Some remain in business through verbal intimidation and violence, particularly with young women they have enticed into becoming prostitutes. A few of them have deliberately created junkies out of impressionable young women in order to keep them engaged in selling their bodies to support their drug habits. It might be noted that many of the streetwalkers in American cities are Euro-Americans. They, too, have Black pimps and almost all of them have drug addictions. Many of them enter the profession to support a preexisting drug habit. They have Black pimps because they are the men who control the sex trade on the streets, are able to physically defeat any Euro-American interlopers, and protect them from unruly clients.

Probably, a large majority of pimps use kindness instead of force to maintain their stable of women. In large part, it is more effective that way since coerced women have the option of escaping to another city. Still, many pimps have a Svengali effect on many ladies of the night. It appears that the pimp receives the lion's share of her earnings. Perhaps the services he provides may be regarded as worth it. Moreover, he applies pressure on her to stick to his rules. Try to rush the "Johns" to completion as soon as possible, meet a quota of a certain number of clients a day and offer certain services, e.g., anal sex, for an extra payment. Still, prostitution is a young woman's trade as many women tire of the problems faced by streetwalkers in twenty-first-century America. They have formed associations such as COYOTE (Call Off Your Old Tired Ethics) to bring about a reform of America's laws regarding prostitution.

The pimp exists because prostitution is an outlaw activity. Calls have been made for the decriminalization of prostitution without much success. In much of the developed world, prostitution has been legalized and controlled. There, women do not need to depend on the protection of a pimp for their survival. Prostitution will continue to be with us as long as there are differential sexual opportunities for men and women. Saying it exploits women ignores the reality of human society. Perhaps the best we can hope for is that women do not need the pimp as a buffer between them and their clients.

Blacks and Pornography

In the national debate over pornography, Blacks are largely irrelevant. Despite their largely sexual image, they are generally excluded from the content of hard-core and soft-core pornography in American society. As a rogue art form, pornography contains a racist content when Blacks are represented. Attitudes toward pornography, defined as displaying graphic forms of sexual intercourse, have varied over the last forty-five years when it was declared legal by the United States Supreme Court. During the heyday of the sexual revolution in the 1970s, pornography almost became mainstream. Society matrons in New York, Los Angeles, and San Francisco attended showings of films such as *Deep Throat*, *Behind the Green Door*, etc. Linda Lovelace and Marilyn Chambers became household names. Over the years, the venues for viewing porno have shifted to private homes with videocassette tapes and the Internet. The so-called soft porn mediums such as *Playboy*, *Penthouse*, and *Hustler* attracted millions of readers, featured articles by best selling writers, and interviews with the most famous from all walks of life. Even cable TV has increased its share of TV viewership because it is unregulated and can show sexually explicit programs.

As for Black attitudes toward porno, it is considerably more liberal than among Euro-Americans. In one survey, Blacks had a more lenient and positive attitude toward erotic material than Euro-Americans. They displayed less concern about the erotic content of novels, TV programs, ads, and movies than comparable Euro-Americans did. And they were less inclined to prohibit erotic magazines and sexually explicit movies.[20] It may be one reason that no Blacks were included on the Meese Pornography Commission established to investigate the effects of pornography.

Most Blacks would agree with Dr. Morris Lipton, one of the experts on the 1970 Presidential Report on Pornography, that "given the major issues of the day, pornography is a trivial issue."[21] And, Blacks would add to that analysis the caveat that pornography is a white man's problem, a particular kind of white man's problem. The Presidential Commission that Dr. Lipton served on found that the typical consumer of pornography was a white male, and that Blacks were underrepresented in the consumption of pornography but they did not harbor particular antipathy toward it.[22] Indeed, many did buy the sex video cassettes, purchase *Playboy* and *Penthouse*, and enjoy risqué jokes, cartoons, etc. As a group that earns only 56 percent of the income of whites, they often do not have the discretionary income with which to purchase erotic publications, films, and artifacts.

As for the Black position on pornography, it certainly differed from the Meese Commission on Pornography. Meese and his minions reflected a particular white worldview that there is something inherently damaging and sinful about sexual activity outside of the marital bedroom, and that any participation in other kinds of sexual behavior should produce enormous amounts of guilt in the errant individual. Blacks have traditionally held a more naturalistic attitude toward their sexuality and saw it as the normal expression of sexual attraction between men and women.[23] Even in African societies, sexual conduct was not the result of some divine guidance by God or other deities. It was secularly regulated and encompassed the tolerance of a wide range of sexual behaviors. Sexual deviance, where so defined, was not an act against God's will but a violation of community norms.[24]

Rather than seeing the depiction of heterosexual intercourse and nudity as an inherent debasement of women, as a fringe group of feminists claim, the Black community would see women as having equal rights to the enjoyment of sexual stimuli. It is nothing more than the continuation of the white male's double standard and paternalism that sees erotica as existing only for male pleasure while women are only the sexual objects that they mentally devour. Since that double standard has never been as strong among American Blacks, the claim that women are exploited by exhibiting their nude bodies or engaging in heterosexual intercourse lacks meaning or credibility. After all, it was the white missionaries in Africa that forced African women to regard their quasi-nude bodies as sinful and placed them in clothes. This probably accounts for the rather conspicuous absence of Black women in the feminist fight against pornography. Certainly, Black men were unlikely to join with the likes of the militant feminists such as Catharine MacKinnon and Andrea Dworkin who treat pornography as discrimination against women.

The Black community represented organic evidence against some of the assumptions of the Meese Commission on Pornography. If pornography is alleged to lead to male sexual aggression (i.e., rape), why are the lowest consumers of pornography so over represented among those arrested and convicted of rape. A pornography commission without a political axe to grind might have concluded that when other expressions of manhood, such as gainful employment and economic success, are lacking, those men will express their frustration and masculinity through sexual aggression against women. This would not go down well with conservative political administrations, whose policies have led to the burgeoning numbers of unemployed Black males, and those who are economic failures.

As for the Meese Commission's view that pornography is related to sexual promiscuity, it is almost a laughable finding in the Black community. One man's sexual promiscuity is the Black population's perception of the definer's sexual hang-ups. In most cases, it refers to keeping women in their sexual strait jackets so that sexual pleasure remains a male's domain. The Black community has exhibited a lusty sexual appetite while obeying certain rules of common sense and propriety in its sexual conduct. The kinds of kinky sexual acts favored by a small minority of whites are almost unknown among the Black population. Group sex, sexual crimes (other than rape) were and are rare in this group.

The omission of Blacks from the Meese Commission on Pornography was all the more understandable given the Black image as a group lacking the more puritanical morals of Euro-Americans. Ranging from the thousands of lynchings of Black men for the dubious sin of lusting after white women, to the segregation of races in the South to prevent interracial sexual contact we have the more recent variant on the theme of Black immorality in the emphasis on teenage pregnancy. While there may be a cause for concern over the high rate of out-of-wedlock births to Black women in their teenage years, the Meese Pornography Commission refused to endorse the best weapon against teenage pregnancy—sex education. The same National Institutes of Health survey discovered that twice as many single Black women as white women are having sex through their 20s without contraceptives. Nationally, many out-of-wedlock births are to Black women.[25] Ultimately, Blacks suffer more and are the chief victims of white sexual guilt. They are denied sex education in the public schools because a white controlled bureaucracy either denies it to the school system or forces it to contain a largely moral content, with the theme that it's okay to say no to male requests for sexual relations. However, in those first public schools that decided to provide contraceptives to its students, only schools with a predominantly Black student body were chosen to do so. Using Black high school students as the first guinea pigs smacks of the same kind of white colonialism that tested birth control products on Puerto Rican women to see if they would be safe for white women.

Blacks in White Pornography

In the fringe hard-core porno films, replete with violence or child pornography, the few Blacks portrayed are as debased as the Euro-Americans in their content. In the porno films largely viewed by the audience for such fare, it is a mostly white world. Pornography addresses the relationship white men and women have with each other. When Blacks do appear, the emphasis is generally on their large penis. Men in these films are always in possession of larger genitalia than the average male regardless of race. Still these films draw an unusual amount of attention to the Black male body and large sexual organ. Students of this film genre note that the focus of the plot, when Black males are involved, is a lust for white women. Moreover, it is the Black male protagonist who shows the least humanity and is portrayed as lacking the ability to be intimate.[26]

The popular men's magazines, *Playboy* and *Penthouse*, refused to feature Black women in their pages. Although *Playboy* publisher, Hugh Hefner donated money to the Civil Rights Movement, advocated racial equality in his column, the *Playboy* centerfold remained lily white, despite the pressures he faced to racially diversify, until the 1970s. Of course, given the experience of Jayne Kennedy, Black women may have preferred to be excluded. Kennedy was a fairly high profile Black woman who was on the *Dean Martin Show* and the NFL pre-game show and who appeared nude in the pages of *Playboy* magazine with her husband at the time. The Black community raised a firestorm of criticism at her for being an embarrassment to Black womanhood and contributing to the stereotypes of Black females as immoral. While almost every major white female actress has displayed some nudity in films and magazines, Blacks felt that one nude Black woman shamed the entire race.

One magazine that regularly featured Blacks was the raunchiest of them all, *Hustler* magazine. It is published by Larry Flynt, who had a feature film made of his life and recently ran for governor of the State of California in a special recall election. Blacks are featured only in the cartoons with the emphasis on their huge penis and appetite for and abuse of Euro-American women. These women are depicted as being in a great deal of pain due to the enormous Black penis doing great damage to their genitalia. Black women, conversely, rarely appear in the pages of Hustler except as a prostitute with oversized lips that give the white client a particularly good act of fellatio.

Most hard-core pornography is produced by and for Euro-Americans. One of the few, perhaps only, Afro-American producer of such films was a man named Tom McKnight of San Francisco. Along with his two brothers, he also owned a grocery store, mortuary, and movie theatre where he exhibited his films. He produced reels, short fifteen-minute movies featuring all Black or interracial casts. His one big goal was to produce a fifty-minute film entitled *Foxfire*, which he finally completed in the 1970s. Despite his participation in what some regard as an unsavory business, Tom was happily married to a Swedish professor at the University of California for more than thirty years, raised two very middle-class sons and was a very kind man. Sadly, he died in 2002 at the age of fifty-eight.

Although published by Euro-Americans, the magazine *Players* was a Black version of *Playboy* with very superficial articles and generous doses of nudity in its pages. Based in Los Angeles, it survived for a number of years and was sold in stores in the Black community and adult bookstores. Even the Titan of Black publishing, Johnson Publishing Company, the publishers of *Ebony* and *Jet Magazine*, has dabbled in the skin trade. For years, *Jet* had the milder version of the *Playboy* centerfold with its Beauty of the Week.

The pictures have revealed a little more skin over the years, with the women now wearing two-piece bikinis, many of them taken by Lamonte McLemore of the singing group, *The Fifth Dimension*. For years, *Jet* magazine published an annual calendar in the 1980s of nude Black women. The late publisher of *Jet* once told this author that it was very difficult finding women to pose nude for the calendar. It is possible that the Black women in porno films, *Players*, and the *Jet* calendar may have worked elsewhere in the sex industry.

Blacks in mainstream erotica have not fared any better than in other areas of American life. Yet they are largely absent from the movement to ban or severely restrict sexually explicit materials, which is populated largely by militant feminists and the religious right. Moreover, media erotica is little more than an extension of mass marketing and the beauty trade in advertising. It is part and parcel of the packaging of the female body to sell products, magazines, and movies. It is used because it works. Women will still be seen as objects of sexual desire because that stimulus is how the species is reproduced. Without erotica in the media, there are enough stimuli in the clothing worn by women to create sexual desire in the ever-sensitive male population. The only remaining question is how that sexual desire will be satisfied and by whom.

Notes

1. Arthur J. Calhoun, *A Social History of the American Family*, Vol. 2. New York: Barnes and Noble, 1960.

2. Fernando Henriques, *Prostitution in Europe and the Americas*. New York: Citadel Press, 1965, p. 254.

3. John Dollard, *Caste and Class in a Southern Town*. New York: Doubleday Anchor Books, 1954, p. 153.

4. *Ibid.* pp. 158–159.

5. E. Franklin Frazier, *The Negro Family in the United States*. Chicago: University of Chicago Press, 1939, pp. 50–69.

6. Walter Reckless, *Vice in Chicago*. Chicago: University of Chicago, 1933, pp. 26–28.

7. Gunnar Myrdal, *An American Dilemma*. New York: Harper and Brothers, 1944, p. 974.

8. Paul Gebhard, et al., *Pregnancy, Birth, and Abortion*. New York: Harper and Row, 1958, p. 187.

9. Harold Greenwald, *The Call Girl*. New York: Ballantine Books, 1958, pp. 15–27.

10. Ulf Hannerz, *Soulside*. New York: Columbia University Press, 1969, p. 55.

11. Judge John Murtagh and Sarah Harris, *Cast The First Stone*. New York: McGraw-Hill, 1957, p. 103.

12. *Ibid.* p. 104.

13. Kingsley Davis, "Sexual Behavior" in *Contemporary Social Problems*, ed. R. Merton and R. A. Nisbet. New York: Harcourt and Brace, 1971, p. 347.

14. John J. Potterat, et al., "Pathways to Prostitution: The Chronology of Sexual and Drug Abuse Milestones." *Journal of Sex Research*, November 1998, 35, pp. 333–340.

15. Iceberg Slim, Pimp, Los Angeles, Holloway 1967. Comments made on TV Show, "Black Journal," "The Black Pimp," January 29, 1972.

16. G. L. Conrad, "Sexually Transmitted Diseases among Prostitutes and other Sexual Offenders." *Sexually Transmitted Diseases*, 1981, 9, pp. 241–244.

17. Claire Sterk, Kirk W. Erickson, and Danielle German, "Crack Users and Their Sexual Relationships." *Journal of Sex Research*, November 2000, 37, pp. 354–360.

18. Richard and Christina Milner, *Black Players: The Secret World of Black Pimps*. Boston: Little, Brown, and Company, 1972.

19. David Kanouse, et al., "Drawing a Probability Sample of Female Street Prostitutes in Los Angeles." *Journal of Sex Research*, February 1999, 36, pp. 45–51.

20. "Gallup Poll on Pornography." *San Francisco Chronicle*, March 10, 1985, p. A-7.

21. Dr. Morris Lipton quoted in Philip Nobile and Eric Nadler, "Ed Meese Gives Bad Commission." *Penthouse*, July 1986, p. 119.

22. *Ibid.*

23. Robert Staples and L. B. Johnson, *Black Families at the Crossroads*. San Francisco: Jossey-Bass, 2004, chapter four.

24. Boris De Rachewiltz, *Black Eros: Sexual Customs of Africa from Prehistory to the Present Day*. New York: Lyle Stuart, 1964.

25. Mark Abrahamson, *Out-of-Wedlock Births: The United States in Comparative Perspective*. Westport, Connecticut: Praeger, 1998.

26. J. Jones, "The Construction of Black Sexuality: Towards Normalizing the Black Cinematic Experience" in *Black American Cinema*, ed. M. Diawara. New York: Routledge, 1993.

CHAPTER TEN

~

Black Sexuality in the Twenty-First Century

It is, at best, a risk to predict the outcome of Black sexuality in the ninety-four years left in the twenty-first century. Any number of unforeseen events could impact sexual patterns in very dramatic ways. Moreover, changes in sexual patterns have been cyclical, not lineal. Who, for instance, could have predicted the level of nonmarital sexual activity among females, the legalization and easy availability of sexually explicit materials, an increasing acceptance and tolerance of homosexuality, abortion, technological innovations that gave us the birth control and male impotence pill in the same century? Yet, we cannot, in good faith, predict a continuing increase in sexual permissiveness and sexual rights further into this century. Already, there are afoot movements and organizations prepared to throw back the clock to an era of sexual repression—at least for women.

Before addressing the specific changes in Black sexuality, we need to concern ourselves with general changes in human sexuality in the United States. No matter what demographic changes occur, it will be Euro-Americans who set the cultural tone and dominate the society as they have for the last five centuries. We expect Euro-American men to hold the reins of political and economic power as they have since this country's formation. Women will make gains as can be expected from their status as a numerical majority. However, their numbers will not be translated into real power as men, white men, monopolize about 85 percent of the political and economic resources. By the end of the twenty-first century, Euro-Americans will be a numerical minority as people of color, by virtue of immigration and higher fertility rates, become the statistical majority.

Accepting the previously mentioned assertions as a given, the basic socio-cultural force in impacting American sexuality will be economic. Although about 75 percent of all women are in the labor force and theoretically will be independent of male economic domination, female sexuality will continue to be a commodity—used by both men and women. We expect capitalism to last the rest of this century and sexuality to be harnessed to capitalist principles. That means sexuality will operate according to the rules of commerce—not morality. With its boom and bust cycles, women may never feel economically secure enough to eschew marriage for a lifetime. They may still desire marriage and to raise a family. While men may want the same thing, perhaps later than women since they face no "biological clock," it may be the necessity to marry in order to "guarantee" regular access to female sexuality that channels most men into that institution. Moreover, women may continue to earn less income than men, despite having more education, and a two-income family may be a requirement for a middle-class standard of living.

Nothing we know, at this moment, will change the basic equation of the demand for female sexual access far outweighing the supply. No matter how liberalized female sexual behavior became in the twentieth century, it never came close to matching male sexual desire. Not only did women's hormonal levels dictate a lower desire for sexual congress, mothers and some fathers continued to socialize their daughters that self-esteem and respectability for them demanded discretion in sexual matters. Males, meanwhile, were unfettered in their sexual drive and further encouraged by all the visual stimuli in their environment. Females continued to be taught that "all that men want from them is sex" and "men won't buy a cow if they can get milk through the fence."

Thus, most women will adhere to the notion that marriage and children must be their ultimate goal and their sexuality must be utilized to entice the reluctant male to go along. However, we expect a large minority of women to reject the conventional marriage model. Already, about 25 percent of American women will not bear children in their lifetime. Those childless women may reject marriage or once married, dissolve it and not marry again. The numbers of permanently single women may increase as our more narcissistic generation try to avoid the responsibilities and sacrifices of parenthood. Some may elect to serially cohabit with a member of the opposite—or same-sex instead of continuing to be free-floating singles in the dating game. Since women can more easily tolerate abstinence from all sexual contact, a life of celibacy may be an option for some as will be a long-term lesbian relationship.

As for men, they will continue to be driven by their sexual instincts, in part, controlled only by female resistance. Because women are a numerical majority, often the largest number of voters, they may strive for the enactment of laws that reduce male sexual opportunities. Sexual harassment regulations may confine all male-female contact to job-related matters. Rape laws may be strengthened so that written consent from a woman may be a male's only protection from accusations of rape. Even women may not like these sexual restraints, but a small minority of militant feminists, allied with the religious right, may impose those constraints on the rest of us. Some men may fall victim to the increasing equality of women. Already, more women are enrolled as undergraduates in four-year colleges than men are and growing close to parity in professional schools. Men continue, on average, to earn more than women do but women are fast narrowing the gap. That means a substantial number of women will earn a higher income than the men in their lives do. Certainly, it will be the end of an era when women had to give into male sexual demands because they were financially dependent on them.

Since men will continue to pursue women for their sexual favors and see success as a form of status, access to female sexuality will retain its allure. However, as many married women find out, once captured, she is often no longer the object of his ardent desire. If a marriage lasts, a couple can expect to remain together for as long as sixty years in the future—forty of those years without children. The male sex drive is capable of being as mental as a woman's is. How much desire he has for an available sexual partner remains to be seen. Unless his sexual options are restricted to only her, how certain can she be of his monogamy. Faith Popcorn, the futurist, has predicted a mass exodus from many marriages once a cure for AIDS is discovered. At any rate, married women will be dependent on the sexual reticence of single women—often much younger—for the stability of their marriage.

Besides the basic gender divide, a number of other factors may alter the pattern of sexual conduct in the United States. One of them could be the demographic factor. Already there are about eight million more women than men in the United States, largely due to the longer life expectancy of women. However, many of those "excess" women will be of an age where they no longer are of sexual appeal to most men. Marriage patterns are such that many women over the age of forty find it difficult to find "desirable" men with whom to marry or cohabit. Still, that does not translate into expanded sexual opportunities for men since those women may be considerably more selective and sexually conservative than women in their twenties. Once these women reach their fifties, they are menopausal and no longer interested in sex for recreational purposes. Another demographic shift may be the increasing number of immigrants from Latin America and Asia. They will compose a large percentage of Americans in the late twenty-first century. Most of them will arrive with more conservative sexual values than the resident Americans possess. Since Euro-Americans will continue to dominate the country's cultural motif, the cultural transmission will be such that the third generation of those newly arrived migrants will have adapted to their new country's sexual values.

We have already mentioned the role of the religious right. Unlike much of the developed world, religious groups participate in a very influential way in partisan politics in the United States. Mostly, they have affiliated themselves with the most conservative political party—the Republicans—and associated themselves with denying rights to gays, women, and libertarians. Their numbers are still too small to have much of an impact although they have been effective in their efforts to censor what we can see and hear in the media. Whether their numbers will grow remains to be seen. Much of the growth in religious membership has come in the fundamentalist churches, the most conservative of the religious groups. Add to their growth the religious values of newly arrived immigrants and they could be a threat to American sexual freedoms, particularly for women.

We can only guess at the role of technology and scientific innovation in impacting our sexual patterns. Already, the invention of the birth control pill and other barrier methods largely freed women from the fear of pregnancy. The "day after pill" has also made nonmarital sexuality even safer. The invention of male impotence pills has prolonged the sexual careers of men over the age of fifty. Who knows where the technique of cloning will lead us in the area of reproductive change. While it is possible that technology could free women from all childbearing responsibilities, we cannot know if it will liberalize sexual behavior. The AIDS hysteria and existence of sexually transmitted diseases meant that the birth control pill became a mixed blessing. Yet, scientific methods largely eliminated the fear of sexually transmitted diseases such as syphilis, which wiped out millions in Europe in previous centuries. It continues to hold our hope for an expanded vision of sexual freedom.

At the time of this writing, gays seemed to have made a dramatic leap in social tolerance from the days when they could be jailed for their lifestyle to gaining legal acceptance of their right to marry. Partly, this has happened due to the public's perception of gays as a white group. If the downtrodden, inferior Blacks could receive civil rights, why can't our beloved white gays? Many white families contain a gay member, particularly the female who is often a pseudo-lesbian. Then, there are any numbers of Euro-American females who have formed friendships with gay males, with whom they have much in common. Moreover, they are not sexually threatening, as are all those straight males with their constant demands for sex. Celebrating the arrival of gay utopia would be premature. Many visible gays are concentrated in large cities with fairly tolerant populations. There are still countless attacks on gays, even murders and chances are that being "out of the closet" still has its drawbacks. Still, with growing tolerance, it is likely the gay population will grow as many will come out of the closet and some will join the gay community because "it's cool to be gay." We can particularly expect an increase in the lesbian population because female sexuality is so malleable and what many women want is companionship—not sex.

We should not expect a decline in sexual violence. The expansion of laws making nonconsensual sex a crime will add to the litany of sex crimes because politicians will pander to advocacy groups who want more and more restrictions on what is legally defined as sexual misconduct. It will not matter that most of these laws are unenforceable. Given that rapes continued to happen when the punishment was death, we can expect little decline with a lesser punishment. Where males are organized into groups, sexual aggression against women will be part of male culture. We do not expect sex education, parental socialization or stiffer laws to have much effect—not as long as female sexuality is sold as a commodity on the TV screen, magazines, and streets of America. All we can look forward to is America to continue having more of its population behind bars than any other country in the developed world.

Somehow, men and women continue to coexist in a nation where they are very much at odds on what they want from sex. We sense a growing lack of trust between the genders. Among the younger generation, there seems to be no moral boundaries. Females may use their sexuality to gain whatever the market will bear while men feel any method of attaining access to female sexuality is fair game—if that means "taking it." At the same time, you have young women being hooked up and having men service them sexually without intimacy or commitment. With the advent of Internet dating, one woman complained that now men can have sex forever without getting married. Yet, men do marry for reasons other than sex and remain fairly content in that institution. In fact, the conventional wisdom among feminists was that men benefited much more from marriage than did women.

The younger generation tends to be acutely aware that about half of all new marriages end in divorce. When and if a cure for AIDS is discovered, the rate of marital dissolution will be much higher. Among the signs of distrust are those hiring private detectives to do background checks on potential lovers and spouses. Others are writing up contracts spelling out the expectations of a marriage or cohabitation. Those who marry for a second time require the next spouse to sign a prenuptial agreement specifying that, in the event of a divorce, each party retains the assets that he or she brought to the marriage. Some contracts may even spell out the frequency of sexual relations although such rules are unenforceable.

Black Sexuality and the Future

At the end of the twentieth century, the following trends continue unabated. Most Black sexual activity does not take place within the boundaries of holy matrimony. That happened because less than half of adult Blacks were married and living with their spouse. As of 2005, only 35 percent of adult Black females and 44 percent of adult Black males over the age of sixteen were entrenched in the institution of marriage. The remainder of that group were never married, legally married and separated, divorced, or widowed. That, in large part, explains why more than 70 percent of all children born to Black women are out of wedlock. Along with other trends related to Black sexual expression, a majority of those infected with HIV was Black males, and Black women composed more than 75 percent of all women diagnosed as victims of AIDS.

It is possible that most Euro-American sexual activity takes place outside of wedlock too. However, a majority of Euro-Americans are married and living with their spouses. What happened to Black Americans to cause their figures to more than double that of Euro-Americans? It has everything to do with the economy. And, it is the position of Black males in the economy that impacts Black female sexuality in America. At the start of the twenty-first century, more than 64 percent of Black males, aged sixteen through sixty-two, were not in the labor force. That is not the same as the annual unemployment rate for Black men that, on a national basis, is currently an official 13 percent. Some Black males are not in the labor force because they are currently students or retired. Others cannot obtain gainful employment because they are incarcerated. Black males compose a majority of those behind bars in the United States. Between the ages of eighteen and thirty, one of every three Black males is in jail, on probation, or parole. Others are not counted in the official unemployment statistics because they are discouraged and no longer seeking work. Members of the armed forces are not counted in the civilian labor force.

Since Black women almost unanimously confine their dating and marriage pool to the Black male population, that low percentage of unincarcerated, working Black males leaves many with slim pickings. The sex ratio is lowered further by the high mortality rate of young Black men—those in the marriageable age ranges—which is three times greater than that of young

Black women. The greatest causes in that age group, eighteen through thirty-five, are AIDS, homicide, accidents, and suicides. Thus, it is understandable why so few Black women are married when the basic requirements for a husband—gainful employment—are met by so few Black males. Even more tragic is the fact that Black married couples are approaching parity, in household income, with Euro-American couples. Marriage, along with a college degree, is the entry into the world of the middle class. Without viable Black marriage partners, Black women are more dependent on a college degree and they achieve those at a ratio of two to one for Black men, and actually earn a higher income than their male counterparts in the younger age ranges.

The institutional decimation of young Black males is accounted for by a number of political and economic forces. In the 1970s, the loss of manufacturing jobs in the United States to other countries began and has rapidly accelerated into the twenty-first century. Black males were more concentrated in that sector of the economy and did not make a seamless transition into the service sector. Often, they lacked the basic literacy skills to compete in information and technology services. Moreover, the greatest increases in jobs, about 75 percent, went to women in the last forty years. Employers, in particular, seem resistant to hiring Black males for jobs that require customer or client contact. When they employed Blacks, they preferred women. Black women also increased their numbers in institutions of higher learning, becoming two-thirds of the Black college graduates by the end of the twentieth century. When welfare reform was set into place, many of the Black women on welfare entered the labor force and competed with Black males for the limited number of low skill jobs.

While some of these are objective economic forces that adversely impacted Black males, the bourgeoning prison population was a conscious political decision that dramatically increased the number of Black men in prison. There is no reason to believe Black males commit more criminal acts than Euro-American men do. Rather, the selective application of the law to mete out prison sentences to crimes committed by Black males is responsible for the dramatic increase in the number behind bars. White-collar crimes continue to be unpunished or lightly punished, certain kinds of drug crimes peculiar to Blacks are more heavily punished, and the Black community is heavily policed, eliciting a greater number of arrests. The political decision to imprison drug users and dealers has made America the number one jailer in the developed world. By imprisoning Black men at a young age, they prevent them from obtaining gainful employment in the future and destabilize entire Black communities. Expanding the definition of sexual crimes increases the number of Blacks in prison.

The aforementioned factors have everything to do with Black sexual patterns. When Black women are faced with a limited pool of dating and marital partners, they are forced to take love and sex on male terms. Many of them are inefficient users of contraception and opposed to abortion when they become pregnant. Faced with a marriageless future, they do not want a childless one as well. Rather than marry a man with no, or irregular employment prospects, they have children out of wedlock and raise them alone. The notion of a future in a tedious, meaningless, service job is not enough to sustain them. At least a child gives them some human relationship and provides meaning to their lives. Nowadays, with a 70 percent out-of-wedlock birthrate among Blacks, there is no stigma attached to such births because they are the norm. It should be noted that the "illegitimacy rate" has increased to such a high level because so many Black women are not married, have no or very few children, particularly in the middle-class.

While we would like to come up with a positive outlook on what will happen in the rest of the twenty-first century, nothing on the horizon beckons to give us hope of meaningful change in the Black situation. In the political arena, the issue of jobs is barely addressed for the disenfranchised. Instead, it is the middle-class issues such as social security, homeland defense, and gay marriage that are being debated by presidential candidates. One glimmer of hope is in the state of California, where increasing amounts in the state budget were allocated to the construction of prisons while less was devoted to making a college education affordable for working-class families. Voters decided that drug treatment and rehabilitation programs were preferable to housing more drug offenders in prison and paying prison guards more than teachers. As a bellwether state, it may presage a reduction in the state's largely Black and Latino prison population.

What about Noneconomic Forces?

There are still millions of Black men and women subject to other forces besides the economic ones. Many Black women, for instance, blame the shortage of dating and marital partners on competition from non-Black women. Many claim that Black men favor all races of women except Blacks. With an intermarriage rate of less than 5 percent, the lowest of all racial groups, most Black men marry within the race. Others point out that the 5 percent are clustered in the highest educated and income group. Where the competition from non-Black women makes a difference is in the realm of sexual partners. While about 20 percent of Black males have engaged in interracial sexual activity, we do not know if it involved a long-term exclusive relationship, multiple sexual partners, or a one-night stand. The distinction between types of sexual relationships makes a difference in their "availability" to Black women.

Theoretically, Black women should have the option of an interracial sexual partner. If not, why not? We hear that Euro-American men do not want to date them because beauty is more important to men and Black women do not fit well the beauty standard as perceived by Euro-American men. It is also possible that Black women reject the sexual advances of Euro-American men due to the historical implications of being sexually abused by that racial group. Black males welcome most sexual opportunities and do not care if their Euro-American partner is only interested in a time-contained relationship. The Euro-American female may be unconcerned that her Afro-American partner is only interested in her body and beauty, not her services as a wife and mother. She may believe the sexual stereotypes about him, just wants to sexually experiment, or faces a shortage of desirable Euro-American males. Whatever the reason, we know their sexual relationship will not culminate in a lifelong marriage most of the time.

What the competition from Euro-American women will do is force many Black women to be more flexible in their sexual practices. Although the percentage of them engaging in oral sex is still lower than the percentage of women of other racial groups, it is a lot higher than in the past. Knowing that Black men could get it from "foreign women" may have forced their hand— or lips—in that area. Even some of the other sexual trends trailblazed by Euro-American women may be emulated by middle-class Black women. Gail Wyatt found a much larger number engaging in group sex than was formerly known to exist. Social lesbianism, pseudo-lesbianism, or bisexuality is increasing among Black women. They possess the same sexual malleability that allows Euro-American women to enter and exit lesbian relationships at will. Some years ago, we predicted a gray lesbianism among Black women when they entered their advanced years. However, the physical pleasures of sex may not be the compelling force as much as friendship, affection, and companionship during those years when there is a severe shortage of available men.

As for future trends in interracial sexuality, we expect it to increase, in a time-contained way, among the very young. Although high schools and even colleges can be very self-segregated, different racial groups manage to find each other. The very young seem willing to breach any number of social taboos and the one on interracial sexual activity is one among many. As time goes by, we expect more sexual contact between Black men and Latino and Asian women. These other two racial groups are located in the same metropolitan areas and often attend public schools together. Asian-American women have generally favored Euro-American males because that was the only interracial relationship acceptable to their families. Many Black men were not that interested in Latino women. We expect those barriers to gradually break down as the third and fourth generation of Latinos and Asians break free from familial control.

Homosexuality and its increase is another social force to reckon with. Black women have often claimed that many "good" Black men have been lost to the gay community. That accounts, in part, for some Black female prejudice against Black men who are gay. This assumes a lot smaller lesbian group among Black women. The available research tells us that is true. All we really know is that Black lesbians are certainly less "visible." Perhaps they are less visible because lesbianism is not as acceptable in the Black community. Many Black women will befriend male gays, particularly since they allegedly represent no sexual threat. The more sexually active Black male stays away from known lesbians or else tries to convert them. Failing to convert them, he may simply "take it." What chance would a lesbian have in pressing a sexual assault claim?

As true of Euro-American males, we expect an increase in the number of Black gays as they receive more legal protection and feel secure in coming out of the closet. We predict Black attitudes toward homosexuality will soften although the militant homophobes will continue to make life difficult for them. At present, straight Black women are being warned against bisexual Black males as transmitters of AIDS. We are told that the percentage of bisexuals is greater in the Black community. Why that should be the case is unclear and it is difficult to get answers to questions about Black homosexuality that are not politically correct. What research that exists shows the proportion of gays in the Black community to be higher than in the Euro-American world. The answers to these questions in the past are no longer acceptable in the community of scholars.

Whatever the reasons, Black homosexuality will be on the rise in the twenty-first century. We particularly expect an increase in Black lesbians. The "authentic" lesbians are acknowledging there are pretenders in their midst, who are bisexuals in lesbian clothing. Since many women can be sexually satisfied by other women, they may resort to that outlet when there are no "desirable" men available. The number of men available to Black women may be reduced if gay Black men feel they no longer need to marry in order to live a "successful" life. As gays find they can marry, have the benefits of straight couples, be protected from job and other types of discrimination, they will remain in the gay community and Black women will be deprived of this source of men that they had in the past. Lesbians may not feel as secure since straight men could make life difficult for them. They may find it problematic to tell their families eagerly awaiting their production of grandchildren. No matter, it will have little effect on the Black male's sexual options. He already has a surplus of women available to him and can always cross racial lines to counteract any shortage of women caused by a surge in the lesbian populations.

The news in the area of sexual violence is not good, no matter your point of view. We expect more and more laws to be passed restricting what sexual acts and gestures are legal for men. Since there is no pro-rape lobby, advocacy groups will encounter no obstacles in getting laws passed. Some, such as marital rape, will rarely be used or result in convictions. Since the crime of rape is rarely witnessed by other than the two parties, it will become a matter of his word against hers. Juries will continue to be arbitrary in their convictions and chances are that most women will not take their chances in court; instead they will pick up the pieces and move on with their life. Increases in rape allegations against Black men will only criminalize an already marginalized group of men. Moreover, they have nothing to lose, as they will go to prison for one thing or the other. Whether women will, or should, change their behavior is an open question. While the response "no" to a request for sexual congress may be sincerely meant by most women, clearly many men do not believe it. Those who do have something to lose may be less violent in their conduct. We must remember that many attempts at sexual activity are accompanied by the use of alcohol or drugs, particularly in the case of Black men. Reticence by a woman may not have much effect on men under the influence of mind-altering substances.

What may be more influential, both good and bad, is the growing reluctance of Black women to be indoors alone with Black men as a response to media reports about date rape. This may solve one problem and create another. First, it stigmatizes all Black male dating partners as potential rapists, a strange perception to have of a man you like enough to go out on a date with. Either he is a man you might eventually marry and become the father of your children, or, he is a man who will act in a sexually aggressive manner toward you and the next time you see him will be in a court of law at his rape trial. One might wonder why most women cannot make the distinction. Moreover, taking separate cars and meeting at a restaurant does not facilitate getting to know a person. A restaurant will not allow you to linger for hours on a busy weekend night. That means a couple can only spend a brief time together before going home in their separate cars.

Furthermore, it can put other women at risk to go inside with a male. Given the number of women who will not venture inside, should he assume that the woman who does go inside alone is tacitly consenting to have sex with him? Visiting a person's home, hers or his, can often tell you much about them and it is an opportunity to relax and get to know that person in an environment they are comfortable with. Refusing to go indoors alone with a male sends a clear message to your dating partner that you are unwilling to have sex with him. Does that mean that the cost of the evening will be equally shared by both parties? Will this clear message discourage him from asking her out in the future? How many times does she refuse to be alone with him before she does agree to? Does this situation have any bearing on the decline of formal dating among Black men and women? Will Black men simply pursue the women of least resistance? It is these thorny questions that will be posed and answered in the future.

We fully expect prostitution to continue as it has for centuries, largely for reasons already mentioned. There is no reason to expect male and female sex drives to be equalized. How many and which men will need their services will be impossible to answer. The really essential question is whether the United States will follow the examples of other developed nations and decriminalize prostitution, or legalize and control it. As with the debate on legalizing now illegal drugs, the issue raises more heat than light. It is still the case that it is the vendor and not the customer who is arrested and prosecuted, another sign of our double standard of sexual conduct. What may change is the manner in which prostitution is carried out. Both pimps and prostitutes may attract workers and clients on the Internet in the future. Continuing to treat paid sex as a crime is a losing war. Many might even claim the difference is not that great between males paying for sex in so many other ways.

Not only is sexual activity something that takes up only a fraction of our waking hours, it has largely been limited to the very young. Once past age fifty, many women facing menopause had their libido dulled or vaginal dryness made sex painful. Men facing health problems such as heart disease, diabetes, and hypertension had erectile difficulties. A combination of male and female problems meant that a majority ceased all sexual activity after the age of fifty-five. The male side of the problem was diminished after the introduction of pills such as Viagra. The same drug manufacturer, Pfizer, tried to find a similar pill, with a similar function, for women only to conclude that arousal did not lead to sexual desire. Their conclusion was that the brain is the crucial sexual organ in women. Because the erectile pills are fairly new, we do not know the effect on the sexual lives of men whose sexual drive had been mostly dormant. Still, they are being sexually awakened at an age when their female sexual partners do not want to be disturbed.

If the drug manufacturers succeeded in creating a pill that generated sexual desire in women, all bets are off. The discrepancy in gender sexual drive is at the heart of sexual conflict between men and women. However, the differential socialization into sexual values and the still strong double standard contribute to that conflict and remains in existence to this day. Such current concerns as the lyrics of rap music may be short-lived as the art form is replaced by something else. At any rate, the lyrics did nothing more than mirror the male sexual culture in the inner city and is being sold to suburban Euro-American males who subscribe to a similar culture. Freedom of speech and the widespread popularity of the music will prevent its immediate destruction no matter how much it demeans women and adds to the sexualization of American culture.

Finally, some progress has been made in the fight against AIDS. New drugs have prolonged the lives of many HIV victims. Because gays, largely perceived as white, continue to press for a cure, the government will continue to devote funds to research on the problem. Although AIDS never deeply penetrated into the drug free, heterosexual world, it had a chilling effect on a dwindling sexual revolution. However, that revolution was slowly fading as women aged and wanted the security of marriage or cohabitation. As history tells us, we shall revisit the sexual revolution sometime in the twenty-first century. It may come about as a result of a cure for AIDS, or disenchantment with marriage on the part of young women who can now support themselves. The only consistency in changes in sexual patterns is they will not be permanent.

~

Conclusion

In concluding our exploration of the Black sexual mystique, we need to address some questions that lead to a summary of Black sexuality's importance to its people. We come to the answer by first looking at its function in American society. The first and most important function is to facilitate the reproduction of the species. Men and women must engage in sexual intercourse to replace the members of the society who die. Given an average life span of about seventy-eight years and a fertility rate below replacement value (2.0) it is obvious that most sexual activity is not designed for that purpose. Moreover, women can be impregnated by artificial insemination and could, theoretically, remain virgins all. While the United States is producing enough children to replace its members through legal and illegal immigration, Western Europe has an average fertility rate of 1.5 children and declining. Sexual activity in the developed world has become largely recreational and not to sire children.[1]

We have already discussed its value as a commodity. It is used in advertising to sell almost everything except cereal, eaten mostly by children. Although it has a far-ranging set of functions, the direct delivery of female sexuality to male customers is a multi-billion-dollar industry that employs millions of women. Closing down all sex industries could bring on an economic depression in the United States. Considering all the businesses that deliver a sexual product, they may be more important than the automobile, oil and communications industries combined. If we add most of the "nonsexual" industries that use female sexuality in some way, the total could be greater than the gross national product of any one developing nation.

As for the importance of sexuality to our Black population, it is one of the few commodities not controlled by Euro-Americans. Blacks had to go to them for housing, food, clothes, cars, television sets, and pretty much every item they consumed. Sexuality resided within their own community and, for the most part, was only accessible to them. It, of course, allowed them to reproduce their own race in a land where they were a statistical minority. It was a source of immense pleasure, at least for men, and cost, on the surface, much less than the other commodities they desired. Alas, they also had to endure the societal stereotype as a "morally loose" people and have that stereotype employed to deny them their civil rights. The White South, for example, used the stereotype to erect an elaborate system of dual institutions to prevent them from infecting the morals of their women and children—and to protect the women.

Thus, their sexuality became a double-edged sword, as a source of pleasure and as a barrier to racial equality. Had they been the chastest of people, the barriers would have remained, only the rationalization would have changed. Moreover, the pain and pleasure derived from sexuality depended on the position one occupied on the great gender divide. For males, there was the physical pleasure associated with the fusion of genitals and ejaculation. Because females were hesitant, sometimes resistant to male pleas for sexual engagement, the pursuit of female sexuality contained its own pleasure when it culminated in a sexual victory. A male prestige system was constructed on the basis of the number and quality of sexual conquests. For some men, the pursuit of female sexuality became a way of life. Some dedicated their nonworking hours to chasing female sexual access, in turn making it the most important goal in life.

The theories abound that sexual pursuits were a compensation for his lack of power in American society. After all, he would not become a captain of industry. During the worst years of the racial caste system, he could not secure any of the titles or respect accorded Euro-American men. Sexual victories were all that was left to him and status enhancement would only come from his Black male peers. While those theories contain some validity, we cannot discount the role of pure physical pleasure associated with these sexual endeavors.

The physical relief from completed coitus can reduce stress, provide emotional enhancement, and pride of accomplishment. Who can say that commanding an industrial empire guarantees more satisfaction? Given the racial codes of the White South for more than a century, achievements in the business world were little more than a fantasy for the overwhelming majority of Afro-American males. The sexual endeavors provided him with some joy when nothing else was possible.

For Black women, sexuality was a mixed blessing. They were not burdened with the guilt and shame that Euro-American women had to bear. For that group of women, the enjoyment of sexual congress was to be denied even when it transpired in the sacred institution of marriage. She was there only to give her husband pleasure and serve her duty. Afro-American women were released from that sense of duty and allowed to give free rein to sexual expression. However, they obtained that sexual freedom at a horrible price. For more than two centuries, they were the sexual vessels of Black and white males. Without their consent, on the plantations of the Deep South, Black women became sexually free because they had nothing to lose. Their right to sexual privacy was not observed in the legal codes nor respected by men of either race in the land of tobacco and cotton. What she could not have, she did not value and sexual freedom became the byproduct of sexual abuse.

Even with the more liberated sexual expression she was allowed, she still fell victim to the hormones that prevent a substantial number of women from enjoying sexual relationships today. Her one saving grace, if you will, was that much of the time she was pregnant with child and unable to indulge her man's passion for her flesh. A woman bearing more than ten children was commonplace in the nineteenth century and for much of the twentieth century. We have only anecdotal evidence for how much even sexually liberated Black women enjoyed coitus in the period after slavery ended. While they were generally not burdened with the Euro-American woman's sense of duty, it is also true that Afro-American men may not have engaged in a variety of sexual techniques to enhance her libidinal strivings. Satisfaction may be contingent on expectations and she may have been content if she was not prey for every male in her environment.

Another question we need to address is how much is female sexuality worth? Framing the question in that way can suggest that female sexuality is put on the market and sold to the highest bidder. We are not suggesting that but sexual bargaining is very common as a function of the differential access to the sexuality of each gender. Sexual attractiveness, for women, is still used as a bargaining resource although in a more complex market than previously existed. For Euro-Americans, the cumulative advantage of males as a group monopolizing higher occupational positions tended to reinforce the need for women to equalize the odds. If you talk with women who are fifty something and happy being single, they will admit that when in their 20s and 30s they used sex as a tool to attract and get a husband.

Certainly, the protest against our employment of exchange theory to analyze sexual bargaining will be answered in the assertion that women enjoy sex and get involved in it only for their personal enjoyment. However, as millions of males are aware, they pay, in some form, sooner or later for sex. With many women, the most obvious indicator of a quid pro quo in female sexuality is that when she becomes unhappy in a relationship her first response is "we should just be friends." Every man knows that means the end of sex with her, at least until there is some reason to believe she will get her desired objectives. Our society still operates on the underlying assumption that a woman should get something out of a sexual relationship other than the sex alone. Her sexuality remains a resource only to the extent that it is not given away. In today's market, she is placing a value on her sexuality that is valid only if a man is willing to pay it. Many women have the same sexual organ but it is contained in widely different packages. Thus, a younger woman can demand more than an older woman, a beautiful woman more than an ugly one.

Examples abound on the price tag attached to female sexuality. In the country of Australia, a union of striptease artists, exotic dancers, and topless bar staff demanded pay rates of up to three hundred and ten dollars for three-minute skimpy lap dancing and six hundred and ten dollars for a three-minute nude performance. The employers responded by saying a full-time nude waitress could expect to earn more than two million dollars a year under their claim.[2] One could only wonder why any woman would ever go to medical school to earn much less money. There are call girls charging as much as one-thousand dollars an hour for her company and use of her body. As recently as the 1970s, a number of states had laws that said if you take her sexuality, the price is your life. It is still life imprisonment in many states for that violation. The Supreme Court of France ruled that no woman could ever be found guilty of rape.[3]

Although both genders were endowed with genitals, male sexuality has absolutely no value whatsoever. Most male prostitutes have gay clients and the scenes we see of women going to see male strippers is actually some female bonding ritual—not a strong interest in the male body. That does not mean women do not have sexual feelings or interest. It only means they rarely have to pay to have them satisfied. Many women may engage in sexual bargaining without a conscious awareness of it, attributing their actions to other reasons. Using sexuality as a tool is effective only if you can get the consumer to pay your price. Sometimes the product is given away free the first time in order to wet his appetite for future sexual trysts. Some females make no effort to hide their bargaining of sexuality for something of value. It can be a material item such as a car, jewelry, clothes, rent payments, or even marriage. The more attractive she is and the fewer opportunities he has, the better the chance of getting her price.

Sometimes the sexuality is bartered for behavior changes. She wants to go dancing on weekends instead of staying home and watching sports on televi-

sion. The most basic exchange for most women, sometimes after a long period of dating, is her sexuality for commitment, cohabitation, or marriage. If
the latter, she may also want children. As unemotional as it may seem, men
confronted with these demands do a cost-benefit analysis. While non-
material forces such as love, sentiment, and loyalty should enter the picture,
he may be thinking of the odds of success in a society where half the marriages end in divorce, paying alimony and child support for twenty years. If
her leverage is her sexuality, he may decide it's not a fair value.

Sexuality can have such an ephemeral value. After engaging in carnal relations over a period of time, there is a point of diminishing returns. The second year of sexual activity will rarely be as exciting as the first. For many
men, even the first time of sexual engagement will produce postcoital depression. Some worldly philosopher said, "Satisfaction is the death of desire."
Men can also lose interest in sexual activity while women still want it. Although he may lie next to an available and willing sexual partner each night,
he is preoccupied with his work and devoting all his energy into his job. If
we are to believe comedian Bill Maher, male sexuality can be explained by
two words, "Young and new." He even claims that being married to or cohabitating with a beautiful woman makes no difference. Once he said, "no
matter how attractive she is, there is a man at home who is bored with having sex with her."

Many men stay in marriages because a tiresome sex life is better than no
sex life. It explains why male celebrities, with lots of options, do not stay
faithful to girlfriends or wives. The late basketball star, Wilt Chamberlain,
was very honest in saying, "I tend to be very fickle. I get tired of a girl fairly
quickly. And, when I do, I 'fire' her. Who knows—I may already have fired
one or two girls who would have made ideal wives for me if I had kept them
around long enough to really get to know them."[4]

We must not be deluded into the notion that every Black woman is out
there hawking her sexuality for some material item. In the underclass, men
may be using their sexuality (companionship) for the resources of women in
that class. They have, in many cases, nothing else to give. The women are
certainly not interested in marrying or living with them. There is little evidence that working-class women are participants in the sexual barter trade.
Even when they ask for assistance, it is for the sake of their children—not
them. Women in this class, who are married, work alongside their husbands
in order to maintain a middle-class standard of living. It is the middle-class,
many of them college-educated where sexual bargaining is most prevalent.
The women of this class may begin as sexual innocents and become jaded as
men fail to make commitments, are unfaithful and unreliable. Whereas the

men may have resources to exchange for their sexuality, there is a pecking or-der of women able to barter their sexuality for something of value. It will be the youngest and most attractive women at the top of the hierarchy. Their motto will be no romance without finance.

The middle-class woman has the command of language to rationalize her attempt to extort something of value from a man. He will be told that if he loves her, it will be arranged for them to take that vacation in the Bahamas and stay at a five-star hotel. Otherwise, he will be regarded as "cheap." In this class, with a top-of-the-line woman, he is expected to take her out to dinner, to give her gifts, help her out in a "pinch," all to demonstrate his concern for her. While he may view her as only after his money and there are plenty of other fish in the sea, there are not a lot of fish as young and attractive as this trader. The sex ratio does not matter to these women because there are lots of men willing to do their bidding.

Second-tier women cannot drive a hard bargain because there is a multi-tude of women with the same attributes. That does not mean these women will not try to sexually bargain, even if it is only for one night at a four-star restaurant. They will not ask for the big-ticket items because he has too many options for her to take that risk. One of the reasons we do not see many Black couples at public places is a Mexican standoff. His idea of a "date" is coming by her house, watching television, and engaging in sexual activity. She wants him to show his commitment by paying for them to go to dinners, nightclubs, plays, concerts, etc. Consequently, we see her in public with second-tier girl-friends who also could not strike a Faustian bargain with a man. While he may be seen with his buddies in the same place, nothing we know of indi-cates that he is going without sexual gratification. Either he is picking up a woman in one of the places they frequent or found a sexual partner among the women staying at home. There is too much of a surplus of women in the Black community to do without.

Women stick to their guns because they have been told they are in posses-sion of something precious and should not give it away. A female Ph.D. once told me that their genitals are the "crown jewels." To her they have great value and must be treated with the utmost care. To her gynecologist, it is a membrane and one of the least important organs in her body. To a male, it may only be a "piece of ass." As W. I. Thomas once wrote, if a person believes something is real, for all practical purposes it becomes real to them.[5] Certainly, the society has placed a strong value on it. Men will seemingly do anything to get access to it. Kings have given up their kingdom for it. Forced entry to it once cost you your life and can still cost you your freedom. Yet, more than half the world's popula-tion has one and the demand can be satisfied by any one of them.

What American society has done is create a mystique around the female sexual organ. Make no mistake. The whole emphasis on female beauty fuels the sexual fantasies of men. That is why they can be seen watching attractive women in public. Their ultimate aim is to gain access to the most attractive women that cross their paths. Very few will act on that impulse or succeed. We know that men think about sex once a day and more depending on what environment they are in. They are always stimulated by the most romanticized image of female sexuality. Our music, movies, and poems all present a vision of sexual attraction that depicts women as the embodiment of their dreams. Women feed that fantasy with the use of perfumes, jewelry, makeup, even plastic surgery. If we lost use of our electricity, toilets, were deprived of perfume, deodorants and makeup, sexuality may be reduced to the bare rudiments of a membrane without all its enhancements and odor masking accoutrements.

While we worship at the altar of the female vagina, who will revere the penis? Freud had said that women envied it and wondered what happened to theirs.[6] Where are the women who will give up everything for access to a penis? France says if a woman forces herself on a penis, she cannot be charged with rape. If the coerced penis does not desire her, it will not stay erect. Other than in Freudian analysis, the penis has no value. Every woman who wants one can have it—as many as she wants. Indeed, that phallus is seen as a potential danger to society, going around and sticking itself in places where it is not wanted. Many feel it is out of control, never satisfied and always striving for gratification among many female members of society. How many female poets write odes to the penis and describe the beauty of its rise and fall? Once, in ancient Rome and Greece, the male body was the admired form. Now we only see it on rare occasions.

It is not only the female body that is shrouded in a façade of perfumes and eroticized clothing. The sex act itself, when seen in movies, is always an emotional fusion in which sentiment outweighs pure pleasure. In reality, it lasts fifteen minutes and, I suspect, less than that time in married households across America. Not only are there no sounds of violins but nothing that resembles laughter or anything emanating from the human voice. Perhaps that is why some feminists have an antipathy for pornography. The cheaply made porno film strips bare the sex act to the intertwining of bodies, penile penetration of a vagina, and ejaculation of fluid. They are made for men and center on male values. It is what sexual engagement is all about for many married couples as the thrill is gone. For the very young unmarried, there is the emotional intensity that mistakes immense physical pleasure for love. Certainly, it is the best kind of sex and a pity it is wasted on the young.

When you talk to unmarried Blacks, there is often a litany of complaints about each other. A central complaint of Black women is that Black men's interests are too narrow. Their interests, according to women, center on their jobs, sports, and music. The women want to explore museums, plays, ballet, opera, the symphony, and books. Men and women are not raised to be very compatible in interests. Not too many women play the major sports, and do not enjoy the competition and violence that go along with them. On the other hand, men see some of the female interests as boring and "sissified."

These conflicts over interests are often played out in the bedroom. She may withhold sex because she is disenchanted with her interests not being included in their joint activities. He prefers being with his male friends. If not for his sexual needs, one might wonder how much time men would spend with women. When they marry, much of their time is occupied by the rearing of children. Leisure time is spent with their families of origin and other married couples. Because she is now likely to work outside the home, there is little time for anything else. We know that her job has caused a decline in the frequency of their sexual activity. Black couples actually have slightly less sexual activity than Euro-American couples do. An interesting finding of some studies is that couples who cohabit have sex more often,[7] maybe the cohabiting couples are less likely to have children or perhaps the female member is less likely to decline his requests for coitus because she does not have the security of a legal marriage.

Complaints about a dissonance in interests are certainly not race specific. The number of single Euro-American women is very high and they have similar grievances. Even in the country of Australia, with similar demographics, single women talk about the difficulty of forming a long-term relationship. In a fairly long article on the topic, the subject of conflict over sex was barely mentioned. One married man, with two children, claimed that "today's young men are ripped off, seduced by lifestyle images involving casual sex, consumer goods, and youth and beauty."[8] What is strange about that analysis is there is every indication young women in Australia are not interested in marriage either. The women who, in the article, wanted marriage and children were all over age thirty.

Others have written about the male flight from commitment in the past thirty years. We cannot be sure what role sexuality plays in that flight. In the 1950s, men were pretty much required to marry for any access to female sexuality. During the 1970s, sexually liberated women blossomed all over the nation. In the 1980s, an economic recession, inflation, and an aging female population brought about a conservative trend. The 1990s and an even older female population really put the brakes on what had been a sexual revolution.

Women over age thirty-five were looking to get married, refusing to casually engage in sexual relationships. It was all chalked up to the AIDS crisis. While Black women, over age thirty, became more sexually conservative, it didn't amount to an appreciable increase in marriage. Still, the increase in the divorce rate was slowed as men remained married due to their fear of AIDS. There was a corresponding decrease in teenage pregnancy among Afro-American females. As the young began to notice that few of their drug free, heterosexual friends were being infected with HIV, they began to liberalize their sexual behavior albeit not with a frequent change of sexual partners.

A predictable trajectory is that as Afro-American females approach the age of thirty, they will be seeking marriage and children, especially women of the middle-class. The chances of them actualizing their aspirations are not good. The imbalance in the sex ratio of Blacks attending and graduating from college show no signs of abating. Not only do Black males marry outside the race by a two to one ratio but their interracial sexual activity is seven times greater than that of their female counterparts. With Generation Y considered the least racist of Euro-Americans, and Latino and Asian females joining them, that difference will only broaden in the future. Only the high divorce rate among middle-class Afro-Americans will make more Black males available to them. Some Black women will cross over the color line in terms of marriage but they tend to be even more conservative when it comes to nonmarital sexual activity with non-Blacks.

If Euro-American males flee from commitment due to the high divorce rate, Afro-American males must really be terrified of a marital dissolution rate that is twice as high. We might ask why Black women are not equally discouraged by the high risks associated with marriage in their racial group. The answer is that some of them are and others have reasons that are more compelling than the high divorce rate. That reason is the desire to have children within the boundaries of matrimony. It has been noticed that some middle-class Black women marry and stay married long enough to have one child and then divorce. Men who father these children face at least eighteen years of child support expenses and college tuition is expected for children of this class. How calculated her decision is to marry, have a child, and divorce is anybody's guess. We do know the number of one-child marriages is fairly high among college-educated Black women.

How do they find the men to father their child? The answer is that the bar is set a lot lower than for men with whom they expect a lifelong marriage and the fulfillment of the American dream. Black men have to worry about forces outside the Black community seeking to curtail their sexual freedoms. Fuelled by an unholy alliance between militant feminists and the religious right, they are antisex in nature and seek to control the expression of sexuality in all forms of media. Somehow, they have managed to equate all kinds of sexual expression as demeaning to women while ignoring the fact that many women do not want censorship of their radio, television, movie, and music programs. Nor do they feel they need protection because they are all potential victims of predatory males.

The religious right, of course, equates sexuality with sin. That is why they want a constitutional amendment to ban abortion and force women to face the consequences of their sexual license. Many of these women will be married and simply feel they cannot afford another child. Despite the fact that many Black women elect to have a child out of wedlock, a large number also choose to abort an unwanted pregnancy. These moral crusaders reside outside the Black community although they have occasionally found some Black woman to head their organization. Militant feminists are not aligned with them on restricting a women's right to choose but instead join them in restricting the sexual freedoms of men.

These conservative forces have introduced terms and concepts like sex addiction to the lexicon of American society. We actually have men going to therapists for treatment of their "sex addiction." If not for the fear of AIDS, an overwhelming majority of men are sex addicts. Their numbers are restricted by the fear of HIV and lack of opportunity because of barriers erected by women. It is only when we look at the past conduct of male celebrities that we see the numbers produced when there is unlimited sexual opportunity. One of the most prolific was the late Elvis Presley who is listed as bedding three women a day in his prime. Some of his obscure sidekicks were paid in sexual opportunities. In a reunion for a television program, one of them recalls that "we got more ass than a toilet seat."

Somehow, women's advocacy groups have managed to associate the liberal sexual attitudes of men with misogyny. Yet, the greatest progress for women occurred during the years of unprecedented sexual freedom. It is a misnomer to label Afro-American men as sexists for their liberal sexual behavior when there is more parity between Afro-American men and women than any other racial group. Twice as many Black women have college degrees, they are the majority of Blacks in professional schools, and they earn a higher income than their male counterparts do. A Black woman, Oprah Winfrey, is the most powerful Afro-American in show business and close to the richest. There are still some inequities among working-class Blacks and women continue to bear the burden of raising children. By almost every statistical indicator, there is greater gender equality in the Black population than among Euro-Americans, Asians, and Latinos. Other than fraternities and sororities, there are few exclusive male or female associations in the Black community.[9]

Many women decry male sexual liberality because they desire marriage, children, and absolute monogamy. While one can understand their feelings about men being more interested in sexual variety than marrying and raising children, I do not know that men need to apologize for their greater enjoyment of sexual activity. Women, if they had the hormones for it, might act the same—and some do. It is tempting to declare that men owe women honesty about what they are doing. Honesty, however, has its consequences and it is not a good thing. Some marriages have survived by her ignoring the obvious and saying, "as long as he takes care of home, I don't mind."

There is no silver bullet for this dissonance in sexual values between men and women. Men have much more in common when it comes to sexuality than do people within racial groups. That is not likely to change in this millennium. Moreover, within the heterosexual world, for every male cavorting with a woman, somewhere there has to be a woman with him. It is not like robbing banks or anything else he can do alone. For every man who commits adultery, he has a willing woman as his sexual partner. Somehow, that gets lost in the female condemnation of male liberality in sexual matters.

At least women now have the same sexual freedom as men—at least in most respects. There is still a residue of the notion that women must be "in love" when they engage in nonmarital coitus. The anonymity of large cities has guaranteed many women sexual privacy. We do not know if she has had one or one thousand sexual partners. It stands to reason that her numbers should closely approximate that of men. Ultimately, a woman has to declare that she has the same sexual rights as men and having sex with more than a hundred men should not stigmatize her anymore than it does a male.

If women can acquire sexual agency, perhaps we can reconsider the draconian penalties for sexual theft (AKA rape) where the injury is mental. In particular, they should rethink regulations like the one at Oberlin College, which require a male to get a female's permission for each level of intimacy he attempts. While few women have used the marital rape laws, it is the height of absurdity to assume a woman can consent to coitus one night, deny it the next night, charge him with marital rape, and consent to sex another night. The divorce courts are for wives who are forced into sex against their will. If it is not worthy of divorce it certainly doesn't deserve life imprisonment. The Ohio legislature considered a bill to define as rape a man who refused to cease sexual activity whenever she says no. It appears that she can consent to having coitus for ten minutes, get tired, and ask him to stop. If he continues on for five additional minutes, he is charged with rape. Simultaneously, we should strengthen the laws for physical violence against women, whether it occurs in the context of a rape or not. It is not fair that a woman can suffer serious physical injuries, be rendered paraplegic or infertile, and endure pain for the rest of her life. As long as it involves no touching or penetration of sexual body parts (i.e., breast, vagina, and anus), he may get a sentence of less than two years.

Other sexual crimes need to be reconsidered, including the ones against males. If we had some rational beliefs about sexuality in this country, maybe people would not be mentally traumatized by sexual acts with them. Indeed, our attitudes toward sexuality are what makes sexually violated individuals think something dirty and horrible has happened to them. We know that some of the statutory rape laws are a function of contemporary child rearing practices. Children are not raised to take on responsibility until they are twenty-two years old and have graduated from college. Whereas a hundred years ago, men and women married as young as age thirteen with plans to have children immediately. Nowadays a person two years or more older engaged in consensual sex with them is charged with statutory rape. Particularly bothersome are the cases of adult women engaging in coitus with fourteen-year-old and fifteen-year-old boys, charged with statutory rape. Instead of suffering grievous mental injury, that will be the fondest memory of his childhood. I dare not suggest the same for teenage girls. After all, the movie "Summer of '42," involving a teenage boy having sex with an older woman, was not especially controversial. The moral crusaders tried to ban *Lolita*, a movie about a young girl's affair with an older man.

The aforementioned suggestions are probably utopian in nature. We live in a nation where many people still believe women must be in love before nonmarital sexual activity is acceptable for them. Love is a social construct and women do not randomly "fall in love" with any decent and available man they meet. White women only fall in love with white men no matter what sterling qualities an Asian man they know may have. Middle-class women typically fall in love with middle-class men and so on. As we have been reminded, a woman is not only choosing a husband but a standard of living. Women of advanced ages have lamented the fact that they often married incompatible men because he was the man with whom she engaged in premarital coitus.

Chances are that we will subscribe to our traditional ideas on sexuality no matter how dysfunctional they are. The final question we must address is what role does sexuality play in the conflict between Black men and women? We have already explained that the problem is structural. The shortage of desirable Black males, the choices it gives them and what they do with those choices. Unless the society does something to address the reasons for the imbalance in the Black sex ratio, little will change. Another problem is the dissonance between the sexually liberal male and sexually conservative Black female. There are indications, for example, that she is more conservative than her Euro-American counterpart is, and he is the most liberal of all males. Is he drifting toward the Euro-American woman because of their perceived sexual compatibility? I doubt it! Many Afro-American women have become competitive and engage in the same liberal sexual practices. Furthermore, Blacks and whites live in very different social worlds with disparate opportunities attached to their membership. Black men and white women may meet in the bedroom but not at the altar. However, Euro-American women do seem to pick off the cream of the crop.

Sexuality becomes important to men only when they have absolutely no access to it. That is not true except for the Black men in prison. What that does for Black men is allow them the freedom to marry or not. Given the odds of marital success, many elect not to marry. That same structural problem is responsible for the high Black divorce rate. Again, some innovative adaptations need to be tried to circumvent an intractable numbers problem. Otherwise, we may be looking at a generation of young, highly-educated, attractive women who will face a lifetime of isolation, hard work, and loneliness.

Finally, we must not lose sight of the fact that a majority of Black men and women have satisfactory sex lives. If you are a college-educated Black male, chances are that you are married and living the American dream. They are the one subgroup in the Black community that does not suffer the hardship of chronic unemployment, imprisonment, low income, or a shortage of desirable mates. Still, graduation from college is not the answer for Afro-American women. Can the Black women who are happily married and enjoying their sex lives be the accidental winners of the marriage lottery? Or do they have something to tell us about how they became the chosen ones. Maybe the unmarried need to look to the models of success. After all, they have nothing to lose.

Notes

1. "Europe's Aging Population Brings about Pension Reform." *The Age*, April 10, 2004, p. 1.

2. "Strippers Pay Claim Threadbare: Employers." *The Age*, April 4, 2004, p. 3.

3. "Court Rules Women Incapable of Rape." *San Francisco Examiner*, June 27, 2000, p. 10.

4. Wilt Chamberlain and David Shaw, *Wilt: An Autobiography*. New York: Macmillan Publishing, 1973, p. 256.

5. W. I. Thomas and Florence Znaniecki, *The Polish Peasant in Europe and America*. New York: Alfred Knopf, 1927.

6. Sigmund Freud, *New Introductory Lectures on Psychoanalysis*. New York: W. W. Norton, 1933.

7. Edward O. Laumann, et al., *The Social Organization of Sexuality: Sexual Practices in the United States*. Chicago: University of Chicago Press, 1994, pp. 294–298.

8. Sushi Das, "It's All Too Hard." *The Age*, April 5, 2004, p. A-3–5.

9. W. M. Blake and C. A. Darling, "The Dilemmas of the African American Male." *Journal of Black Studies*, 1994, 24, pp. 402–415.

Index

~

About the Author

Robert Staples (Ph.D., University of Minnesota), one of the leading authorities on Black sexuality, is professor emeritus of sociology at the University of California, San Francisco, and a visiting research fellow in the Centre for Australian Indigenous Studies at Monash University, Melbourne, Australia. He has written or edited fifteen books in the area of the Black family and race relations. His articles on Black sexuality have been published in *Ebony*, *Essence*, and academic journals. He has served on the board of directors of the National Council on Family Relations and the Sex Information and Education Council of the United States (SIECUS). A widely traveled speaker, he has lectured at more than five hundred colleges in the United States, Latin America, Europe, and Asia. At present, he divides his time between residences in San Francisco and Melbourne, Australia.